A CRY FROM
THE STREETS

Slum in the Seven Dials area of London, 1873. After Doré.

A CRY FROM THE STREETS

The Boys' Club Movement in Britain
from the 1850s to the Present
Day

FRANK DAWES

"In helping to run a boys' club I learned more practical economics and more practical sociology than I ever learned through any books." (Clement Attlee, Prime Minister, in a speech at the Grocers' Hall, London, in November 1945.)

Wayland Publishers

Also by Frank Dawes:
Not in Front of the Servants (Wayland)

SBN 85340 441 0

Copyright © by Frank Dawes
First published in 1975 by
Wayland (Publishers) Limited
49 Lansdowne Place, Hove, Sussex
Made and printed in Great Britain by
The Garden City Press Limited
Letchworth, Hertfordshire SG6 1JS

CONTENTS

LIST OF
ILLUSTRATIONS

FOREWORD

by

HRH the Duke of Gloucester GCVO

IT GIVES ME great pleasure to write a foreword to the History of the Boys' Club movement, which has been specially written by Mr. Frank Dawes to mark the Golden Jubilee of the National Association of Boys' Clubs.

The story not only concerns the fifty years since the NABC was formed but also describes the achievements of the pioneers of the boys' club movement in the nineteenth century.

The need for boys' clubs is as great today as it was then. Any boy who joins a club can benefit from the experience of other boys who undertake a similar activity or sport. He, in turn, can pass on his experience in the form of the leadership he shows to those who follow him—a process which will inevitably give him a self confidence that will help him throughout his life.

There are many boys' clubs throughout this country, and they are all different in many ways, but they all have this special quality because the membership is limited to a certain age group—an age group that covers those formative years when boys develop into men.

In many cases boys' clubs have provided opportunities for real creativity in areas where ambitions and natural talents are all too often frustrated by lack of suitable shared facilities.

I hope this book, highlighting the contribution which boys' clubs have made, will encourage people to come forward and provide boys' clubs with the help which is always urgently needed.

Richard,
the President of the NABC

PREFACE

FIFTY YEARS AGO, on 24th October, 1925, a meeting at Toynbee Hall in the East End of London formed the National Association of Boys' Clubs. The eighty people present had come from towns spawned by the Industrial Revolution. In these towns working class life in street upon street of box-like little houses, crouching in the shadow of belching chimneys, revolved around the pub on Saturday night and the pawnbroker on Monday morning, the fish and chip shops and the music hall or the local "picture palace."

The only playgrounds for the youngsters in these towns were all too often the same streets, sandwiched between factory walls and the railway; dingy backwaters shut in by soot-grimed brick and overhung by a pall of smoke, where no grass grew. They found their own amusements in discarded lorry tyres used as hoops, or tennis balls thrust into old stockings and used bolas-fashion on their enemies. Little girls skipped to the same sing-song rhymes their mothers and grandmothers had used, while boys formed street football teams, kicking a punctured rubber ball about, or an old tin can, the goals marked with folded jackets or chalk marks on the wall. As they grew older, the boys found more sophisticated excitement in pitch-and-toss or dice in back alleys or on tenement roofs, or in battles with rival street gangs.

There was, let it be said, a *camaraderie* and neighbourliness in some of these mean streets which is still remembered by people who grew up in them. Some of the most famous professional footballers learned to play in the street. But it was not enough for men who had survived the holocaust of the 1914–18 war with their spirit still unbroken and who had been promised by Mr. Lloyd George a "Land Fit For Heroes." There were some of these men among the eighty who met at Toynbee Hall and they wanted something better for the rising generation than a life on the streets.

At that time boys' clubs were the only educational and social agency for the vast majority of lads who were unable to continue their schooling beyond the statutory age of fourteen. They had to go out to earn their living as soon as they put on their first long trousers, or "long-uns." Many found themselves on the dole at sixteen, the age at which employers were compelled to pay insurance for them. The boys' club was then the only constructive alternative to the street corner and a means of directing the gang-spirit to a socially useful end.

Boys' clubs had begun in fact much earlier, in Victorian England, an England where the conditions in the industrial towns were infinitely more vicious and degrading than anything experienced by the men who formed the National Association of Boys' Clubs in 1925. Their story is part of the social history of England, with its roots in the slums of the last century.

ACKNOWLEDGEMENTS

I WAS ASKED to write this book to mark the Golden Jubilee of the National Association of Boys' Clubs in 1975 and I owe thanks to the Association for access to their library and archives at Bedford Square. The sources are detailed in the text but I was particularly helped by C. E. B. Russell's *Working Lads' Clubs*, first published in 1908 and revised in 1932 by his widow, Lilian Russell, and W. McG. Eagar's *Making Men*, his history of boys' clubs and related movements in Britain, published in 1953. It is also worth mentioning *The Shaftes*, Leslie Bibby's fascinating account of the historic Shaftesbury Boys' Club at Birkenhead, which was published by that club in 1974, James Butterworth's *Clubland* (1932) and B. P. Neuman's *The Boys' Club* (1900).

The journals of today are the very stuff of history and a great deal of detail about club life and the social climate in which they operated comes from *The Chronicle*, a monthly record of St. Andrew's Home and Club from 1883 on, the London Federation's *Boys' Club Chronicle*, which had a short span of life from 1888–89, and more enduringly *The Boy*, which was the journal of the NABC from the late 1920s to the 1960s when its name changed to *Challenge*. The association's file of the NABC Newsletter from 1947 to the present day is another fruitful source although it is more difficult at short range to select from it what is significant.

Apart from published material I gained much by talking to veterans of the boys' club movement like Sir Reg Goodwin, Neville Goodridge and Captain Sammy Cole. Others now dead, such as Sir Hubert Llewellyn Smith, Sir Basil Henriques, Sir Alec Paterson and Barclay Baron, were prolific writers and researchers in their day, and I have been able to draw on their reflections and memoirs. It is a pity that more of the boys themselves did not write about their lives in the clubs—only here and there do we catch an occasional glimpse of their view of things. We have E. M. S. Pilkington's *An Eton Playing Field* from the year of 1896, but alas no account from any grimy-faced boy in that Hackney mission district about what *he* thought of the Etonians who came among them.

I have tried to relate the story of the boys' club movement in Britain to the social history of the country and as far as the Victorian period is concerned there is no difficulty: the massive research carried out by Henry Mayhew, Charles Booth and Seebohm Rowntree into the lives of "the lower orders" provide more than enough background detail, together with the reports of the Children's Employment Commission (1863–64) and the annual reports of the Ragged School Union for 1877 and 1881.

In the opening years of this century indictments of the callous exploitation of boys as workers poured forth from individuals with a social conscience and official bodies such as the Poor Law Commission (1909). The Lewis Report on *Juvenile Education in Relation to Employment after the War* (1916) shows a well-intentioned attempt to put an end to this abuse.

But the bleakness of the inter-war years for many of those who grew to maturity in them is all too clearly shown by Sir Hubert Llewellyn Smith's *New Survey of London Life and Labour* published in 1932 and *Wasted Lives* by W. F. Lestrange (1936). Extracts from broadcasts by the BBC reflect a feeling of hopelessness among the legions of unemployed, while J. B. Priestley's *English Journey* in 1933 underlines the contrast between the depressed areas and the relatively prosperous south-east. *The Needs of Youth*, Dr. A. E. Morgan's specially commissioned study for the King George V Jubilee Trust, came out in 1939 just as England awoke (too late) to the threat of Nazism and Fascism.

The post-1945 story of the boys' club movement is bound up with official reports on education and the social services—Albemarle, Newsom and lesser-known treatises such as *Eighty Thousand Adolescents*, Bryan Reed's study in 1950 of young people in Birmingham. The NABC produced its own thoughtful analysis of the new order of society in *Boys' Clubs in the Sixties* in 1962.

Unlike boys' clubs, the related movements of the boys' brigades and the Scouts had individual founders who created them in their own style. The story of *William Smith of the Boys' Brigade* was told by F. P. Gibbon in 1934, while in 1942 E. E. Reynolds produced his *Baden-Powell*; B-P himself wrote *Scouting for Boys* (1908) and *Scouting and Youth Movements* (1929). Biographies of boys' club leaders are few and far between, but in *Lex* (1937) Frank Whitbourne produced a colourful account of the Manchester pioneer, Alexander Devine.

Thanks are also due to the following for permission to reproduce copyright illustrations: The Radio Times Hulton Picture Library, *frontispiece*, 1, 2, 24; St. Andrew's Home and Club Westminster, 5, 6; Dr. Barnado's, 7; The Mansell Collection, 9, 13, 14, 17; The London Federation of Boys Clubs, 10; the NABC, 12, 16, 20, 22, 23, 26–31; Keystone Press Agency, 25. Other photographs reproduced are the property of the Wayland Picture Library.

Last, but not least, I owe thanks to Kathy Rochford for typing the script.

PART ONE

"Better perhaps than any other social effort of the Victorian age the Boys' Club Movement proved the democratic argument for equal opportunity for all children."

WALDO McGILLICUDDY EAGAR

I

A Cry from the Streets

IN THE NINETEENTH CENTURY, while London was spreading outwards, devouring green fields and woodlands, in the Black Country of the Midlands and the industrial North other cities were expanding overnight in the manner of gold-rush towns. Even by 1851, the census returns showed that for the first time in history there were more people living in the towns of England and Wales than in the country and by the end of the century three people out of every four lived in towns.

The population of the city of Salford, for example, grew by 72 per cent in just twenty years between 1861 and 1881. The town of Middlesbrough, which in 1831 had only 383 inhabitants, had a hundred times as many by 1871 through the development of its iron and steel works.

There were rapid improvements in sanitation, lighting, transport and the provision of public baths, libraries and parks in the closing decades of the century, but as Trevelyan says in his *English Social History* (volume 4):

"The State had permitted the landlord and the speculative builder to lay out modern England as best suited their own private gain, too often without a thought given to amenity or to the public welfare. In vast areas of London and other cities there were no open spaces within reach of the children, whose only play-ground outside the school yard was the hard and ugly street."

While the pall of smoke spread from the chimneys of the mills and dyeworks, the tanneries and the boneworks, hard-headed Manchester business-men proclaimed; "where there's muck, there's brass." The River Irk was black with refuse to prove it.

And if this meant more "brass" to the millowners, it also meant a grim environment for the workers living on the river's banks in ghettoes like the one in Manchester called Gibraltar, where 15,000 people were crammed into dank cellars. Whole families lived cheek by jowl in a single room, throwing their slops into the open sewers. Since there was no tapped water —a standpipe would serve a whole neighbourhood and from it women and children would draw their water in tubs, buckets and pitchers—and not even the most rudimentary sanitation, the stench can be believed but scarcely imagined.

There were, of course, plenty of rural slums, too, but it was in the towns, built to serve the hungry mills with cheap labour, that hell on earth became a reality for the toiling masses and their children. A country child could at least find escape in the woods and meadows, whereas in the towns, as a clergyman told the Children's Employment Commission in 1843: "You will find poor girls who have never sung or danced; never seen a dance; never seen a violet, or a primrose, and other flowers; and others whose only idea of a green field was derived from having been stung by a nettle."

It would hardly be an exaggeration to say that childhood had been obliterated. The division between learning and earning which came with the spread of State education from 1870 onwards did not exist in the mid-Victorian period. There were dame schools in country districts where the widows of discharged soldiers and undischarged bankrupts gave instruction in the Bible and the "three Rs," using the brighter of their pupils as unpaid assistants. In one parish school in East Anglia a boy of thirteen was left in charge while the schoolmaster was away ill.

Enlightened Victorian millowners like Robert Owen and John Bright provided a thorough schooling for the children who worked in their factories but in other factory schools the teacher himself was illiterate and the school-room was often a cellar or a garret without books, desks or chairs. In towns the education of those who were too dirty and ill-kept to attend charity or church schools was in the ragged schools.

The anonymous diary of the master of a London ragged school, published in the *English Journal of Education* in 1850 gives us some idea of the problems he faced when to his pupils:

"... the very appearance of one's coat is to them a badge of class and respect-ability; for although they may not know the meaning of the word, they know very well, or at least feel, that we are the representatives of beings with whom they have ever considered themselves at war."

Assaults on teachers, not only by parents of the pupils but by the pupils themselves, were routine. This particular schoolmaster interpreted his role as seeing that the boys and girls were well washed and scrubbed, trying to get prayers said decently and teaching them the rudiments of reading, writing and arithmetic. After a few months he had his class singing nicely and obeying orders, but: "I cannot boast of the means adopted—they have been frightened into subjection."

The Ragged School Union was started in 1844 to cater for children whom other schools refused or whose parents could not afford even nominal school fees. Its aims accorded with Victorian principles of helping the *deserving* poor with nourishing bowls of soup and quotations from the Good Book.

The ragged schools, to do them justice, prided themselves on never turning away a child, however ragged. Indeed, Quintin Hogg (grandfather of the present Quintin Hogg, Lord Hailsham) found when he started a ragged school in 1865 that some boys were sent to him not only without boots but with no clothes at all apart from their mothers' shawls pinned around them.

For untold numbers of our great-grandfathers and great-great-grandfathers even the minimal education provided by the ragged schools was lacking. In 1850, according to census returns, 40 per cent of the population could not sign their names. As soon as a child was old enough to walk it was old enough to start work down the mines, in the mills, on the land and at scores of other occupations.

The early nineteenth century was a period of repeated legislation to mitigate the hardships of working women and children. The Factory Acts of 1819 and 1820 limited the working hours of cotton mill employees under sixteen years of age to *twelve a day*. The Act of 1831 extended this restriction to all those under eighteen, while the Act of 1833 drew a distinction between children (those aged between nine and thirteen) and "young persons" (those between thirteen and eighteen). Adolescence was thus officially recognised.

What was started in the textile mills spread to the mines, the foundries, the glassworks and the printing works after the Children's Employment Commission of 1843 revealed shocking abuses. But despite new laws, the efforts of teams of inspectors and other well-meaning attempts at reform, the abuse of child labour continued throughout the Victorian period and even into the twentieth century. A Children's Employment Commission in the 1860s found in the Potteries small boys aged between six and ten carrying moulds from the potters to the stoves in temperatures of 120°F for up to sixteen hours a day. They were earning 2s. 6d. a week.

In the hosiery and lace industries centred in Derby and Nottingham all members of the family were essential breadwinners. While men and women worked the machines, children threaded them or were employed in "seaming and footing." In the factories where Lucifer matches were made children as young as nine years old suffered from the horrible ravages of the phosphorous which so impregnated their clothing that it glowed in the dark. After a few years of such work their jaws began to rot away, a condition known as "phossy jaw." At home, even at the end of the century, babies of four were employed helping their mothers to make matchboxes for 2¼d.

a gross, fitting the drawers into the covers while an elder brother or sister made the drawers and another pasted on the sandpaper.

There were many such "unregulated occupations" outside the scope of the factory regulations. The cruel exploitation of boys as chimney sweeps, forced to climb up long, twisting, soot-encrusted flues with their brushes, was brought home to the drawing room in Charles Kingsley's *The Water Babies*. Middle class conscience was salved by Lord Shaftesbury's Chimney Sweep Act of 1840, but it was ignored by employers and twenty years later the Children's Employment Commission reported that the evil was "decidedly on the increase." Mr. Ruff, a master sweep in Nottingham, declared:

"No one knows the cruelty which a boy has to undergo in learning. The flesh must be hardened. This is done by rubbing it, chiefly on the elbows and knees, with the strongest brine, close by a hot fire. You must stand over them with a cane, or coax them with the promise of a halfpenny, etc., if they will stand a few more rubs. At first they will come back from their work with their arms and knees streaming with blood and the knees looking as if the caps had been pulled off; then they must be rubbed with brine again."

Even in 1875, by which time several laws had been passed prohibiting the practice, there were still plenty of boys earning pennies crawling up chimneys.

Young boys employed in the hot, smoky and airless nail-making smithies of the Black Country were distorted by having to wield hammers which they were scarcely big enough to lift. Not only boys, but girls too, worked in these dens and in his novel *Sybil*, Disraeli wrote of a file-maker who had a back like a grasshopper from her cramped occupation. She married without ceremony an apprentice boy who did not even know his own name. Small wonder that Disraeli wrote: "There are great bodies of the working class of this country nearer the condition of brutes than they have been at any time since the Conquest . . ."

It was the threat of utter destitution and admission to that grimmest of Victorian institutions, the workhouse, which kept men, women and children harnessed to the most back-breaking labour for a few pence in wages. A barefoot homeless urchin might easily die of starvation in the streets, yet those with the wits could survive in the urban jungle. At Greenwich and Blackfriars the boy mudlarks prospected for the droppings from barges and other treasures left by the river at low tide. In his *London Labour and the London Poor*, published in 1861–62, Henry Mayhew reported on those who made a living collecting dogs' droppings to sell to the tanneries, for use in processing leather, and others called "toshers" who could make as much as £2 a week (more than skilled artisans and clerks were paid) by combing the London sewers.

There were other less exotic, if less potentially rewarding, ways in which a boy could earn his bread on the streets. He could be a match-vendor or a newsboy, an errand boy or a shoe-black or he could join the great army of crossing sweepers whose job was to clear a path, especially for ladies with long skirts, through the dirt left by a constant stream of horses pulling carts and carriages, cabs and buses.

James Greenwood, a journalist who made a name for himself in the 1860s with a stream of newspaper articles and books about such lads, wrote in *The Seven Curses of London*:

". . . when Tom has reached the ripe age of ten, it is accounted high time that he 'got a place', as did his father before him; and as there are a hundred ways in London in which a sharp little boy of ten can be made useful, very little difficulty is experienced in Tom's launching. He becomes an 'errand boy', a newspaper or a printing boy, in all probability. The reader, curious as to the employment of juvenile labour, may any morning at six or seven o'clock witness the hurried trudging to work of as many Toms as the pavement of our great highways will conveniently accommodate, each with his small bundle of food in a little bag, to last him the day through."

Domestic service in a comfortable household, with its guarantee of meals and a roof, was the refuge of the majority of girls from poor homes but there were relatively few openings for boys. Less than a tenth of well over a million servants employed in private houses were male and the chances of a lamp-boy or a knife-boy (both very necessary in houses where there was no electricity and no stainless steel cutlery) becoming a footman, much less a butler, were slender. There was, however, a great increase in the numbers of people aspiring to the status of "carriage folk," or those who maintained their own equipages, in the prosperous years between 1850 and 1870. This led to more employment of "tigers"—small boys dressed in livery—as assistants to the coachmen. In late Victorian days, Lord Salisbury had a "tiger" to help him push the tricycle which he was fond of riding in the grounds of Hatfield House up the steeper slopes. On descents this small boy jumped up behind and rode with his hands on the great man's shoulders.

In 1872 the French artist Gustav Doré and the English author Blanchard Jerrold set down for posterity some fascinating glimpses of the city's teeming boy-life in *London: a Pilgrimage*. At The Ship at Greenwich, where Londoners went to eat whitebait, they noted the local boys "busy in the mud below, learning to be vagabond men by the help of thoughtless diners flushed with wine, who were throwing pence to them."

At the annual Oxford v. Cambridge University Boat Race, Jerrold wrote:

". . . the boys of London are seen in all their glory, and in all their astonishing and picturesque varieties. To watch them on the parapets of the bridges, dangling from the arches, swinging from the frailest boughs of trees, wading amid the rushes, paddling in the mud; scrambling, racing, fighting, shouting along the roads and river paths or through the furze of Putney Common, is a suggestive as well as an amusing sight. We studied them in all the rich picturesqueness of rags—poor, hungry, idle little fellows!—as they worked valiantly, trying to earn a few pence by disentangling the carriages and leading them to their owners, after the event of the day was over. Little rascals whose heads could hardly touch a man's elbow had the deep-set voices of men. On our way home we paused a long time, watching them and speculating on the waste of brave spirit that was going on within them. They were all pale, and, nearly all, lean; they were babes tossed—their bones hardly set—into the thick of the battle of life. The cockney *gamin* was the constant wonder of my fellow-pilgrim. It appeared terrible, indeed, to him, that in all the poverty-stricken districts of our London, children should most abound; that some of the hardest outdoor work should be in their feeble little hands; that infant poverty should be the news-distributor; that, in short, there should be a rising generation, hardened in its earliest years to vagabondage, and allured to grow to that most miserable of human creatures, the unskilled, dependent, roofless man."

As Thomas John Barnardo, the Irish medical student who opened his first home in Stepney Causeway in the East End of London in 1870, had discovered a few years earlier, large numbers of boys slept out on roofs, in sheds or even in barrels. Twenty years before that Lord Shaftesbury, the founder of the ragged schools, had given Members of Parliament an account of "the curious mode of life" of London street-arabs who slept out at night under arches and viaducts, in porticoes, sheds and carts, in sawpits and outhouses, on staircases and in the open. One boy slept every night in relative comfort inside the iron roller of Regent's Park, since he was thin enough to squeeze through the park railings.

Henry Mayhew reports in *The Criminal Prisons of London and Scenes of Prison Life*, published in 1862, on a meeting of boy vagrants he had called a few years earlier. Some 150 attended and the youngest was only six years old, a self-styled "cadger" who said that his widowed mother had sent him into the streets to beg. The majority were aged between fifteen and eighteen and eighty of them had neither father nor mother alive. According to Mayhew, the uproar before this meeting started was best compared to "a public menagerie at feeding time". He noted that many of the boys were not only good-looking but "had a frank, ingenuous expression, that seemed in no way connected with innate roguery," yet the hair of most of them was cut very close to the head indicating that they had recently been in gaol. Indeed, the comparative length of hair showed the time that each boy had been out of prison. In their rags and filth, they were nevertheless remarkably cheerful. Answering questions from him about the number of times they had been in gaol, a boy of nineteen who had notched up a score of twenty-nine was greeted with shouts of "Bray-vo!" which lasted for several minutes "whilst the whole of the boys rose to look at the distinguished individual." Entering into the spirit of the thing, some of the boys chalked on their hats the number of times they had been in gaol.

Of the sixty-three present who said they could read and write, most were thieves. The favourite reading of the majority were the lives of Jack Sheppard, Dick Turpin and the notorious criminals and pirates. When they were asked what they thought of Jack Sheppard, several bawled out "He's a regular brick." Twenty said they had been flogged in prison.

A policeman in plain clothes who was at the meeting was quickly identified and his withdrawal demanded. The departure of the "Peeler" was greeted with hisses, groans and cries of "Throw him over!"

Thirteen of the 150 boys at the meeting said they had taken to crime to get money to go to "Penny Gaffs" and other low theatres and one lad said this had cost him a good job on a Birmingham railway.

Blanchard Jerrold said that the Penny Gaff, unlike the respectable music halls which grew up and flourished in the latter half of the nineteenth century, was the place where juvenile poverty met juvenile crime:

"We elbowed our way into one, that was the foulest, dingiest place of public entertainment I can conceive; and I have seen, I think, the worst in many places. The narrow passages were blocked by sharp-eyed young thieves, who could tell the policeman at a glance through the thin disguise of private clothes. More than one young gentleman speculated as to whether he was wanted; and was relieved when the sergeant passed him. A platform, with bedaubed proscenium, was the stage, and the boxes were as dirty as the stalls of a common stable. 'This does more harm than anything I know of,' said the sergeant, as he pointed to the pack of boys and girls who were laughing, talking, gesticulating, hanging over the boxes—and joining in the chorus of a song the trio were singing.... The odour—the atmosphere—to begin with is indescribable. The rows of brazen faces are terrible to look upon. It is impossible to be angry with their sauciness, or to resent the leers and grimaces that are directed upon us as unwelcome intruders. Some have the aspect of wild cats. The lynx at bay has not a crueller glance than some I caught from almost baby faces. The trio sing a song, with a jerk at the beginning of each line, in true street style; accompanying the searing words with mimes and gestures, and hinted indecencies, that are immensely relished. The boys and girls nod to each other, and laugh aloud: they have understood. Not a wink has been lost upon them: and the comic ruffian in the tall hat has nothing to teach them. At his worst they meet him more than half-way. For this evening these youngsters will commit crimes—the gaff being the prime delight of the pickpocket."

In his search for "copy," the journalist James Greenwood mixed with thieves and ticket-of-leave men, tramps and beggars, visited every kind of low-life entertainment, and under the name of "The Amateur Casual" described from the inside a casual ward in Lambeth which he had entered disguised as a tramp. He applauded Barnardo's efforts to give shelter and work to London's outcast and ragamuffins and publicized other philanthropic institutions such as an Errand Boys' Home, but he was not blind to the fact that a proportion were inveterate cadgers and loafers. In fact the streets teemed with Artful Dodgers, boys of thirteen or fourteen who stood no taller than 4 feet 6 inches, yet wore men's clothes with sleeves and trouser bottoms rolled up, smoked clay pipes and drank beer or gin with the air and manner of grown men.

Greenwood was among the first to see the folly of leaving the young of the poorer classes to steer their own way through the "middle passage" between childhood and adulthood. After more than a decade of elementary education the situation seemed little improved in 1883 when he identified in *Odd People in Odd Places* this most critical period in a boy's life:

"It is at the time when he becomes a 'hobbledehoy,' as it is called—neither a man nor a boy. . . . There is always a demand in London for boys of from fourteen to seventeen, and the wages paid them are not illiberal. A sharp youth of sixteen can command as much as ten shillings weekly, boarding at home; and in the way that poor folks contrive to live, such a sum leaves a considerable margin of profit for a thrifty mother to eke out of general housekeeping expenses. But, unfortunately, this satisfactory condition of affairs does not last very long . . . it is a melancholy fact that in our great metropolis young fellows of from seventeen to nineteen are a drug on the unskilled labour market. They are too big to be classed with boys, and not old enough or sufficiently able-bodied to elbow their way in the already crowded ranks of the lower order of adult labourers. . . . In numberless cases it is a terribly hard time for the poor young fellows. Half-fed, shabby and penniless, it is no great wonder that many even of the best disposed fall into evil habits, and those who are at all viciously inclined are almost sure to do so. The ranks of the detestable army of 'roughs' are no doubt largely recruited from this source, or the evil may develop into the milder social difficulty represented by the comparatively harmless vagabond who begs his bread, and resorts to the workhouse casual ward for his bed. . . ."

Pitch-and-toss, cards or dice on tenement roofs and in the back alleys was the only entertainment apart from the penny gaff available to working class youths. Since organized football and other sports were rare, they found an outlet for their combative instincts in street gangs, fighting other similar gangs on any trivial pretext. Every major town had its gangs of ragamuffins and hooligans, local roughs with studded belts and bell-bottomed trousers, with razors in their sleeves, who terrorized shopkeepers and plagued the police. Manchester had its Scuttlers and Ikes, Birmingham its Peaky Blinders, Bermondsey its Dockhead Slashers and Yoboes. Charles Russell, one of the founding fathers of the boys' clubs in Manchester, wrote in *Working Lads' Clubs*, first published in 1908:

"It was not until the latter decades of the nineteenth century, when the ruffianism of youths had reached such a pitch as to become an absolute danger to the community that attention was thoroughly roused, and men who had the welfare of their city and country at heart grew apprehensive and began to cast about for some means of checking so alarming a development."

Respectable Victorians were shaking their heads and asking where had these young monsters sprung from, why were they behaving in this outrageous way. Russell himself suggested that the spectacular growth of industrial towns, dedicated to producing more and cheaper goods for everyone, had forgotten about providing decent housing, open spaces or facilities for recreation.

Beatrice Webb writes in *My Apprenticeship*, looking back on her Victorian youth from the year of the General Strike, in 1926:

"Commodities of all sorts and kinds rolled out from the new factories at an always accelerating speed with an always falling cost of production, thereby promoting what Adam Smith had idealized as the Wealth of Nations. On the other hand, the same revolution had deprived the manual workers, that is four-fifths of the people of England, of their opportunity for spontaneity and freedom of initiative in production. It had transformed such of them as had been independent producers into the hirelings and servants of another social class, and as the East End of London in my time only too vividly demonstrated, it has thrust hundreds of thousands of families into the physical horrors and moral debasement of chronic destitution in crowded tenements in the midst of mean streets."

As the Prince of Wales heard in 1885 when he sat on a Royal Commission on Housing, people who crowded the stairs and passages of East End tenement houses at night were known as " 'appy dossers". But it was far from a happy existence in those narrow grimy streets, far from any fields or parks, where the streets were the only playground for the young.

It was not until the twentieth century that the State took any active intervention in the welfare of those in that awkward stage of transition between boyhood and manhood. But, as we shall see, there were a large number of middle class and upper class Victorians who made it their own business and went out of their way to make contact with those who had none of their privileges.

2

A Helping Hand

THERE WAS AN IMMENSE GAP between the haves and the have-nots in Victorian society and it must be counted as one of the wonders of the age that so many men of privilege and position gave up their spare time and spent their own money to organize the leisure time of working boys or provide homes for those who were destitute. Since the poor lived in ghettoes, physically separated from the civilized amenities of those who could afford boots and new clothes for their children and comfortable homes with servants, their problems might have been swept under the carpet and forgotten. But respectable Victorians were church-goers and saw it as much their duty to dispense charity coupled with religion to the poor at home as to the poor of the countries within the Empire. Indeed, contemporary reports on conditions in the East End of London sometimes sound as if they had come from a foreign land inhabited by savages. In some senses, of course, the two were alike. Decent people like clergymen who went to live in areas swarming with prostitutes, thieves, beggars and destitute children, where cholera acted as nature's pruning form and from which the only temporary escape was the beer-house and the gin-palace, were little different from missionaries going to Africa.

Charities abounded, providing free dinners, free education, free nursing, free medicine, free soup, free clothing; but always with the message "Know thy place". In any case, charity was but a drop in the vast ocean of poverty in the big towns. Boys like those described in the previous chapter at the meeting called by Henry Mayhew needed more practical and sustained help than a bowl of free soup or a pair of second-hand boots. Thomas John Barnardo was only one of those who provided it, but his flair for publicity and organization ensured that his name would live when the others had been forgotten, and that the term Barnardo Boy would go into the language.

When he opened his Labour Home for Destitute Youths in Stepney Causeway in 1870, Barnardo was determined to have no bar against any child on account of race, creed, sex or physical condition. Instead of doling out charity, he set them to work chopping wood. Together with his beadle, a former detective policeman whose "past experience with the criminal classes is of the highest service to him in prosecuting his present employment," Barnardo combed the alleyways of East London for waifs and strays. But his practice of having "before and after" photographs taken of them for advertising purposes brought him under attack. A local parson, the Rev. George Reynolds, alleged:

"The system of taking and making capital of the children's photographs is not only dishonest, but has a tendency to destroy the better feelings of the children. Barnardo's method is to take the children as they are supposed to enter the Home, and then after they have been in the Home some time. He is not satisfied with taking them as they really are, but he tears their clothes, so as to make them appear worse than they really are. They are also taken in purely fictitious positions. A lad named Fletcher is taken with a shoe-black's box upon his back, although he never was a shoe-black...."

Barnardo defended himself against these accusations in the Arbitration Court in 1877. He won his case and the Homes went from strength to strength, although they no longer sent out cards and pamphlets bearing the pictures of children. Instead he relied more on his house journal *Night and Day* and his books to publicize his work. However, the process of photographing children admitted to the Home went on. Valerie Lloyd, of the National Portrait Gallery, who organized an exhibition entitled *The Camera and Dr. Barnardo* in 1974, wrote in the *Sunday Times Magazine*: "The faces of thousands of destitute children, otherwise totally unremembered, some suffering from eye disease or other deformities, are recorded. Many are intelligent, beautiful or display extraordinary strength of character."

This was the great discovery of the clergymen, the missionaries and the ragged school teachers who went to live and work in the ghettoes, that the poor were not necessarily a sub-species, but human beings like themselves. In conditions of the utmost degradation and almost unbelievable suffering as a result of unemployment and sickness, many of them managed somehow to remain human.

Men like Dr. Barnardo and William Booth, who started the Salvation Army—the last great evangelical revival in England—from a tent in the wastes of Mile End in 1865, won fame through philanthropy. Booth struggled for the souls of the homeless and unfed drunkards, criminals and harlots. Others performed their good works on a more modest scale and their names are forgotten, like those they served. Men like one J. McGregor who in 1851—nearly twenty years before Barnardo's first home was set up— established the Shoeblack Society as a dormitory for the homeless. The idea started with the employment of out-of-work boys to clean the shoes of foreign visitors to Queen Victoria's Great Exhibition and the service caught on with the British public. At that time seven refuges for boys and girls were available as off-shoots of the ragged schools and in 1865 the Reformatory and Refuge Union was formed.

Blanchard Jerrold described a visit to an establishment with one of those formidably verbose titles which were much in favour with Victorian gentlemen: the *Boys' Home for the Training and Maintenance by their Own Labour of Destitute Boys Not Convicted of Crime*:

"...a humble little Home which has the tone of a happy united family, the master, his wife and their family living with the boys who are taught to be gentle and forgiving with each other. To it is attached a farm school at Barnet, to which boys suitable for country work are sent."

There was usually a practical side to Victorian philanthropy. Mr. Bromley, a superintendent of Sunday schools who opened in the 1850s a refuge at Maida Vale for "boys who had lost both parents actually or virtually" was able to find them useful employment in printing and making paper bags.

Indeed, such establishments commended themselves to the parish authorities as being a more economical way of dealing with destitute boys than the workhouse. As the *Illustrated London News* reported in 1870 on a boys' home which had been set up by "a few earnest men" to save such boys from a life of crime:

"The boys are taught habits of order, cleanliness and industry. The average cost of maintenance for each boy is £15 1s. 2d. . . . the average net cost in the reformatories of Great Britain is £18 19s. 3d., and that of London pauper children never less than £24 10s. . . ."

The Victorian code exalted the virtue of honest toil, and was loud in its condemnation of the Demon Drink. Drunkenness among boys and youths was widespread up to the 1870s because the beer-houses and gin-palaces were not governed by any licensing laws and there was no restriction whatever on young people using them. The Temperance Movement in England had began as the young Queen Victoria ascended to the throne and gathered momentum as her reign progressed, reaching its climax in the 1860s and 70s when distillers and brewers were reviled as living on the wages of sin. But before the century was out they and their shareholders had captured the Conservative party.

Reformers were anything but temperate in their demands for total abstinence, their calls for people to "sign the pledge," their Blue Ribbon armies (takers of the pledge wore a blue ribbon on their breasts), their Bands of Hope and large numbers of youths' associations. They clearly recognized that adolescence was a crucial period in forming the drinking habits of a lifetime.

After 1870, when the State accepted responsibility for elementary education and set up School Boards with powers to compel children to attend school between the ages of five and twelve, the numbers of ragged schools declined and the union tried to find ways of using premises which had not been taken over. The Union's report of 1877 said that night schools were prospering, and added:

"There is a strange fascination in some of these young arabs; they are shrewd, quick, and brimful of life and sport, having in them the germ of future greatness if they be but influenced aright; precious stones that need but polishing to shine with lustre, or if led astray, to become leaders in the way of crime."

In the 1880s the Ragged Schools Union emphasized the need to provide for what they described as the "young Toilers of London from the age of fourteen to eighteen . . . who have profited little by the new order of things educationally." Associated with night schools was the "somewhat novel movement" for providing recreation in youths' institutes as an alternative to the garish attractions of the gin-palace and the penny gaff. Institutes had been set up in Castle Street, Old Pye Street, Brewer's Court, Clare Market, Ernest Street, Exeter Buildings, John Street, Love Lane, Ogle Mews, St. Peter Street, Wagner Street, Whitecross Street and elsewhere. Members paid a penny a week and the attractions included a drum-and-fife band and reading and coffee rooms. The older boys "subscribed a small sum to purchase papers, periodicals, coffee and cake."

At Latimer Road in Notting Dale, where a temperance public house called the Magdala Castle had been built, a ragged school became a shelter for the local youths in 1880. One of the attractions was a fortnightly cocoa concert, of which the *Quarterly Record* of the Ragged Schools' Union said: "The admission is one penny, which is returned in the shape of hot cocoa and a piece of cake." As early as the 1850s a number of Church of England parishes ran institutes for boys who attended church—they did not admit "rough boys". Boys' clubs grew out of the pastoral work of the Church and were the start of the youth movement in Britain, but no one knows who started the first club as distinct from an institute. In 1858 a man named Charles Baker opened one in Bayswater, but he left no known record of why he started it, or how, and what manner of boys came to his door.

General Charles Gordon, famed in history as Gordon of Khartoum, where he was killed in 1885 in an heroic but unsuccessful attempt to relieve the Egyptian garrison, has been credited by some as the founding father of the boys' club movement in Britain in the mid-1860s. At that time he was the officer commanding the Royal Engineers reconstructing the defences of the Thames. But it seems his military duties were not over-demanding because he found time to teach in the local ragged school and keep open house for boys for whom he found jobs or sent to sea. While they were abroad he wrote to them and made a point of welcoming them on their return. Already a military hero after the battle of the Taku Forts in 1865, Gordon was nonetheless a stern Victorian moralist who shunned personal glorification and believed in good works for their own sake. However, he left no club or organization for boys behind him in Gravesend when he moved on to other duties after four years.

At the same time that Gordon was taking a friendly interest in the boys of Gravesend, Quintin Hogg was starting a ragged school class in Of Alley, Charing Cross, with some of his friends from Eton. He had set out on his missionary work by teaching a couple of crossing sweepers to read by the light of a candle stuck in a beer bottle under the Adelphi Arches. As a way of getting to know these street arabs better, Quintin Hogg bought a suit of shoe-black's clothes, brushes and blacking, and disguised himself. After blacking boots he curled up in a barrel or under a tarpaulin with the ragamuffins and shared their diet of tripe and onions or pig's trotters. But during the day, after a hot bath, he reported for his dull routine as a junior in a tea merchant's office in the City.

He was the fourteenth child of a wealthy Irish barrister, Sir James Hogg, popular and good at games at Eton with a highly developed social conscience based on religion. His attempts to bring learning to the roughs in Of Alley were not all that gratefully received. One night when he was in bed with a feverish cold he was summoned urgently to the ragged school:

"On arriving there, I found the whole school in an uproar, the gas-fittings had been wrenched off and were being used as batons by the boys for striking the police, while the rest of them were pelting them with slates, and a considerable concourse of people were standing round in a more or less threatening way, either to see the fun or to help in going against the police. I felt alarmed for the safety of the teacher, and rushing into the darkened room, called for the boys to instantly stop and be quiet. To my amazement the riot was stopped immediately, in two minutes the police were able to go quietly away, and for the first time in my life I learned that I had some kind of instinct or capacity for the management of elder boys. . . ."

Quintin Hogg threw himself with great dedication into his work for street boys: a dilapidated house next door to the ragged school in Of Alley was restored and fitted out as a dormitory by the boys themselves and their leader. He was also involved with the Shoeblacks' Brigade, played at half-back in the first England v. Scotland football match (which he and another old Etonian organized) and opened another dormitory for forty boys in Castle Street, Long Acre. This last venture developed into the Christian Youths' Institute and ultimately into the Regent Street Polytechnic in 1881, an entirely new kind of educational opportunity for working lads providing gymnasia and playing fields on the public school pattern, as well as technical training.

Apart from all this, this prodigiously active man managed to be successful enough in business to finance his ideas out of his own pocket. He was so devoted to what he called "his boys" that he even took with him as a valet on his honeymoon one of the Long Acre lads whom he did not trust to leave to his own devices.

If it cannot be stated definitively who started the first boys' club, it *can* be said that they grew naturally out of homes and refuges for the destitute and institutes opened in the evenings with a mainly educational purpose in view. Men like Quintin Hogg were, therefore, the true founding fathers of boys' clubs, although they could not be expected to foresee which form the movement would eventually take. He had done something different by living among street boys as one of them and trying to find out what they needed. As the Reverend Dr. Clifford put it:

"He saw that recreation was absent; that the life for which the Christian churches were catering was a life fragmentary, one-sided—providing a prayer-meeting but no gymnasium, giving opportunity for the study of the Bible but no chance of joining a cycling, a swimming or a rowing club, nothing that related to man's body, as though, forsooth, a man could be lifted out of himself by touching just one part of his nature. . . ."

The need for somewhere to go other than the beer-house or the penny gaff was not confined only to shoe-blacks and crossing sweepers. In a paper read to the Social Science Association at Edinburgh in October 1863 the Rev. Arthur Sweatman, who later in the century became the Archbishop of Toronto, called for youths' clubs or institutes for boys between the ages of thirteen and nineteen who had left elementary schools. He had in mind junior clerks and office boys, errand boys and apprentices earning between 5s. and 18s. a week:

"Their peculiar *wants* are *evening recreation, companionship, an entertaining but healthy literature, useful instruction* and a *strong guiding influence to lead them upward and onward socially and morally.* Their *dangers* are the long evenings consequent on early closing, the unrestraint they are allowed at home, the temptations of the streets and of their time of life and a little money at the bottom of their pockets."

Sweatman had started just such a youths' institute at St. George's Hall, Richmond Road, Islington, in 1860. Even earlier, in 1857, another clergyman, the Rev. Henry White, had started the Dover Youths' Institute for boys of fourteen to nineteen who were too young for Mechanics' Institutes and far too well dressed for the Ragged Night Schools.

Youths who joined the Islington Institute paid 3d. a week for the use of a well-lit and warm reading room hung with pictures and equipped with more than three dozen periodicals, including the daily illustrated and local newspapers, various boys' magazines and "serials of a higher class." Or they could play "chess, draughts, solitaire, tactics and any similar drawing-room amusement that may be found" at tables cheerfully covered with red baize. Every evening there were classes in a variety of subjects ranging from bookkeeping to biblical study and elocution, and lectures were given on alternate Tuesday evenings. The institute also offered a penny bank and a lending library with eight hundred volumes.

In the first season 236 boys and youths joined the institute and the nightly attendance was between fifty and seventy-five. By 1863 there was a waiting list for membership and the nightly attendance was up to ninety even though the members' subscription had been raised from 3d. to 4d. a week. A cricket club had been formed.

This institute, in many ways similar to a modern boys' club, if somewhat on the intellectual side, was entirely self-supporting. The total members' subscriptions of £95 a year more than covered the cost of rent, gas, lighting, cleaning and fuel (£65) and printing, classroom materials, periodicals, postage and so on, which amounted to less than £20.

Edward Tabrum, a clerk in the Public Record Office, who was twenty-five when he became honorary secretary of the Islington Youths' Institute, was to be found every evening sitting at a table in the social room, shaking hands with every member as he came in and addressing them all by name. He gave the whole of his spare time to the boys of Islington for twelve years until his death at the tragically early age of thirty-seven. He was also connected with the London Shoeblack Brigade and a member of the London School Board, which laid the foundations of education for all.

Perhaps the best tribute to his efforts is that several other institutes were set up in London in imitation of the one at Richmond Road, and there was friendly rivalry among them at chess or in recitation contests, as well as summer outings by rail and river.

By the 1870s concern for working lads of thirteen and upwards who had nothing to do when their work had finished but loiter around the pubs and music halls was being noticed in high places. In September 1876 a deputation waited upon the Lord Mayor of London to urge the setting up of "Working Lads' Institutes." It came about because Henry Hill, a businessman in the City, chanced to find one of his office boys reading a "penny dreadful" when he should have been working. Evidently a humane and understanding employer, he listened while the lad described his abysmal home life in Whitechapel, and took the trouble to go down there to see for himself a penny gaff into which four hundred working boys were crammed for want of any better amusement.

As a result of the deputation the Lord Mayor called a public meeting at the Mansion House to discuss the problems of boys who finished at seven in the evening and were left to their own devices until bedtime. At the meeting Sir Robert Carden, a magistrate, talked of honest boys who had ended up in front of him because of bad associations they had formed in the streets, and Bishop Claughton appealed for funds.

The upshot of all this high level concern was the founding of the Whitechapel Institute in 1876, and in the following decade the Prince of Wales opened imposing new premises for a combined institute and home offering Bible classes, temperance society, savings bank, brass band, drum and fife band, gymnasium, refreshment bar and even a swimming pool. None of the worthy people concerned appeared to be aware that institutes had flourished, admittedly on a somewhat less grandiose style, in North London in the previous decade. This lack of communication and co-ordination goes a long way to explaining why efforts to provide facilities for adolescents were so slow in coming. Yet progress had been made by the mid-1880s. The Regent Street Polytechnic was a long way from Quintin Hogg's ragged school in Of Alley, just as the brand new Whitechapel Institute was worlds apart from General Booth's tent in Mile End.

The debate about popular education assumed an even higher priority as Queen Victoria's reign wore on. Would education mitigate the danger of violent social upheaval, or would learning to read and write make the working classes, as the middle classes feared, even more of a threat to the established order? Encouraged by high churchmen and university dons, youths' institutes such as the Albert Institute at Cambridge began to widen their appeal to attract drapers' apprentices and the like. Games were introduced by the public school men as a means of inculcating moral discipline.

Institutes and polytechnics were all very well, but what of the great unwashed, the dispossessed and demoralized masses? As it turned out, the institutes with a purely educational purpose were gradually absorbed into the developing State school system, while boys' clubs were concerning themselves more and more with games and character-building than with formal learning.

3

Opposite Sides of the High Road

From 1801 to 1891 the population of England and Wales grew from under 10 million to 29 million, and the population of London grew faster than that of any other town or city in the land. The rash of little redbrick houses and shops was spreading outwards all the time, creating new estates alongside the already decaying tenements thrown up in the early years of the industrial revolution.

This was happening along the Camberwell New Road, south of the River Thames, in the late 1860s, as it was happening elsewhere to the south, east, west and north of the metropolis of the Empire so grandly described in the report of the 1871 Census as "the seat of the Legislature, the primary Home of Justice, Medicine and Religion, the theatre for the fine arts and the sciences, the great centre of society; the emporium of commerce, the warehouse of England, the great Port in communication with the sea."

Such sonorous phrases can have meant little to the people living in Nelson and Pitt streets on the north side of Camberwell New Road, an area given notoriety by Charles Booth twenty-five years later in his *Life and Labour in London* as the most miserable slum in all the capital. But on the other side of the high road, where until lately strawberries grew in the market gardens, long streets of almost exactly similar houses had been built to accommodate the respectable commuting classes in the beginnings of suburbia.

The high road was the frontier dividing two distinct social classes and, interestingly enough for the purposes of this social history, on the south side a youths' institute was set up by the Rev. Daniel Elsdale, curate to the newly created parish, while on the other side of the road a boys' club was started in 1872.

The parish magazine recorded:

BOYS' CLUB

This club has now been opened for three weeks, in Beulah Hall, for 1½ hours on Thursdays and Fridays, and 2 hours on Saturday: and from the number that attend seems to be much appreciated. The boys have a few games and, by the kindness of some friends, a Bagatelle Table was bought last week. There are 25 or 30 boys who generally attend. Tea and coffee, bread and butter are supplied. The club is free to Sunday and Night School boys, also to the Band boys:

others are charged 1d. a night. Two gentlemen kindly superintend each night and have little or no trouble with the boys.

The writer of that brief paragraph could not have realized that he was celebrating the birth of the first boys' club, plainly named as such, in England. It catered for the rougher boys, with whom the middle class who lived to the south of Camberwell New Road, destined for office employment in the City, did not mix. For *their* benefit an "Institute for Boys and Youths from 14 to 21" was opened at 149 Camberwell New Road in the following year. Like other youths' institutes described in the last chapter it offered classes, a reading room and library and a variety of indoor games for a subscription of 4d. a week. According to a note in the parish magazine when the subscription was raised to 6d. (a sizeable unit of coinage at that time) this establishment combined "the luxuries of a West-end club with the benefits of a first-class Educational Establishment."

Whether or not this was something of an exaggeration, the youths' institute clearly was not catering for what one clergyman described as the "dear wicked boys" from the other side of Camberwell New Road. This man, the Rev. Green, who came newly ordained to what was in 1867 still technically a missionary district, recalled fifty years later how these boys tried to smoke him and his congregation out of a room by setting fire to faggots piled against the door and how one picked his cassock pocket while he was preaching, but returned the contents later.

They were the children of washerwomen and navvies like the one who came to join the Temperance Society and opted for "partial" rather than "total" abstinence. When he was asked what limit of beer he wished to impose on himself he replied: "Two gallons a day." Four gallons was his usual intake. Another navvy, earning 36s. a week, said he gave £1 to his wife and spent the other 16s. on beer and tobacco.

Perhaps it was to be expected that a high proportion of the children of Nelson Street and Pitt Street would turn out to be liars and thieves. But behind their facade of bad language and bravado lurked a desperate urge to please and to be loved. When the parson went on holiday six or seven of these "rough street boys" came with their push-carts to take his luggage to Euston Station, miles away on the other side of the river, to save him the expense of a cab. And: "Jemmy, a little boy of 10 or 11, whose home was a big sewer pipe on the Thames side, and whose sole covering was a jacket, shirt and a pair of ragged trousers, sold his jacket for 6d. to put to the memorial given me when I left." Sixpence was the price of a week's subscription at the Youths' Institute in Camberwell New Road, but to this barefoot child it was the price of a coat. Clergymen had rewards greater than money in their pastoral work in districts like this one in Kennington. In the new parish of St. John The Divine as it became in 1872, two years after the passing of Forster's Education Act, they had built a National school for boys and girls from the north side of Camberwell New Road as well as schools for the middle class boys and girls on the south side and an infants' school at Westhall Road. They started Sunday schools and catechism classes, reading rooms, an athletic club devoted to the dumb-bell and exercises on the parallel bars for the office boys and a "drum and fife band for our working lads." Penny readings—meetings at which adventure stories were read aloud— were always crowded. In the midst of all this social activity the class barriers were strictly maintained: "Two cricket Clubs are now formed: the one called St. John the Evangelist; the other for working boys"—parish magazine, April 1873.

But the clubs on both sides of the high road were flourishing in their own different ways. By the mid-1880s the institute's programme included a wide range of sport including cricket, rugby and soccer, running, swimming, rowing and bicycling on "penny-farthings." As yet, the latter pastime was something beyond the reach of poor boys, but a social conscience was developing among their better off brothers. In 1878 the youths' institute gave an entertainment to aid the funds of the Cyprus Boys' Club, in Kennington. Why the name Cyprus was chosen is not altogether clear, except that at the time that island in the Eastern Mediterranean had just become a bastion of the British Empire, having been purchased from Turkey as a military and naval base. In any event, it made a distinctive name for a club which now boasted its own Christy Minstrel Troupe. At the time the club met in a school in Westhall Road, in association with a home for destitute boys which was being set up in the adjoining mission house. The downstairs front room of the mission house was being "magnificently fitted up as a Coffee Tavern," as part of the then fashionable temperance movement.

Given the chance the wood-choppers, cab-washers, crossing-sweepers and costerboys who made up the membership of the Cyprus Boys' Club knew how to enjoy themselves. In 1879 they were driven in charabancs to Thornton Heath (still not engulfed at that time by the outward spread of housing) for a Boys' Own Bean Feast. At another beano a few years later they displayed appetites which would not have disgraced Billy Bunter of Greyfriars fame: having downed 124 lb. of beef, they were still shouting for more. Fortunately for the caterers, they had ample supplies of plum pudding to follow.

Some of the members missed that particular treat because, as the parish magazine explained, they had: "... suffered from over-caution, for being shy of trusting us with their right address they had given us the wrong one and, in consequence, their invitations never reached them so that, to use their own expression, they 'caught a fox'...."

In the early 1880s the Cyprus Boys' Club had seventy names on its books and offered gymnastics on the horizontal bar two nights a week, boxing on two other nights, and classes on Friday nights. "On Saturday nights money is received for the Penny Bank and an effort is to be made to have Temperance Meetings on the first Thursday in each month"—parish magazine, 1882.

1. *Above*. Scene in a London street on a Sunday morning. From the *Illustrated London News* of 1856.

2. *Below*. Crossing sweepers race for a coin; "The Dead Heat," 1865.

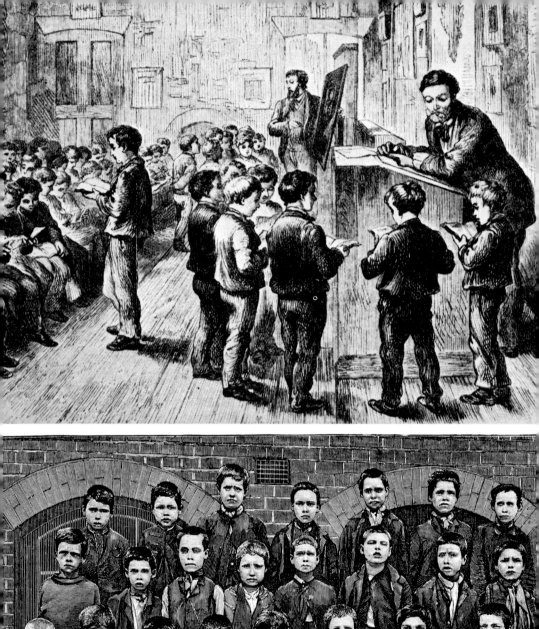

Opposite page: 3. *Top.* A schoolroom near Regent's Park, London, in 1870.
4. *Bottom.* "Waifs and Strays of London"; from the *Illustrated London News.*

This page: 5. *Top left.* A group from the St. Andrew's Home and Club for Working-boys, founded in 1866, on the club's annual camp at Hayling Island in 1889. 6. *Top right.* The crew of the *Merry Andrew* at Sunbury-on-Thames in 1889. 7. *Below.* "Before and after" photographs taken by Dr. Barnado in the early 1870s.

E. E. J. M.
Home for *Working & Destitute Lads.*

No. 27.—ONCE A LITTLE VAGRANT.
(The same lad as on card No. 28.)

E. E. J. M.
Home for *Working & Destitute Lads.*

No. 28.—NOW A LITTLE WORKMAN.
(The same lad as on card No. 27.)

8. *Left*. A display of gymnastics at the Glasgow headquarters of the Boys' Brigade in 1911.

9. *Below*. The Burgess Hill Company of the Boys' Brigade.

In the following year the magazine commented:

"It is of first importance to keep working-boys out of the streets now that the evenings are getting dark, and much pains are needed to make the light of the Club preferable to the outer darkness. Moreover, successfully to manipulate these somewhat rough-and-ready customers no small share of tact is needed, for they can be led by firm and judicious kindness but are by no manner of means inclined to be 'druv' by anybody. It may seem rather a paradox but no work in the parish requires more delicate treatment than has to be exhibited at the Cyprus Club."

It is a tribute to voluntary workers that they had the kind of personality and understanding of boys that was needed and were able to offer bright fires, comfortable chairs and tables arranged with books and games to attract boys into the club out of the night. A circle of perhaps dirty, but bright, intelligent and happy faces as they were read to from some book of adventure was reward enough for these dedicated men.

What was happening in the outer fringes of the capital, as they were then, was also happening in the city centre. In 1878 the St. Andrew's Home for Boys moved to better premises in Dean Street, Soho, which were opened in the evenings as a club for the boys in the neighbourhood. The home had been started twelve years previously after a group of young men of the high Church of England on a mission in the area found a boy sleeping in a sack under a railway arch. It was in the same year that the young Dr. Barnardo discovered boys sleeping out on shed roofs in the East End.

The first St. Andrew's Home for Boys in Market Street, Soho, was a poor place and the project might have perished but for the fact that it captured the interest of George Biddulph, a banker, who was instrumental in getting the Dean Street premises and remained actively connected with the home, and the club which it fostered, for sixty years.

In 1885 home and club moved to a new building on a site given by a benefactor, Mrs. Nathaniel Montefiore, in Great Peter Street, Westminster, where it thrives to this day. At the same time the Dean of Westminster collected £5,072 to pay for the building, and the cheque for this amount which he handed to George Biddulph meant that the home and club started life in its new home free of debt.

St. Andrew's was the pioneer of many boys' club activities. In 1867 it acquired for £11 a ship's cutter and christened it *The Merry Andrew.* Its eight oars were manned by lads in blue jerseys and navy-style caps, who rowed it merrily indeed up river on Saturdays and on camping weekends at Sunbury-on-Thames at Whitsun and later in the century became a familiar feature of the Oxford v. Cambridge Boat Race. The idea of camps under canvas at Hayling Island over the August Bank Holiday weekend was another innovation of the young gentlemen who ran the home and club and believed that fresh air, exercise and adventure were good for the boys.

The club was probably the first to put a soccer eleven of working lads into the field when, on Boxing Day 1875, they played the Hanover Club at

Primrose Hill, yet for the next nine years little football was played because the game had not yet become popular; there were few boys' teams to play against and there was no such thing as a cheap pair of football boots. In an effort to stimulate the game, Mr. Biddulph provided jerseys in stripes of black-and-blue—somewhat reminiscent of bruises, as some wag remarked. By 1890 it was the club's most popular game.

Cricket flourished too, from 1879 onwards, although in the early days most of the fixtures were internal ones like Gentlemen v. Boys—the members of the committee versus the members of the club. Team sports suffered from the lack of playing fields. As one of the members of the Junior Cricket Club put it:

"Now we can get away, after our day at the desk or in the work-shop, from the atmosphere of Soho; oftentimes the reverse of invigorating or refreshing; and breathe fresh air while we stretch our legs. . . . But open spaces in London are few and still fewer the spaces where games may be played. Battersea Park is too far for us and the steamer fare too much for our pockets.* What about Regent's Park? Hundreds of clubs play there so that there is hardly an inch of ground that is not covered with cricketers; and who plays there must expect a few knocks from a friendly (i.e. belonging to your own match) or an unfriendly ball."

But the St. Andrew's cricketers were luckier than most, for the Archbishop of Canterbury let them play in the grounds of Lambeth Palace.

All these activities were reported in *The Chronicle,* first published in July 1883 and probably the first ever boys' club magazine. When club membership started dropping from its original two hundred at about that time, George Biddulph regarded it as a sign that his leadership was becoming too autocratic and promptly handed over the management to a committee of boys elected from among themselves. In an authoritarian age when youngsters were expected by the middle classes to be "seen and not heard," Biddulph's action was not merely far-sighted. He was seventy or eighty years ahead of his time: it was not until after the Second World War that the National Association of Boys' Clubs started recommending boys' committees as a means of managing clubs.

* River bus services were used much more in Victorian London than they are today.

4

What's Brave,
What's Noble

WHAT WAS HAPPENING IN LONDON in the 1870s and 1880s in the development of boys' clubs was mirrored in other towns and cities of England,
although arguments have raged ever since about who did what first. As in
other matters, there was a particular rivalry between the capital and Manchester, the centre of the northern cotton industry. When in 1889 the *Manchester Echo* published an account of Alexander Devine's "first camp for
working boys," the St. Andrew's Boys' Club *Chronicle* in London tartly
commented: "The *Echo* ought to know that St. Andrew's have been camping out for at least twelve years, Whitsuntide at Sunbury and in August at
the seaside."

In 1886, fourteen years after the boys' club was started in Camberwell
New Road in South London, Alexander Devine, who was half Irish and half
Greek, had started a club in Manchester on very similar lines. But although
not a Mancunian himself, he evidently agreed with the local view that Manchester led the world. As late as 1927, in a letter to the editor of *The Boy*,
the journal of the National Association of Boys' Clubs, "Lex", as he was
known, wrote:

"I was acclaimed by the *Daily Chronicle* as the Father of the Boys' Club Movement. It is just a question whether I started the first Boys' Club in England. I
fancy that George Biddulph of the St. Andrew's Boys' Club was before me, and
I think a man named Hill had a Boys' Club in Whitechapel, but I don't know the
nature of these Institutions. But it seems certain that the first real Boys' Club in
England was started in 1886 by myself in Manchester, followed in 1887 by the
Hugh Oldham Boys' Club, and then generally in Lancashire were others almost
immediately. Whether I am the Father of the Boys' Club Movement or not I
don't quite know, but certain it is that I was one of the first men to organise a
Boys' Club, and I was certainly the first man to take boys to camp from Boys'
Clubs in 1887."

Whatever conflicting claims were laid to being first in the field, there can
be no doubting the *need* for boys' clubs in the industrial towns of Victorian
England, as we have already seen.

It was Alexander Devine's experience as a reporter in the Manchester
police court, horrified by the suffering and deprivation which he saw in
daily procession there, which moved him to start his boys' club. He himself

35

had been brought up in a large house whose nursery had a nurse for each child. But his Irish father lost his money and fled from one house to another in London and Manchester pursued by creditors and the bailiffs. Lex was taken away from his preparatory school at fourteen and apprenticed to the printing trade. It was a sad but all too common fate in Victorian times.

But Lex was not the sort to sit about feeling sorry for himself. As a Sunday school teacher at the Rusholme Institute he discovered a talent for the leadership of boys and in 1886, when he was twenty-one, he circulated a letter drawing attention to the need for something to be done for working lads in their early teens: ". . . the most important space in human lifetime . . . the years during which the rest of the life is practically lost or won, a springtime of character at which the mind is most receptive and plastic, in which habits good or evil are being formed for life."

A committee was formed to set up a Working Lads' Institute complete with reading room, gymnasium, evening classes, penny savings bank, Saturday concerts and cricket clubs. A site was found in a disused organ-building works in Mulberry Street, Hulme, and the corporation's Open Space Committee fitted it up with a gymnasium.

On 11th November, 1886, Lord Aberdeen, who had consented to be president, opened the Hulme and Chorlton-on-Medlock Lads' Club, as it was called. Within two years he had opened in Livesey Street his second club, named after Bishop Hugh Oldham, the founder of Manchester Grammar School, and before long he had opened a third club, the Gorton and Openshaw Lads' Club, with all the expense paid by the Crossleys of the famous engine-building firm, one of whose members, Frank Crossley, had vacated his suburban mansion to live in one of the most wretched districts in Manchester. Such behaviour, extraordinary by present standards, was symptomatic of the guilt caused by living in wealth in the midst of squalor. This, combined with evangelical fervour, was the driving force of so much Victorian philanthropy.

As Frank Whitbourne says in *Lex*, his biography of Alexander Devine, the three clubs, co-ordinated by the newly-formed Manchester Working Lads' Association, centred on the founder: ". . . happy, irresistibly charming, sublimely egoistic, worshipped by the boys, 'his boys', gloriously indifferent to the feelings and ideas of his Committee, a heroic worker, a generous master but a very difficult colleague."

Unfortunately, Lex's career with boys' clubs was not without its problems. He could bring in donations and have aristocrats at his feet but he simply could not keep accounts. And with his Boys' Home for Delinquents, named after General Gordon, he over-reached himself. The brave experiment ended in a sordid legal squabble over who should pay the bill for the luncheon served when Lord and Lady Compton opened the home. Lex resigned and spent the rest of his life up to 1930 in various unorthodox phases which included starting a college for public school misfits and being for a time Minister Plenipotentiary in London for Montenegro.

But in Manchester he left behind a lasting monument to his vision and energy. By 1893 fifty boys' clubs were active in Manchester, Salford and neighbouring milltowns like Stockport and Bolton. Moreover, the ten lads' clubs founded in Manchester and Salford between 1886 and the end of the century are still active today.

Another Manchester lads' club, the Adelphi, was founded by Walter Southern in 1888. He taught for an hour a week in a ragged school, and he arranged to meet the boys in his class every Wednesday evening in more informal surroundings. He thought that this way he might get to know the nineteen boys better and "become better acquainted with their everyday life." It turned out to be something more than that and Mr. Southern lived to see the sixtieth anniversary of the club, together with several of the original nineteen members. Their motto was "What's Brave, What's Noble, Let's Do It."

The first meeting place was an old mill whose rusted shafting was still in place at the end of an upper room. The programme for those Wednesday evenings was simple: first a hymn and a prayer, followed by draughts and dominoes and the reading of the illustrated papers, and to close at 9.30 p.m. another hymn and prayer. It sounds simple enough, yet before long the club was open several nights a week and 156 lads had joined. The subscription was 1d. a month.

But Mr. Southern did have his problems. When he tried to hold a singing class the voices of those within the old mill were drowned by the catcalls of the urchins without, shouting through the boards put up to replace the windows they had already broken. Sometimes the roughs broke in and had to be bodily ejected.

Southern seems to have been a stern disciplinarian. Lads who arrived with dirty faces and hands were obliged to wash themselves, or pay a fine. But early boys' club leaders had an uphill task. In *Working Lads' Clubs*, for many years the classic manual of the boys' club movement, Charles Russell wrote:

"Boys liked the clubs well enough, but did not care about paying their membership fees, and there seemed no means of holding them when the attractions of their native street-corners called them back. They did not understand discipline, still less what it meant to be quiet, and where all were 'new boys' there was no foundation of established custom and opinion to support the efforts of those who were trying to keep order. Rough horseplay was common, and general riots, when the excited members broke windows and furniture, blew down the gas-pipes, and pommelled and pelted their officers in the darkness, were by no means unknown. There seemed no reason why draughtsmen should not be used as handy missiles to be hurled at one another on the slightest provocation or why billiard-cues should not be used to poke the fire. And surely there could be no better amusement than to goad to desperation some kindly individual who was anxious to do his best but who failed to appreciate the fact that a lad requires ruling, and generally despises rather than respects a man who fails to punish him when punishment is deserved."

Indeed, Russell prefixed his book with: "Quit you like men, be strong." His own experience of managing boys was gained at Heyrod Street in Manchester, a model for many other clubs. It was founded in 1890 and was still in its infancy when "Jim," as he was known to the boys for some long forgotten reason, became involved in its activities. He was a doctor's son who had to leave Dulwich College and find a job when his father died. Employment on the railways took him first as a clerk to Accrington (where with some of his wild friends he was expelled from the Conservative Club after wrecking the furniture) and then to Manchester as a "business-getter."

How he managed to find time to get business for the railways in the midst of all his other activities is something of a mystery. Apart from rapidly becoming the driving force at Heyrod Street, he was honorary secretary of the Manchester Boys' Brigade, investigated the condition of the poor, wrote books on young gaol-birds and social problems, and campaigned for playing fields. In later life he went to London to become Chief Inspector of Reformatory Industrial Schools.

His ideas about discipline as set out in *Working Lads' Clubs*—"the iron hand in a velvet glove"—make a sharp contrast with George Biddulph's advanced ideas of self-government in his London boys' club. But then Manchester clubs were much larger—Heyrod Street had nine hundred lads on its books—and therefore perhaps more difficult to control.

There was a flowering of boys' clubs in the northern milltowns in the last two decades of the nineteenth century. Indeed, the same was happening all over the country. It was as if clubs were springing up throughout England by some form of telepathy. In 1891 as many as 182 runners from the Livesey Street, Hulme, Bolton, Levenshulme, Adelphi, Salford, Pendleton and Openshaw clubs took part in an inter-club run, and 420 lads sat down to a tea and entertainment afterwards. Different clubs were also looking towards links with each other, and in 1888 twenty-eight London lads' clubs and institutions formed themselves together, in the first federation of such organizations.

In the North, Manchester was not the only city where clubs were springing up. In Liverpool, boys' clubs founded in the 1880s owed much to the generosity of the city merchants, like William Cliff, who built at his own expense a working lads' institute in memory both of a son who had died at the age of eleven and of General Gordon of Khartoum. The foundation stone was laid in 1886, the same year that Alexander Devine opened his first club in Manchester, yet by his own account he knew nothing of what was happening in Liverpool.

Across the River Mersey in the town of Birkenhead, where many of the earliest steam-driven iron ships were built, something else was happening in the year of 1886: the opening of the Shaftesbury Street Boys' Club.

The club grew out of Chester Street, in the shadow of the great shipyards which enabled Britannia to rule the waves. The street was teeming with ragged, barefoot children. Those who lived on the side of the road near the parish church were known as St. Mary's kids, and those on the other side were the Gasworks Gang. William Arthur Norrish, an optician who taught at Sunday school at the Chester Street Mission, could see why they fought one another in the midst of their poverty and squalor. Entirely on his own he started a kind of boys' club which met once a week in a shop in Ivy Street. But he knew it was not enough, and he gathered round him a group of like-minded people who leased from the Chester Street Mission a few rooms above a store which distributed ice to the local fish and meat shops. The Craven Rooms, as they were called, were up two flights of stairs, with a little window on the first landing from which the identity of all comers could be checked.

The new club was named in memory of the Earl of Shaftesbury, one of the greatest of Victorian social reformers, and within a year or two its full title, resonant with the pious overtones of the period, became the Shaftesbury Club for Street Boys and Working Lads. It survives to this day, although in a very different form, in a new building at Mendip Road, Prenton. Published in 1974 was *The Shaftes*, by Leslie Bibby, its president, which tells the story of the Shaftesbury Boys' Club in vivid detail from the beginning. He quotes Norrish from the very first annual report:

"The large and increasing number of half-clad boys whose occupations keep them on the streets in cold or wet weather, without the prospect of a comfortable home to spend their evenings in, and the many poor working lads seen loitering about at night, led to a meeting being held on the 4th December, 1885, to consider what steps should be taken towards opening a club for street boys.... The Club was opened on the 5th January, 1886, by Wm. Laird, Esq.,* who expressed pleasure it gave him to open such an institution, from which the boys would receive so much benefit and afterwards addressed a few words of kind advice to them. About 80 boys were present. The name and address of every one was taken and a ticket of membership given, which is shown every time they enter the Club. It has since been open every Friday for fifteen weeks, from 7.30 to 9 p.m. The number of members is now 270. Their average attendance was 105. The greatest number present on any night was 200. The staff of Helpers, including nine of the Committee, numbers fifteeen, and their average atttendance nine."

The report goes on to mention a reference library with fifty-four volumes donated by well-wishers, and hopes of starting a lending library with an appeal for "suitable books which would be eagerly read by the poor boys (as well as by their toiling parents), who otherwise have few opportunities of reading literature of a healthy character." The games offered ranged from draughts and dominoes for the older lads to quoits and toy building bricks

* The Mayor of Birkenhead and grandson of the founder of Lairds shipyard, later merged with another famous shipbuilding name to become Cammell & Laird.

for their younger brothers, most of whom had never seen such objects before. But the star attraction was the bagatelle board "for use of which the Committee are greatly indebted to Miss Laird." Miss Alice Laird also suggested "Merry Musical Pastimes" and provided free buns and oranges.

The attractions of free buns and oranges to half-starved boys must have been a powerful inducement to attend the club, and no less an attraction were the bright gas lighting and blazing coal fires. "Patching classes" were held where boys were taught to mend their own clothes and boots (if they were fortunate enough to possess a pair). Another popular event was the weekly visit to the Corporation baths, preceded by an obligatory scrub. Most of the members first came to the club dirty and often verminous too.

As in other clubs, Temperance lectures and meetings were a regular part of the programme in that age when gin was the only cheap solace available to working people and the pubs were open from six in the morning until midnight.

Norrish himself, who was only twenty-four when he started the club, was a devout chapel-goer who had vowed never to touch alcohol or tobacco, and he never did throughout his long bachelor life. He was a slenderly-built man with a short, pointed beard. He became in his lifetime almost an institution, deliberately threadbare in his cloth cap, well-worn tweed jacket, knee breeches, long stockings and down-at-heel boots, pedalling his old bicycle about the town. Yet he maintained close contact with the Town Hall (annual meetings of the club were usually held in the Mayor's Parlour at that Victorian edifice) and had a remarkable talent for cornering not only the time but the money of wealthy shipbuilders and merchants.

He kept a store of second-hand clothes, defended his boys when they went before the magistrates for petty thieving and helped them to find jobs in Birkenhead or even—for a few—a new life in Canada. He lived with his parents in a comfortable mid-Victorian semi-detached villa at 29 Bratton Road, Birkenhead, but his heart was in the much less salubrious Chester Street. By the 1890s the club was open six nights a week, concluding every night at nine o'clock with the club song:

> Whatso-er you find to do,
> Do it then with all your might,
> Let your prayers be strong and true,
> Prayer, my lads, will keep you right.

At the annual festival tea party the ladies were in attendance, led by the faithful Miss Laird, distributing button-holes of primroses and prizes of pen-knives, books, footballs, boots or even new suits of clothes, followed by a concert given by "Madame Makin's talented orchestra." It was very much part of the contemporary mood of self-conscious do-goodery, yet as far as Norrish was concerned there were no barriers between the helpers and the boys. He tried to live up to the club's mottoes, first: "See that ye despise not one of these little ones" (Matthew xviii, 10) and from 1889 on: "Bear ye one another's burdens, and so fulfil the law of Christ" (Galatians vi, 2). He had no desire to exclude the very poorest, and fought to keep the admission fee at just 1d. per season (it remained so, in tribute to his memory, until after the Second World War). And in a period of rigid sectarianism, he refused to close his doors to members of denominations other than his own. Many of his boys were Roman Catholics, despite the hostility of local priests to their being members of a non-denominational club.

In Birmingham, on the other hand, the first boys' clubs were Roman Catholic, and indeed the movement started around the cathedral church of St. Chad's. Tom Manning recalled in the late 1940s at the age of eighty-eight how he joined the St. Chad's Club—called the Confraternity—in 1874 when it had been in existence for some years:

"German-style gymnastics were taught in a rackets court in a pub called *The Rackets* next to the Cathedral. A French priest by the name of Father Turin taught fencing, and I remember playing handball against another Catholic boys' organization. St. Chad's School was used as well as the rackets court. No outdoor games were played at the time, but we had a drum-and-fife band, a popular pastime with lads in those days—particularly when a free uniform was provided."

In the latter half of the nineteenth century clubs for boys were springing up in many towns throughout the country, their origins and eventual fate now long forgotten. Tom Manning's memories are all that survived of the history of St. Chad's Club, and how many others were there of which we know nothing? Yet we do know that the same green shoots were sprouting in black cities all over the land: in Birmingham, Nottingham and Bristol, no less than in London, Manchester and Liverpool. Alexander Devine was not, as he liked to believe, the father of the boys' club movement in Britain, but just one of many toilers in the same vineyard.

The story of the Shaftesbury Boys' Club runs parallel with most others of its kind and it is fortunate that its founder kept meticulous records of its early life. No less fortunate is the fact that Leslie Bibby, an official of the club eighty years on, has put the whole story together in such detail, and we shall return to it in the later chapters of this book. It is the story of just one club in a northern shipbuilding town, but in many ways it is the story of the boys' club movement as a whole.

5
An Eton
Playing Field

WEALTHY VICTORIAN PARENTS sent their sons to public schools as much to
mix with other boys of their own class and to develop their characters as
for education in its narrower sense. Seven or eight years acquaintance with
Greek and Latin grammars and healthy participation in cricket and rowing
produced the public school man, easy in the assurance that he was by right
a leader of men, and not ready to be questioned by his inferiors.

Developing a social conscience was not part of the formal curriculum but
there were headmasters who made it their business to impress upon their
top-hatted, stiff-collared boys that they were a privileged minority kept at
school well into their teens, unlike most boys, who had to start earning their
bread as soon as they were physically able and certainly by the time they
were thirteen. One of these was Dr. Arnold, the reforming headmaster of
Rugby School, who wrote towards the end of his life: "I would give anything to be able to organize a Society for drawing public attention to the
state of the labouring classes throughout the Kingdom." But it was the
Rev. Edward Thring of Uppingham School who originated the idea of Public
School Missions in the belief that "the rich boys must learn to help the
poor boys." From 1864 onwards his school contributed towards the support
of a boys' home in Regent's Park and adopted parishes in the East End
of London, first in North Woolwich and later in Poplar. In 1876
Winchester founded an East End mission at All Hallows, in the London
docks area.

But new impetus was given to the movement by Eton in 1880 when it
undertook in the East End a mission district "about the size of Eton Playing
Fields," and containing six thousand people, mostly of the very poorest.
On one side lay the archways of the North London Railway, on the other,
Hackney Marshes. The Rev. Billy Carter took over a little house and under-
taker's shop in Mallard Street which had to serve as church, Sunday school,
meeting place and rough boys' club—the first boys' club set up in London
by a public school.

It seemed that all the Old Etonians who came to help run the club were
"wet bobs," as the lads called the rowing enthusiasts, and as it happened
the River Lea was at hand for rowing practice. E. M. S. Pilkington, who

wrote of his experiences in Hackney Wick in *An Eton Playing Field*, published in 1896, said in a message to Eton boys:

"There are lots of boys who have just as good a right to amusement and instruction as you and we have, but at the age of 13 they start to earn their living by long hours of work at wretched rates of pay, and at 18 they settle down to hard work for a bare existence. Come along and make friends with them. Then you can do almost anything with them and a lot for them. You'll learn a lot that will be useful to you whatever you are going to do in life and you'll probably enjoy it. We have, anyway."

Those who took up the invitation were perhaps surprised to discover that East End boys of their own age, however different their accents and conventions might have been, were, in the jargon of the age, "decent fellows and good sports."

Pilkington and other OEs lived in a small house in Hackney Wick for part of the year, having first destroyed the inevitable bed bugs. Apart from rowing, Pilkington was keenly interested in swimming, but to teach the boys to swim involved getting up at four o'clock in the morning, since that was the only time available to them. Three days a week in the summer months his window was pelted with pebbles at that unearthly hour by pupils eager to plunge into the heavily polluted Hackney Cut, the only place that was available to them.

Pilkington was the very best type of Old Etonian, a "proper Toff" as East Enders would say, generous with his time and money to people less fortunate than himself. He was also active in the St. Andrew's Boys' Club in Soho where it was his habit to give any promising boy swimmer a book of a hundred tickets for Westminster Baths and tell him to ask for more when he had used them. He knew that a boy couldn't possibly develop his potential if he could swim only on the one night a week allotted to the club.

Not all men of his class found it as easy as he did to get along with Cockney boys, with their scant respect for their social superiors and their cheeky manners. The Rev. Carter recalled:

"We found that during the winter after a time the indoor games began to pall, and the boys became somewhat restive and rowdy. One not uncommon form of this rowdiness was blowing down the gas-pipe, and so putting the whole house into darkness. This happened not once or twice only and then there was a general bally-rag, the result being what can be imagined under such circumstances. On two or three occasions it was found necessary to close the Club for a few days, when the boys came round again expressing their penitence for what had taken place."

Members of the Cadet Corps at Eton passed on their uniforms when they left school to the boys in the drum-and-fife band at Hackney Wick. The club library was started by an Old Etonian who also happened to be a member of the Macmillan publishing family. In many such ways the links between Eton and the East End were formed. Etonians learned to sing

"Break the News to Mother" and "The Ship Never Returned" as well as their own Boating Song.

Where Eton led Harrow was not far behind. Preaching in the University Church at Oxford in 1883, the headmaster of Harrow School, Montague Butler, brandished from the pulpit a copy of *The Bitter Cry of Outcast London*, a searing pamphlet published by the London Congregational Union, and thundered: "God grant it might not startle only but be read and pondered by thoughtful brains as well as by feeling hearts. . . . God grant that *here* in this great home of eager thought and enlightened action and generous friendship the bitter cry of outcast London may never seem intrusive or uninteresting but that year by year her choicest sons may be arrested by it."

In fact earlier that year some of London's choicest sons wearing Old Harrovian ties and dog collars had ventured into Notting Dale, not far from the school in distance but light years away in other respects, William Law, a famous cricketer of the day, was appointed missioner to this "low-lying, low-living area" inhabited by Gypsies and hard-drinking Irish brick-makers, whose children were veritable savages. The Hammersmith & City Railway had been built across it in the 1860s with the inevitable further desolation of an already dreary landscape, but there were still large numbers of piggeries in the area. Indeed, the new station at Latimer Road was known as Piggery Junction. The rough women of Notting Dale eked out their meagre family budgets by taking in the dirty linen of the more prosperous neighbouring areas, earning their particular area the nickname of Soapsuds Island.

The Harrovians quickly established a plethora of clubs, including one for Small Boys as well as Just Boys. Arthur Bryant, an Old Harrovian who wrote a booklet about the mission, made this appeal:

"There is no philanthropy at the Harrow Mission: we are all very proud and independent. If you can teach dancing or piano-playing, or coach our young Meads and Hendrens in the summer, or help to improve the standard of our little boys' billiards, so much the better. That will be only putting back a few of the good things Harrow gave you. But if you are a mere fool, like the present writer—and possibly you are—there is plenty to do. You can get beaten at ping-pong, you can amuse the audience by your ignorance of voice production at our concerts, and you can enliven our dances by your presence; if you are a good dancer you will be most popular; and, if bad, you will provide plenty of quiet and innocent amusement. You might also pursuade your clever sister or cousin to come with you and teach piano-playing or dancing, or whatever it is that you—a mere male—are incapable of teaching. But what is needed above all is friendliness; and that anyone, however unaccomplished, who has a human heart inside him can give. It is an easy thing for Harrovians to learn to know and appreciate the men and boys of the Dale: they are so simple and loyal and lovable. Unless you are a prig or a snob, or an ardent young reformer casting out motes—and Harrow does not produce many such—you will find plenty in common with the 'Mission' folk—perhaps, if you are very fortunate, you will find everything. It is not the mixing of 'Classes' that is needed, but the oblivion of class, if only for one hour in the week, in the light of a common humanity. Any evening will do—just come down and see for yourself. Probably you will want to come again. It is Harrow's work; the one place where Harrovians can be certain of meeting on common ground in London. True, there is no hill, no bill-yard, no first or second bell: yet the spirit of Harrow is here all right, among the mean streets and alley-ways of this forgotten region. *Stet Fortuna Domus.*"

From 1880 onwards public school missions, with their attendant boys' clubs, multiplied vigorously: Marlborough moved into the newly developing area of Tottenham in North London and later into the railway town of Swindon, which was nearer the school; Charterhouse interested itself in the Tabard Street area in South London, an area which had a death rate nearly twice that of the rest of the city (over 22 per 1,000 of population, which in itself was appalling enough), and Wellington tried to civilize the costerboys around East Street, Walworth; Tonbridge School, Felsted and Trinity College, Oxford, started other missions and towards the end of the decade Rugby School Home Mission came into being as a boys' club, later adding an "Old Guard Department" for the club's old boys and acquiring a seaside weekend and holiday home at New Romney. The boys' club was moved into premises in Birmingham.

In Bristol, where the slave trades of sugar and rum gave way in the nineteenth century to thriving chocolate and tobacco industries, a new public school was founded in the 1860s on Clifton Downs high above the teeming slums of the city. The prosperous merchants' families lived on the heights, too. No tradesmen's sons were admitted to Clifton but the boys were encouraged to take an interest in lads who were literally, as well as socially, at a lower level than themselves. The first headmaster, Dr. Percival, selected a mission area—part of the parish of St. Barnabas beside the River Frome—which defeated the first curate. He resigned within a year.

But in 1881 the college found the right man for its mission in the Rev. Thomas William Harvey. He was a grammar school, not a public school, product and he did not make a particularly good impression at his interview for the post. But many other candidates who had come forward had gone quickly away again after one look at the place, so Harvey was appointed.

As a Christian Socialist, the new curate was very keen that the mission should serve as a real link between the public school and the working class community around it, where people were suffering from low wages, over-work and bad housing. The market gardens of his district were being swallowed up by yet more bricks and mortar, jerry-built little boxes liable to flooding when the waters of the Frome were swollen with rainwater. But at least some of the more intractably lawless elements were being replaced by hard-working and God-fearing people, although the inevitable coffee shop in the cause of Temperance quickly became a haunt of thieves and other ruffians.

Yet Tommy Harvey, as he was known, was not the only remarkable character sent out by the public schools in the 1880s to bridge the gulf between them and the common streets. Another was Robert Radclyffe Dolling, a portly Ulster man with the ability to make contact with ordinary boys. As warden of the St. Martin's Postmen's League house in Southwark he was known as "Brother Bob" not only to the postmen but to all the shoe-blacks, newsboys and urchins of the surrounding streets, for whom he found hot baths, teas and clothing. To him their rags suggested wings and he called them his "angels."

In the mid-1880s "Brother Bob" was appointed by the headmaster of Winchester to take over the school's mission in Landport, a poor area of Portsmouth noted for its slaughterhouses, brothels and a high ratio of fifty-one pubs for five thousand people. He brought home to the boys of Winchester the reality of life in such a deprived area, vividly described in the book *Ten Years in a Portsmouth Slum*, which he wrote and published in 1897 to pay off the debt on St. Agatha's, the church he had built. Alas, at that time he was not allowed to officiate in it, having incurred the wrath of the Bishop with the "third altar" which he had set up for Masses for soldiers and sailors killed in far-flung parts of the Empire. The Church of England was strict on matters of doctrine and procedure and Father Dolling had not made things any easier for himself by allowing a *Socialist priest*, Stewart Headlam, to talk politics from the pulpit of St. Agnes. He had resigned twice in his ten years in Portsmouth and his second resignation was accepted.

Dolling had charisma, and he was as much of a success with the Winchester public school boys as he was with the slum boys of Landport. Like Tommy Harvey in Bristol, he was on the side of the underdog, encouraging the shop assistants of Portsmouth to form a union and fight the few greedy shop-keepers who would not agree to early closing and kept young girls and lads working for sixteen hours a day. He had a fierce hatred of people who sought profit from the degradation of other human beings: the publicans, pimps and slum landlords who thrived and grew fat in a city where sailors freely spent their pay when they came ashore.

His special pride was his gymnasium, converted from a disused Baptist chapel, "a splendid property ... a gallery all round, square pews, three-decker pulpit, a font for immersions and two dead ministers buried in the middle." He hadn't a penny, but he had to buy it. The departed congregation refused to pay for the reinterment of the ministers, so the boys using the gymnasium "stamped over their heads as they lay fast asleep."

The gymnasium became the headquarters of the various clubs of lads and young men in Portsmouth and Dolling wrote:

"How many has it won from the awful fascinations of the public-houses, from the vulgarity and worse of the sing-song room, from the delirium of gambling, from hideous forms of sin, impossible for those who desire to achieve a wholesome mind in a wholesome body! From all parts of the world strong, healthy, self-respecting men bless and praise God for the old gymnasium in Clarence Street."

By the 1890s the great wave of public school evangelizing in the slums had passed its peak, although Haileybury launched a "rough boys club" in Stepney and, finding that somewhat too condescending, they then converted it into an army cadet company of which the future Labour Prime Minister, Clement Attlee, was an officer.

In the "Naughty Nineties," the *fin de siècle* when Victorian complacency reached its zenith, snobbery became rampant in the public schools. The old school tie exclusivism which did their image so much damage in the next century became an article of faith and few schools continued to impress on their boys that other lads of their age who happened to be born in Bethnal Green or Bermondsey were of the same race as themselves. There was a drift away from the church-going, family prayers and ascetic Christian morality which had been the moving spirit behind the public school missions.

Like many boys' club leaders Alexander Devine, although he had not been to a public school himself, much admired this system of education. In the running of many of the early clubs it is possible to see an imitation of the system introduced by Dr. Arnold at Rugby, based on self-government, thereby placing a responsibility for leadership in the hands of the senior boys. There was also in the early clubs a mild form of "fagging," which required the new boys to sweep the clubroom floor, make the fires and so on. Until the first clubs were formed, the majority of boys had no such "character training."

The public schools played a significant part in the formative years of the boys' club movement from the highest of motives but they worked in isolation from the rest of the movement and failed to build many lasting bridges between themselves and the back streets of the industrial towns. In retrospect, it appears that they failed to seize a golden opportunity to play their full part in the coming social revolution.

Yet their influence was undoubtedly felt, as is shown by the closing words in Charles Russell's *Working Lads' Clubs*, written in 1908:

"It will probably have struck some of our readers that many of the results which we claim for boys' clubs are precisely those which have made our public schools the special pride of the country. The significance of this in relation to the Nation may be appreciated when we reflect that if our rulers in the nineteenth century were educated at Eton, our rulers of the twentieth century are being educated in the elementary schools. If it is largely the public-school spirit which has made England great in the past, any means by which a similar spirit may be fostered in the boys who leave the elementary schools at the very age when some of the monied classes are entering on the most valuable years of their school career, is of incalculable importance."

6

The Oxford Connection

To THE ORDINARY WORKING BOY in Queen Victoria's time Oxford and Cambridge meant little more than an annual boat race on the River Thames, a hugely popular event well into the twentieth century. He knew that Oxford were Dark Blues and Cambridge Light Blues but the chances were that he had never met anyone who actually went to either of these ancient seats of learning, where the emphasis seemed as much on rowing and games as on scholarship. Oxford and Cambridge, like the public schools, were for the sons of gentlemen, and as such were strongholds of upper class male privilege.

The right to high living was regarded as part of this privilege. In the 1870s a Royal Commission reporting on Oxford had referred to the expensive tastes of undergraduates who spent £40 a year at the tobacconists, dined lavishly at inns and clubs and gave more of their time and energy to riding and hunting, gambling and "sensual vice" than they gave to their books. This life style was worlds apart from the poverty and deprivation of the backstreets of London. For most Victorian undergraduates at Oxford a visit to the East End was "slumming," with its connotation of a visit to the zoo to observe the curious habits of the strange animals there. Others, however, when they came down from the university, went to live among the East Enders and started to colonize places like Stepney as early as the 1860s. Thus was born the Settlement Movement, defined with Teutonic precision by a German academic, Dr. Werner Picht, in a book published in England in 1914 as "a colony of members of the upper classes, formed in a poor neighbourhood, with the double purpose of getting to know the local conditions of life from personal observation, and of helping where help is needed."

At the start the movement was not so much the conscious colonization of the East End as a flowering among Oxford men of the social idealism preached by Carlyle and Ruskin. Some of the upper class newcomers to the slums lived more or less as their poor neighbours did. Others, who liked to perform their good works in comfort, set up house in the East End, complete with their own servants.

This sort of thing had been fashionable for twenty years before the decision was taken at Balliol in January 1884 to found a permanent universities' settlement in Whitechapel. This was the birth of Toynbee Hall, a memorial residence built in the Elizabethan style on to a portion of a disused boys' industrial school in Commercial Street, within easy reach of the newly completed Inner Circle underground station at Aldgate. The Reverend Barnett, vicar of St. Jude's, Whitechapel, moved into Toynbee Hall with his indomitable wife, Henrietta, and fourteen young university men, five of them wearers of dog collars.

It is difficult to assess what the local populace made of them at first, although an obvious criticism was that the "varsity" men had set themselves up in Whitechapel like missionaries in an African village.

Barnett's aims were clear. He wanted to harness the rising tide of Socialism which had so alarmed the middle classes in Herne Hill, Clapham and Tooting. If he did not succeed (and it might have been argued that he helped Socialism forward) at least he played no small part in channelling it away from the bloody revolution.

Waldo McGillicuddy Eagar, an Oxford man who played a large part in the formation of the National Association of Boys' Clubs, recalls in *Making Men*, published in 1953 to mark the first twenty-five years of that organisation, a conversation with Alfred Salter, the leader of the Labour Party in Bermondsey, just after the First World War: "He jumped off his bicycle to say: 'Hallo! Back again to the club? Delighted to see you!' Then hesitated and added, with his enormous laugh: 'But I don't know that I ought to be—you Oxford men have made the class-war impossible in Bermondsey.' "

But that was a World War and a lost generation later. In 1884, the same year that Toynbee Hall was established as an undenominational effort of both Oxford and Cambridge, the high churchmen set up Oxford House in Bethnal Green and put their intention uncompromisingly in their first annual report:

"... to supply a headquarters for those University men who are anxious to understand the real condition of the artisan and labouring classes in East London, who are ready to devote a certain amount of time and trouble to studying the problem on the spot, and who are prepared to take part in the furtherance of Christianity and education and the bettering of the moral and sanitary conditions of the various neighbourhoods.

"Colonization by the well-to-do seems indeed the true solution of the East-end question . . . . for the problem is, how to make the masses realise their spiritual and social solidarity with the rest of the capital and of the kingdom: how to revive their sense of citizenship, with its privileges which they have lost, and its responsibilities which they have forgotten. Among these privileges should be education, rational amusement and social intercourse; and these can be best supplied by Local Clubs, with their various guilds, classes and societies. Among the duties, on the other hand, which require to be revived, thrift and prudence stand pre-eminent; and thrift and prudence can only be taught by men who will associate with the people and thus induce them to face the elementary laws of economy. The sympathy and example of educated people living in their midst does more good in all these ways than the foundation of any number of new charitable institutions. Destitute London requires their personal help . . . what is especially wanted is a living contribution of energy, pluck and enthusiasm from the imperishable youth of Oxford to a work which grows and expands with every honest effort to perform it."

Bethnal Green was the scene of more activity in the 1890s. In 1889 the Prince of Wales came down to open a furniture factory converted into a boys' club and named in memory of a well-known cricketer, Herbert Webbe, who had also lived and worked among the people of the East End. Membership was limited to a hundred of the grubby and noisy lads who besieged the place and from among those a committee was selected. Two of the boys' committee had the nighty task of supervising the others and reporting any insubordination to the club leader.

The managers of the Webbe Institute quickly found that gymnastics, cricket, swimming and outings had a greater appeal to the boys than history and writing classes. They persevered, however, and in the second winter added shorthand and arithmetic, the passports to office employment, to the subjects taught. There were also the inevitable drum-and-fife band and Bible classes. The manners and general appearance of the boys was markedly improved and at the same time the Oxford men started talking naturally of "we" instead of "us and them."

The club worked on the principle that few boys were interested in everything, but all were interested in something, and by the end of the century it had a band, cricket, football, gymnastic, swimming and boxing clubs, harriers, life-saving classes, lectures and Shakespeare reading societies, discussion groups, reading, writing and carving classes, chess and draughts clubs, a black and white minstrel troupe and a company of army cadets, as well as camps and outings. There was a penny bank and a sick fund.

According to Eagar, "Whit-Monday outings to Oxford, where undergraduates entertained the Webbe boys in their rooms and took them out on the river, broke down class consciousness on both sides. Oxford men found the Bethnal Green boys to be decent, friendly youngsters and the Bethnal Greeners found that the supposed stand-offishness of the 'Oxford gentlemen' or the 'Oxford blokes'—both phrases were current—was largely shyness, which soon yielded to their Cockney wit and matter-of-factness." In *Making Men* he describes how on Whit Monday 1904 he entertained three such boys:

"As the tenant of two of the smallest rooms in the College I was surprised when, on going into the bedroom to brush their hair, one asked how many people slept there; *he* was surprised when I said that I had it to myself. That boy sent me afterwards a cardboard box of his own making, encrusted with seashells and with a photo of himself glued to the lid. When I inquired for him on paying my first visit to the House, he was untraceable; his family had 'flitted by moonlight' to escape the rent, a common family exercise in those days. Another was an extremely likeable, athletic lad who talked to me of the differences between Bethnal Green and Oxford, and in later years became strongly political. The third boy, a wiry, good-looking 14-year-old, told me that his job was in a fur factory; when I went to Bethnal Green at the end of the year, he had gone to hospital with phthisis, said to be due to his work. He died of the disease the following year. Indignation sharpened my dawning interest in social conditions, as it undoubtedly did that of many men of my generation, some of whom found satisfaction in social work, while others, such as C. R. Attlee,* looked for political remedies."

In the 1880s, Oxford was taken from Whitechapel and Bethnal Green across the newly-opened Tower Bridge into the waterfront area of Bermondsey by the University's Evangelicals. The driving force behind the mission of the 1890s was a little man with a pointed beard, John Stansfeld, who had begun his working life as an office boy, become a clerk in Customs and Excise and by a great deal of late night reading by gaslight and candle had qualified as a doctor and achieved a Bachelor of Arts degree at Oxford.

His Oxford Medical Mission set up a number of boys' clubs in Bermondsey, a crowded, ugly place of wharves and warehouses, tanneries and food factories, with tenements and miserable little houses in between. Stansfeld was known to everyone as "The Doctor", and Alexander Paterson describes him and the Oxford Medical Mission in Abbey Street in *The Doctor and the O.M.M.*, published in 1910:

"The streets were full of boys every night, whose spare time was being wasted, whose characters were being formed by any chance combination of instinct, passion or convention. Every evening from the Mission windows (and especially when they were broken) could be seen a processsion of boys in noisy gangs on their way to the Star Music Hall at the top of the street. A Boys' Club was declared essential, a pair of gloves and a bagatelle table were hurriedly procured, and the ground-floor was invaded by a crowd of ready members. Now and then the Doctor would think the tumult beyond the limits of family life, and would dodge round the partition, wave a thermometer, and eject two of the biggest without mercy. Even in these early days it was the custom to close the Club each evening with family prayers and the Sunday Bible-class grew to such a size as to make these first headquarters seem very small. A shed was built at the back, but this was in turn too small for the number of boys who were taking refuge in this small Mission. Opposite was an old corset factory, big and ugly, with strong floors and large rooms. The rent was stiff, but the Doctor was inexorable, and a move was made to the new building, which was six times as large and quite as uncomfortable. Here the big Abbey Street Club sprang into being, every room humming with life, and the Doctor in a white coat dealing with a growing stream of patients on the ground-floor. On the top floor, wooden partitions grew up, and produced a small number of bedrooms. Oxford men began to trickle down a little faster, and soon counted themselves lucky to secure a bed."

The Doctor still earned his living as a clerk in the Civil Service, going across the bridge every day from Bermondsey wearing the top hat which was at that time the badge of City men, and returning in the evening to

* Clement Attlee, who in 1945 became Prime Minister of the first Labour Government in Britain to achieve a working majority.

attend to the dispensary and the club, visiting the sick and the dying in the small hours, to plan extensions and dream of camps and convalescent homes.

Having civilized the boys of Abbey Street who at first broke the windows of the mission, the Oxford men moved into Dockhead, the home of Bill Sikes and Nancy in *Oliver Twist*. Two other boys' clubs came into being. Behind the rough exteriors of street boys, character and spirit was discovered. As one society woman who occasionally visited the club reported to a no doubt astonished luncheon party in the West End: "Bermondsey boys have *poise* —as much poise as Eton boys. They put you entirely at your ease from the moment you enter the Club."

But not all the good work in the slums south of the Thames was done by Oxford men. Cambridge colleges, not to be outdone, deployed their missions all over South London in the 1880s and 90s, venturing into Walworth, Rotherhithe, Camberwell and Battersea. The Cambridge Medical Mission was an off-shoot of its Oxford counterpart.

Some of the more radical Cambridge men objected to the term *mission*, with its patronizing overtones, and wanted instead to call themselves the Friends of Labour or even Union of Workmen. But missions they remained. And like their friendly rivals from Oxford they discovered the value of boys' clubs in civilizing the heathen. Canon Peter Green, recalling St. John's College Mission in Walworth in the *Church Times* in 1950, wrote:

"The Mission had a large hall fitted as a gymnasium with a platform at one end.... The members fell into five classes, recognizable by their smell. The 'layers-on' and 'takers-off' from the big printing works smelled of printers' ink; boys from the boot factories smelled of blacking; those from the jam and pickle works smelled of raspberry jam for two months and of aromatic vinegar for ten; lads from the market smelled of fish and were covered with rough salt—a visitor said that sitting next to one at a boxing match was 'like clinging to the supports of a pier'—and the fifth class of nondescripts, errand boys, van boys, beer bottlers and workers at the tan yards would and did smell of many things."

Whatever their distinctive odour, these South London boys, as the worthy canon discovered, faced life with "courage and cheerfulness and unfailing humour and a wonderful capacity for loyalty and affection."

7

Play up! Play up!
And Play the Game

THE CULT OF ORGANIZED TEAM GAMES spread rapidly through the public schools in the mid-Victorian period: in the early 1860s a boy at Harrow might spend fifteen to twenty hours a week on the cricket field. It then spread to the middle classes and artisans, and in the last two or three decades of the century it was transmitted, as we have seen, to working class boys in their clubs by the missionaries from the public schools and universities. By that time the playing of games loomed large in the forming of character and what was widely recognized as that indefinable public school spirit. Phrases such as "It's not cricket" and "Play the game" had become the very epitome of Englishness.

"Play up! Play up! And Play the Game," a line from Sir Henry Newbolt's poem *Vitai Lampada*, summarized the orthodox Victorian view of public school and university. But the missionaries who ventured into the slums in the latter half of the nineteenth century found boys who had no chance of learning to play the game in its literal sense; no swimming baths, no gymnasia, no playing fields, no place of their own in which to meet.

These amenities had to be provided before a start could be made on introducing town boys to the cult of games. As Charles Russell rightly claimed, without the lads' club movement there would probably have been no playing fields movement either. It certainly did not occur to the merchants and industrialists who created the towns as places for the working classes to sleep in when they were not at work, that they might also need somewhere to play. Nottingham, an honourable exception, as early as 1845 set aside 130 acres for public recreation, and the first public park in England was opened at Birkenhead in 1843.

But the movement to provide playing fields for boys really got under way in London. The London Playing Fields' Committee, formed in 1890, had among its members such distinguished and far-sighted men as the Earl of Aberdeen, Canon Barnett of Toynbee Hall and Quintin Hogg, the founder of the Regent Street Polytechnic. They brought together a variety of clubs and open spaces committees, as well as the Surrey and Marylebone Cricket Clubs.

The committee found that for every acre of open field there were a thousand youths clamouring to play on it. As one of the members, Alfred Lyttleton, said at the first public meeting:

"Enthusiasm is dulled when clubs fail week after week to get a pitch, when square leg of one match collides with point in another, or when players have to decide which of three footballs on one ground is their own. Playing-fields are as essential for the boys of the London streets as for the Public School boy or the undergraduate. The physique of the town-bred man is deteriorating; the figures of acceptance for the Army and Police prove that. Lack of opportunity for healthy exercises produces the loafer and the gambler. Playing-fields are not a magical cure-all for all the evils of modern civilization, but of their benefits no sane man can raise a question."

If anyone doubted the truth of Lyttleton's remarks, their complacency was shattered at the end of the decade when one in three volunteers for the Army in the Boer War had to be turned away from the recruiting offices because of their poor physique and low state of health. The clerk and the shop assistant, as well as the legions in the factories, had wasted their youth in badly ventilated, ill-lit workplaces.

In the golden sunset of the nineteenth century, when the British Empire was at its zenith, boys in the capital of that Empire had to play their games (unless, like the lads of St. Andrew's Boys' Club, they were able to borrow the grounds of Lambeth Palace by kind permission of the Archbishop) on pitches that were, according to Lyttleton, "more fit for chamois or goats than for cricketers."

The main problem of public school men who interested themselves in developing sport in working class areas was, according to Eagar, to "overcome the Win, Tie or Wrangle spirit, and inculcate the basic idea of sportsmanship to be taken up later by the elementary schools. That they did so is perhaps the greatest achievement of the Boys' Club Movement, for it was a vital necessity of the democracy then in formation."

The beginnings of that democracy were apparent even in the 1880s when, a few weeks after the traditional Eton v. Harrow cricket match at Lord's, another Eton v. Harrow match was played, but this time between teams drawn from the "rough lads" in those schools' respective mission clubs in Hackney Wick and Notting Dale. Public school and university matches on that hallowed turf were thought to be a model of what all such matches should be and were watched by crowds of mustachioed and monocled young men in beribboned straw boaters and college blazers. The handful of Old Etonians and Old Harrovians who watched the second match on a warm August day must surely have felt a shiver of apprehension of the social changes which would erode their traditional exclusiveness.

But, of course, it was football, the kind played with a round ball, that became the main sporting passion of working boys, not cricket. As late as 1855 the *Boys' Own Book* rated football as worth only a brief mention, as a game played with a "large ball made of light materials—a blown bladder or an india-rubber ball cased with leather is the best," while the rules and history of cricket—"a sport paramount"—ran to more than twenty pages.

At that time, country lads used a pig's bladder, blown up by mouth and without any covering of leather, as a football. They also had a habit of putting dried peas and beans inside the bladder, so that it made a loud rattling sound as it was kicked about.

The game was played at Eton and Harrow and at Cambridge—the latter combining with a number of Sheffield clubs to form the Football Association in 1863—but it was not until the 1880s and 1890s that the watching of professional football on a Saturday afternoon caught on with the British working man. For him it was not something to play but something to watch, to gamble on and to discuss in the pub in the evening. For his son it provided a new set of heroes and the dream that one day he might himself reach the same pinnacle. Thus, despite the efforts of police and magistrates to stop street football, which could be dangerous to both private property and to life and limb where there was heavy traffic, it was in the street that most working boys' games were played. There was nowhere else. These hooligans, as they seemed to the respectable Victorians, had neither a proper football nor boots; their goalposts were lamp-posts or dustbins, and in the absence of a referee, the game would more often than not degenerate into a pitched battle between the two gangs. Yet they identified themselves with particular professional teams and individually famous players in their street games.

The boys' clubs alone provided a way for working boys to play football in a proper jersey and "nicks," on a field with real goalposts. By the early 1900s inter-club competitions were well established and Charles Russell at the Heyrod Street Lads' Club in Manchester had nine or ten football teams. More than a quarter of a century had passed since eleven lads of St. Andrew's Boys' Club trooped on to a field at Primrose Hill in their black-and-blue striped jerseys.

The Big Game—that other kind of football described in *Tom Brown's Schooldays* which later was named after the school which invented it— retained its upper class image in London and most other parts of England. In Bristol, however, the Broad Plain Lads' Club, founded in 1894 by a local accountant, played rugger with distinction, as well as soccer and cricket. Unlike soccer and the rugby league game, rugby union remained an amateur game played by enthusiasts as much for its social aspects as its intrinsic values, and perhaps for that reason failed (at least until it became popular on television a hundred years later) to attract a substantial following outside the clubs, certain public schools and universities and, of course, in Wales, Scotland and Ireland.

For the most part, the sports and pastimes taken up by the largely working class boys' clubs mirrored the rather curious class divisions of English sport as a whole. Lawn tennis, an invention of the 1870s, remained well into the twentieth century the preserve of the middle classes, accompanied by tea in the leafy shade of suburban tennis clubs or country gardens and the well-known cry of "Anyone for tennis?," while the more leisurely croquet was positively aristocratic. After an initial burst of upper class enthusiasm, cycling became—with the advent of pneumatic tyres, light frames and acetylene lamps in the 1890s—an essentially working class pursuit.

Athletics, track events and cross-country running were as popular in boys' clubs, most of whom had their harriers, as they were in the public schools and universities in the second half of the nineteenth century. Boys' clubs held paper chases from Notting Dale and Kensington to Harrow on August Bank Holidays, at the time when Winston Churchill was pursuing his undistinguished early career there, and were entertained at the school afterwards.

But of all team sports played in England, cricket was the one which most successfully spanned the class barriers, whilst at the same time managing to maintain the proper distinction of Gentlemen v. Players. On village greens, or the new playing fields, tradesmen's and labourers' sons were able, if not to appear immaculately clad in white, at least to pit their skills at batting, bowling and fielding against the sons of gentlemen from the public schools.

Money was not the least of the reasons why so many outdoor pursuits retained an air of exclusivity. "Huntin', shootin', and fishin' " were pastimes of the rich. So, too, were golf, ski-ing and yachting. Rowing, despite the efforts of E. M. S. Pilkington and the St. Andrew's Boys' Club in the *Merry Andrew*, was still monopolized by Eton, Oxford and Cambridge, cheered on at the Henley Regatta—one of the great social events of the Season—by nostalgic Old Boys in college caps, straw boaters and striped blazers, escorting sylph-like young ladies under parasols. Swimming, on the other hand, was for everyone, as the Hackney Wick boys proved on their early morning dips in the filthy Cut. All that was needed was a pair of bathing drawers, or if the place and time were right, nothing at all.

Indoor games tended to polarize among the various social classes, too. Squash and fives, which both require a specially built court, did not spread far beyond the public schools and universities. Billiards, snooker, draughts and table tennis were the most popular recreations in boys' clubs. A second-hand billiards table costing from £25 upwards was a sizeable investment for a poor club, but by charging 2s. a night in fees from the boys the club leader could make it eventually pay for itself, and at least it kept them away from the low billiards halls and saloons which were a feature of the age. Skill at snooker and billiards was held, in some quarters, to be evidence of a mis-spent youth.

The chronic lack of open spaces and playing fields in the cities led to some ingenious solutions. The Bernhard Baron Jewish Settlement founded by Basil Henriques in London had a miniature football pitch on the roof, surrounded by a high wire fence to keep the ball from falling to the street below. Some clubs in the north of England went in for netball, an imported version of the basketball popular in many of the large American Boys' Clubs. The advantage of netball was that it could be played in any reasonably sized gymnasium.

One indoor sport which proved to be peculiarly adaptable to boys' clubs and which they fostered on a wide scale, becoming a veritable nursery of professional champions, was boxing. Since fighting came naturally to most working lads, the provision of boxing gloves and a punchball or bag was quickly discovered by most clubs to be a natural outlet for the excess energy and combative instincts of their rougher members. As with snooker, the promotion of boxing contained a moral element, for it was felt desirable to keep boys away from sleazy gyms where the hangers-on and touts associated with professional boxing gathered. As Dr. G. Stanley Hall put it in his book *Adolescence*, published in the early 1900s:

"Like dancing, it should be rescued from its evil associations and its educational force put to do moral work. . . . At its best, it is indeed a manly art, a superb school for quickness of eye and hand, decision, force of will, and self-control. The moment this is lost stinging punishment follows. Hence it is the surest of all cures for excessive irascibility, and has been found to have a most beneficent effect upon a peevish or unmanly disposition."

Singlesticks, a cheaper version of the foils used in the noble art of fencing, were popular in many Victorian boys' clubs, although Charles Russell warned, presumably from experience at Heyrod Street: "Amongst boys, however, it very often degenerates into horseplay, and for this reason foils are preferable, if a selection has to be made between the different 'weapons'. . . ."

In the gymnasia of the early boys' clubs, exercise with dumb-bells and Indian clubs and on horizontal and parallel bars all helped to improve the physique of the lads bred in the streets, while weight-lifting appealed to those who fancied becoming "strong men." Town boys revelled in muscle-building.

Throughout all these activities which provided an escape for under-privileged boys from the unnatural environment of the towns ran the belief that games taught them fair play, self-reliance, endurance and how to take a beating—lessons which would endure for a lifetime. From the public schools came the practice of bestowing "colours" on those who excelled: a cap for cricket, a jersey or shirt for soccer, an embroidered badge on the vest for physical training, boxing or running. To the boys who won them, they undoubtedly meant as much as they would to an Oxford or Cambridge Blue.

But the lessons of "playing the game" were not always easy to teach. Charles Russell observed:

"Unless and until a fine tradition has been established, junior teams should always be picked by the officers of a club themselves. Young boys—and very often young men too—do not know how to be impartial, and may not hesitate to keep in a team a totally inefficient player if he happens to be a chum of its leading spirits. The cunning with which they will try to get into their team a boy they like personally is often extraordinary, whilst they persistently decry the merits of a better player who does not happen to be one of their set, or, as they say in the North, is not one of their 'click', meaning *clique*. Efficient officers do their utmost to break up these 'clicks', for they often do great harm in a club. In most cases outdoor games furnish the best means of putting an end to them, since a wise officer distributes members of a 'click' among different teams, in which fresh associations and friendships will be formed. For example, a daring, reckless, perhaps evil-living youth of sixteen, the 'cock' of a number of boys of fifteen years of age, and an intolerable nuisance to his club, if put to play with a team whose average age is seventeen, will feel the honour of playing with his elders, and begin to associate with them. He will be no hero to them, and will soon find his right level."

The flourishing of sport in the early boys' clubs was especially important against a background of poor facilities for games in schools. In the 1880s, when education in England became compulsory, local School Boards built new schools up and down the country. The late Victorian board schools, grim and barrack-like, had no playing fields, and only a patch of asphalt where as many as a thousand children had to find an outlet for their energy. The efforts of a few teachers to introduce drill and exercises were frustrated by the extreme poverty of the children. Their parents could barely afford to give them hand-me-down clothes and second-hand boots for everyday wear, let alone gym-vests or football boots for games. When a thousand of them were officially recorded as attending school in want of food, how could they be expected to respond to physical training?

So the elementary schools did the best they could, but teachers and pupils had to wait for half of the twentieth century and two world wars for amenities like playing fields, swimming baths and gymnasia which made sports days on the public school pattern possible. In the meantime the boys' clubs continued to supply the children of the towns with recreation and the occasional breath of fresh country air on outings up the river and to the seaside, or an annual holiday under canvas.

8

The Military Impulse

THE MILITARY PANOPLY of uniforms, arms, marching and drum-beating, brass-sounding bands has an irresistible appeal for some boys. Victorian boys' clubs had drum-and-fife bands, some of them had drill instructors and parades, but they had no uniform. The Boys' Brigade had no proper uniform but it provided a cap and accoutrements which amounted to the same thing, and within a few years of its formation in 1883 with three officers and twenty-eight boys it had recruited thousands of boys in companies up and down the country and spread to the United States and New Zealand.

It started in Glasgow and Henry Drummond, who was Free Church Professor of Natural Science in that city's university, wrote of it:

"Amazing and proposterous illusion! Call these boys 'boys', which they are, and ask them to sit up in a Sunday class and no power on earth will make them do it; but put a fivepenny cap on them and call them soldiers, which they are not, and you can order them about till midnight."

Unlike boys' clubs which were started by a variety of men in a variety of places, the BB was the creation of one man, a stiff-backed Scottish Nonconformist called William Alexander Smith. He was a young businessman who "sat under" the Rev. George Reith (father of Lord Reith of the BBC) at a mission, taught Sunday school and was an officer in the Volunteers, the forerunners of the Territorial Army, which were run as private clubs with their own distinctive styles and uniforms. Smith fused his two interests of the Church and the Volunteers together with the 1st Glasgow Company of the Boys' Brigade when he was twenty-nine years old.

From the start it was a success in a nation which was still religious but at the same time was becoming increasingly militaristic. Perhaps the late Victorians had had enough of peace—several decades of it—and were in need of a little excitement. The Crimean War and the Indian Mutiny were far away and half forgotten. Books like W. H. Fitchett's *Deeds That Won The Empire* emphasized the virtues of a sense of duty and the preference of death to dishonour while at the same time treating campaigns against primitively armed savages in the Sudan and elsewhere as a more exciting form of blood sports. The Victorians greatly admired the manliness which military training developed.

In the 1860s thirty-five cadets of the Queen's (Westminster) Rifle Volunteers paraded in Hyde Park in front of Queen Victoria at the head of the men taking part in the review. A member of the regiment, "fully conscious of the value of gymnastics and military exercises for improving the general health and physique of boys," had started the experiment by dressing his two sons in a cut-down version of the regiment's colourful uniform. After some initial ridicule, the London Rifle Brigade, the South Middlesex Rifle Volunteers and other Volunteer regiments took up the idea seriously of putting boys into uniform in the manner of the drummer-boys and powder-monkeys in the wars of long ago. Cadet Corps then spread to the provinces and the Huddersfield Volunteer Battalion boasted a company turned out in red jackets and grey trousers.

Small boys as young as nine years old were admitted to cadet corps armed with old Irish Constabulary rifles and led by drum-and-fife bands. In some cases, according to the *Boys' Own Volume* of midsummer 1862, they were in charge "not of paid army sergeants, who are not always the best judges of the treatment a boy requires, but of gentlemen who were sergeants in the regiment."

The *Boys' Own Volume* was not alone in being impatient with the general unpreparedness for war of England in the latter half of the nineteenth century and realizing "the imperative necessity for the systematic practice of manly and martial exercises, by English men and English boys of every grade and age."

Smith was in tune with this mood and outlook. Many of the new elementary schools and lads' clubs had compulsory drill but they lacked the *esprit de corps* of the public schools with their Houses, games, teams and cadet corps. Smith set out to teach boys drill, physical exercises, obedience to the word of command, cleanliness, neatness, punctuality, self-respect and reverence for God, but even that was not enough. They must have *esprit de corps*, too.

His way of achieving this objective was characteristically direct and uncomplicated. He gave his boys a badge bearing an anchor and the words "Sure and Steadfast" and the motto "Remember Now Thy Creator In The Days of Thy Youth." Any doubts about whether the brigade was a church organization was dispelled by the stating of its object in just twenty-six words:

"The advancement of Christ's kingdom among boys, and the promotion of habits of reverence, discipline, self-respect, and all that tends towards a true Christian Manliness."

The very first Boys' Brigade company in Glasgow laid down a formula which was to remain virtually unchanged for the next nigh on a hundred years: drill and gymnastics, ambulance, swimming, clubroom, cricket, a summer camp and a band. It was basically very similar to other kinds of boys' clubs except for the emphasis on drill and, of course, the motto and the badge on the "fivepenny cap." It was found that boys liked polishing the brasses and pipeclaying and webbing of the accoutrements which set them apart from the fellows in the streets. They liked drill and they liked marching to the sound of brass bugles and drums. If they had a big bass drum, the boy who was allowed to take it home to practice on had been accorded a great honour, however much his family and neighbours might have suffered as a result. There soon developed a sound quite unlike any other in the world; the sound of the local Boys' Brigade band.

The 1st Glasgow Company was pursued when it marched through the streets by stones and taunts from the crowds of street urchins. It would be pleasant to record that many of them were converted but, alas, the BB did not cater for the lowest elements, but was confined to the more respectable town youths, aged between twelve and seventeen, who were churchgoers.

For them the brigade was much better than Sunday school and Bible classes alone (although they were an essential part of the new movement). The number of companies multiplied within a couple of years to forty-four, with precisely 1,999 boys enrolled. Forty of these companies were in Scotland, which had played little or no part in forming other kinds of lads' clubs, and the remaining four were in London, Manchester, Armitage Bridge, and (somewhat surprisingly) in Penzance, as far away as possible from Glasgow at the opposite end of the British Isles. After four years, the brigade had formed 124 companies, meeting in draughty gaslit church halls, many of them far beyond the boundaries of Scotland. The Americans enthusiastically adopted the idea but insisted on kitting out their boys with a complete and resplendent uniform, something which Smith had carefully avoided. He did not want the military aspects of the BB to overshadow its religious side, and after a time gave up the use even of dummy weapons at drill sessions.

Coincident with the founding of the Boys' Brigade, the cadet movement started to recruit working class boys as well as the sons of gentlemen, but not of course in the same companies. A colourful military gentlemen named Francis Fletcher Vane, who later became a baronet and wrote an autobiography entitled *Agin' the Governments*, formed in 1886 what he claimed was one of the first companies of working boy cadets from among the members of the Whittington Club attached to Toynbee Hall, thereby shocking some of its Liberal residents. And three years later Octavia Hill, who worked so hard to improve housing and general conditions of working people in Victorian London, sponsored a cadet unit in the belief that boys who lived in dismal Courts and Buildings would benefit from "exercise, discipline, obedience, *esprit de corps*, camping-out and manly companionship with the gentlemen who would be their officers."

Note, yet again, the use of *esprit de corps*, the talisman phrase of the age. In Octavia Hill's view the Boys' Brigade was mere military make-believe and the cadets should appeal much more as the real thing to boys who had passed beyond the stage of childish games. Yet from the start, the Boys'

Brigade ran into opposition from the strong pacifist elements in the Non-comformist church. Some were frankly horrified by what they saw as Smith's militarism of youth. The Peace Society exhorted its members to do their utmost to

"Crush this young praying and fighting monster—the masterstroke of Mars. . . . dragging true religion into the gutter of corruption."

In retrospect, this reaction seemed almost hysterical, and yet in the light of what happened in Nazi Germany in the 1930s, perhaps the late Victorian pacifists were right to be apprehensive of a movement which put boys into something very like uniform and taught military-style discipline.

As it turned out there was clearly little harm in a movement which attracted tens of thousands of boys from each succeeding generation and, if nothing else, discouraged dirty talk and encouraged them to brush their hair, wash behind their ears and keep a neat crease in their trousers. Of course, it taught a great deal more than that: perhaps most importantly the ability to submit to, as well as exercise, authority. The Constitution of the Boys' Brigade laid down that:

"All boys between the ages of twelve and seventeen shall be eligible for membership of the brigade, and in applying for their membership cards they shall fill up a form of application, agreeing to comply with the Rules of the Brigade, and expressing a desire to be true to Christ in their lives, and to help other boys to be so. Strict discipline shall be enforced, and all members must submit to the Authority of the Officers and Non-Commissioned Officers placed over them."

Some boys' club critics of the brigade claimed that it encouraged vanity and a love of "bossing" and that shouting "Quick march!" and "Shun!" at a crowd of boys was no way of teaching them anything. A few clubs, like the one at Heyrod Street in Manchester, included a Boys' Brigade company. In Nottingham, boy's clubs grew out of the brigade started there in 1888 by Johnny Dixon, a famous cricketer in his day, and still remembered through the Dixon Gates at Trent Bridge Cricket Ground.

The launching of the Boys' Brigade undoubtedly stimulated church interest in the boys' club movement as a whole, but the Victorians were very conscious of religious denomination as well as class differences. Before long, the Anglicans broke away from the Noncomformist mainstream and started the Church Lads' Brigade, adapting Smith's rules for the Kingdom of Christ for lads "to make them faithful members of the Church of England." It was for a time affiliated to the British National Cadet Association, which was avowedly militarist in that it encouraged the use of real weapons, not merely dummy ones for drill purposes. A Roman Catholic Boys' Brigade was formed, but somehow the Irish immigrant youth in the industrial towns failed to respond to the formula of drill and band practice which had become established by the end of the nineteenth century. Yet the Jewish Lads' Brigade, using its own version of the Christian ethic, gave the children of that perse-

cuted race who flocked into Britain from Russia and Poland from 1880 onwards and settled in their ghettoes in London, Manchester and other large
towns, the approved English public school sense of discipline, duty and
playing the game of life according to the rules of cricket.

Even the pacifists who so much objected to William Smith's "amazing and
preposterous illusion," managed to borrow some of his ideas by coupling
drill with instruction in lifesaving from fire, drowning and accident in the
Boys' Life Brigade to make it clear that it was not a militarist organization.
Dr. Paton, its founder in Nottingham, said: "I do not object to the military
forms of the Boys' Brigade, but it is useless to ignore the fact that many
people do."

All these off-shoots had sprung from Smith's original idea before the end
of the Victorian age. Professor Drummond, quoted at the beginning of this
chapter, also had this to say about this particular form of muscular
Christianity:

"What interests young men in the Boys' Brigade is the naturalness of the work.
It is absolutely natural for a young man to be mixed up with boys. It is natural
for him to take up their cause, to lay himself alongside their interests, to play
the part of the elder brother to them; he knows their ways and dodges, and has
been in all their scrapes. A mother does not really know a boy in the least. She
has never been a boy. So the young man is in his place when he offers a kindly
hand to these his younger brothers."

This was why so many young men volunteered to be Boys' Brigade officers,
although later, more sophisticated and less charitable generations might
suspect that an interest in "Christian manliness," drill and gymnastics, was
but another name for latent homosexuality. The Boys' Brigade, like the
boys' clubs, developed in total isolation from the opposite sex, who had to
be Girl Guides or join girls' clubs if they wanted similar opportunities for
recreation as their brothers. More than a million in domestic service in
private homes had an opportunity to join clubs, but relatively few were given
the necessary time off.

Because they were exclusively male societies, the brigades and clubs, (and
indeed the public schools), were suspected of not being interested in girls,
and all which that implied. It is probably significant that in a later age when
co-education and mixed youth clubs had long ceased to be a rarity, the Boys'
Brigade and the boys' clubs continued to attract boys to whom girls with
their flirting ways and eyes ever open for a potential husband were nothing
but a "bloomin' nuisance" and creators of trouble among friends. Although
there is no evidence on the subject, no doubt there were homosexuals among
both officers and boys. It was not then a subject for public discussion as it
is now.

It is reasonable to assume that the majority of boys had a healthy interest
in the opposite sex, did their courting outside the club but did not let it
interfere with their boxing or billiards or their game of football on their one

half-day off a week. In the case of Boys' Brigade lads, it is likely that their pillbox caps (modelled on those soldiers "walked out" in) and brasses, belts and drums made them doubly desirable in the eyes of the girls down their street, since Victorian females were notoriously susceptible to the attractions of a uniform.

William Smith, that dour son of the kirk, would not have put this very high on his list of reasons for starting the Boys' Brigade, if, indeed, he would have considered it at all. But perhaps the author does him an injustice. He unashamedly liked boys and the ways of boys and liked to encourage their high spirits and sense of fun. He was no prim deliverer of texts and homilies, despite the high tone of his mottoes and rules. More than anything else he wanted elementary school boys to acquire that much-prized and oft mentioned *esprit de corps,* or as one of his men expressed it: "The readiness to act in unity, to obey and trust a leader, and the authority and responsibility given to the NCOs provide a wonderful substitute for the 'public school spirit' which working class boys have so little chance of acquiring."

Before the 1880s were out, Smith gave up his business activities to devote his whole time to the affairs of his beloved brigade and build up a nation-wide system of companies. He was able to keep for the church in adulthood many of the boys who were members, while most boys' clubs could offer nothing to *their* outgrown members but Old Boys' Clubs. His only failure might have been that he failed to do anything for boys who did not come from decent working class families where church and chapel-going were already a way of life.

April 10. 1888

The Federation of the London Working Boys Clubs and Institutes

At the 1st meeting of the Council of the Federation of the London Working Boys Clubs and Institutes held in Northumberland Chambers on April 10. 1888 at 5 p.m. Rev. W M Carter was elected into the chair, and an executive Committee to consist of 5 members exclusive of officers was formed to serve until Oct 1.

The Committee to be represented by 4 members in the London diocese and one in the Rochester.

The following were elected to serve
Hon Thomas H W. Pelham
as chairman of the Executive Commi[tee]

Rev. W. M. Carter   Rev. Wm Law
Rev. I Denison   G. T. Biddulph Esqr
Evelyn Murray Esqr — and { A L Baselie Esq
                     as Hon Sec { H. Hoare Esq

10. The report of the first meeting of the Council of the London Federation of Boys' Clubs, 10th April, 1888.

11. *Above*. The Drum and Fife Band of the Hugh Oldham Lads' Club, 1890.

12. *Below*. The Dordon Miners' Welfare Boys' Club in the 1890s.

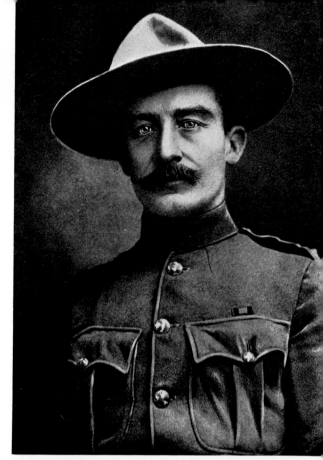

13. *Right*. General Robert Baden-Powell (then Colonel), hero of the relief of Mafeking in 1900.

14. *Below*. Baden-Powell talking to a group of Scouts round a camp fire in the autumn of 1908—the year the Scout movement was formed.

15. *Above*. The founders of the National Association of Boys' Clubs at the Coleshill conference, 1924.

16. *Below*. The Duke of Gloucester, first President of the NABC, visiting a Boys' Club in Edgbaston in February 1932.

9

East End, West End,
South of the River

UNLIKE THE BOYS' BRIGADE, started by one man with an urgent moral impulse and based in church halls, the boys' club movement had no head-quarters, no simply stated creed, no arresting motto, and no single national leader. As the nineteenth century drew to its close, and so, too, the sixty years' reign of Queen Victoria, individual club leaders drew their bands of boys around them in quarters ranging from Walter Southern's old mill in Salford and the Hollington Club's old bakery in South London to the splendid new Webbe Institute in Whitechapel with its gymnasium and swimming pool. They drank their toasts to the Queen from commemorative diamond jubilee mugs, and while the crowned heads of Europe paraded in splendour, even in the meanest courts and streets there were bonfires and bunting.

Only a handful of these boys' club leaders seemed to be aware that they were part of any great movement; these were the men who had met in April 1888 for the first executive committee meeting of the London Federation of Working Boys' Clubs and Institutes. It was, in the phrase of Waldo Eagar, "confessedly at the start an Old School Tie organization—with a liberal sprinkling of dog collars." No creed or common purpose had emerged from this meeting. According to one of the numerous Old Etonians connected with it, the object of the newly-formed Federation was "to give London boys an insight into the true meaning of games and such-like pursuits," which sounds a very modest aim for an organization which was (and remained for another twenty years) the only one of its kind in the country.

The Earl of Chichester's son, Tom Pelham, who had been junior to Quintin Hogg at Eton and had helped him in the boys' club in Castle Street, Long Acre, London, became chairman of the new Federation's executive committee. In 1889, the year after the committee's first meeting, he published his *Handbook to Youths' Institutes and Working Boys' Clubs*—a title reflecting the class differences between the two types of organization. Indeed, the list in the book is a monument to Victorian passion for hierarchy and fine shades of definition. It includes: Boys', Lads, Working Lads' and Youths' *Institutes* and one Institute for Rough Youths (which seems to be a contradiction in terms); Boys', Lads', Working Boys', Youths', Youths' and Lads', Young Men's, Choir-Boys', Youths' Friendly and Rough Boys' *Clubs*;

Boys' and Youths' *Guilds*, and, with splendid originality, just one *Club &
Gymnasium*. Pelham was a gentleman of his time, a barrister who held a
number of Civil Service appointments, and in his ample leisure hours he
served on innumerable committees (homes for working boys, playing fields,
polytechnic and Borstal institutions, as well as the Federation) and wrote
appeals for good causes. Much of his writing lacks any glimmer of humour
and is as dry as an over-long Sunday sermon. He repeatedly emphasized the
need for Bible classes and prayers in the clubs. He approved of chess and
draughts, quoits, dominoes, bagatelle and some long forgotten game called
Cockamoroo—but not billiards, which encouraged gambling. He was very
keen on cricket and thought that boating, although not as good morally,
was good exercise. He was rather cautious about camping, having heard that
even Volunteers were apt to catch pneumonia when sleeping under canvas,
although he thought it was a very "healthful holiday" and probably all right
for working boys.

Since the *Handbook* was published by arrangement with the Diocese of
London, the list of clubs confined itself to the three hundred parochial institutions for young men and boys in that diocese, and ignored those in
another diocese south of the River Thames. The federation, even though
it enrolled clubs south as well as north of the river, had an initial membership of only twenty-eight and for several decades never managed to exceed
fifty. Its stated objects were threefold: to foster the interchange of ideas
about the best ways of conducting boys' clubs, to provide lectures and help
to set up classes, and to promote competitions between the clubs in both
indoor and outdoor games, generally, in Pelham's words, "to make the life
of the working boy as real and human as that of the average public-school
boy."

The *Boys' Club Chronicle*, a monthly journal which was started in October
1888 but which survived for less than one year, showed that most of the
federation's efforts were devoted to the last of the three objectives mentioned
above. Pelham, who also wrote a long-extinct manual entitled *The Laws of
Cricket*, regretted that the game was not as popular with London boys as
football. Even so, there was a Cricket Challenge Cup, which the Harrow
Mission Club won in the first season. There were competitions in football,
gymnastics, chess and draughts. Clubs used the public swimming baths at
Poplar and Lambeth, as well as outdoor bathing spots, like the Welsh Harp
at Hendon. Swimming races for a cup were held in the West India Dock,
which at that time was crowded with merchant steamers carrying the commerce of the world.

Inevitably, the posher type of club tended to win the cups in competitions.
The Kensington Boys' Club, patronized by the nobility and gentry of that
royal and ancient borough, had harriers who paper-chased to Harrow and
its two cricket teams were allowed to practice regularly "on the Palace field,
through the kindness of H.R.H. the Princess Louise." The Club was
honoured by invitations from the rich; on an outing to Lady Wolverton's

stately home at Coombe Wood three brakes were needed to transport the members. There was a strong religious influence in the Club, and communicant members had an annual tea with the vicar, followed by a "grand entertainment."

In complete contrast were the Maurice Hostel, founded by the Christian Social Union in Hoxton in 1898 (when the district was terrorized by the "cockhorse boys" and the belt and pistol gangs) and the St. Christopher Boys' Club in the district around the north end of the Tottenham Court Road where the Judd Street Gang, famous for its belts and coshes, held sway. Both these clubs were outside the Federation, but were extremely vigorous and supported by influential and wealthy people: the former by Lord Haldane, founder of the Territorial Army, and the future Liberal Prime Minister, Mr. Asquith, and the latter by a cohort of aristocratic ladies led by the Dowager Countess of Pembroke.

It was in the Maurice Hostel Boys' Club that the idea of industrial welfare work was generated through a young curate who later became, as Sir Robert Hyde, a senior official at the newly-formed Ministry of Labour. He was a noted authority in the 1920s on the problems of boys in industry and he was among the first to realize that a boy's working conditions had the greatest influence on his life.

St. Christopher's on the other hand was a strictly West End effort, operating from a house in Fitzroy Square which was reputedly at one time a male brothel. The club's pantomime party performed with admirable ease in parish halls and stately homes alike. Indeed the tradition of making your own entertainment, which has survived in boys' clubs despite the alternatives of radio, television and the cinema, began with these Victorian Saturday night concerts and "glees," the "grand entertainments" and melodramas, the Shakespeare Reading Circles, the black and white minstrel troupes and the drum-and-fife and brass bands.

Yet by no means all Victorian club leaders were devoted to providing sport, and fun and games generally, for their members. Paul Neuman, a barrister who in 1887 opened a club in the hall and vestries of New College Chapel in north-west London, expounded his own, highly individual ideas, in *The Boys' Club*, published in 1900. He was a stern prophet and he toiled on in isolation, joining no federations, for another forty years until he died at the age of ninety. Neuman strove to create his ideal club, one that would provide not only games and entertainment, but also a comprehensive training of body, mind and character. He found most existing clubs badly organized, badly equipped, dingy lounging places for the young, lacking any education motive; the Boys' Brigade was merely playing at soldiers, with dummy guns and a ridiculous uniform.

Neuman was something of a pedagogue who believed in "head-work"—his expression for mental activity or study—and in "whacking" as a punishment for breaking the rules. He believed that forming character meant making boys do what they didn't like, as well as what they did like. He had a membership examination in his club by which boys could become Associates, first or second class, and Fellows. He was keenly aware of the tragedy of boys educated in the elementary schools, degenerating between the ages of fourteen and sixteen into ignorant, foul-mouthed louts. He felt that although scores of boys' clubs had sprung into being in the last quarter of the nineteenth century they were not fully aware of the possibilities of post-school education. A boy transferred from learning to earning at the age of thirteen or fourteen quickly forgot all his learning. Neuman called this "the break in the aqueduct," which let the stream of boyhood run to waste. Polytechnics were pitifully few in number, but they were the only way up from the bottom rungs of society for the few who had the necessary gifts and determination to use them. Evening schools were run by tired, overworked teachers supplementing their earnings after their day's work in overcrowded elementary school classrooms.

All too often the club atmosphere savoured of Purity, Temperance and No Smoking. Neuman was antagonistic towards pompous Church of England parsons and the church attendance enforced by many of the church-run clubs:

"It draws a line of demarcation between sheep and goats, with this startling result that, while among the sheep will be found the well-mannered, easy-tempered, acquiescent boys, the goats will include those of strong character, blunt, master-ful, independent, suspicious of patronage, resentful of coercion—the very lads who, wisely treated, are the salt of the Church. The unwisdom, the impatience, sometimes the intolerance, of the official representatives of religion too often make it appear an ulterior object for which all that is attractive in the Club is offered merely as a bait. And the interpretation which the shrewd but irreverent errand-boy puts upon the parson's policy is simply this: ' 'E wants to fill 'is shop'. . . ."

Although the London Federation was a creation of the Church of England and run by the high Anglican public school elite, it should be said that two Jewish boys' clubs founded in the late 1890s—Brady Street in Whitechapel and West Central in Fitzroy Square—were admitted to membership. In fact the Jewish clubs made a notable contribution to the whole movement. They were well-run and their members were particularly successful in chess, essay-writing and drama competitions as well as, by contrast, boxing.

The Catholic Church was comparatively slow to realize the value of boys' clubs and the first one in London was not started until 1894, in a school-room of the church of St. Francis in Notting Dale. The condition of the poor Catholic population can be judged by the fact that only one in ten of the 136 boys and young men, aged from fourteen to twenty-two, who were members had a regular job. They were too poor to pay more than 1d. to take part in cricket matches and Neuman said of them in 1900: "They are very desultory in their habits, even a gymnastic squad being too great a demand on their patience."

In the closing years of the nineteenth century, the youths' and boys' institutes, with their greater emphasis on educational classes than the clubs, were dying out, and this was another reason why Neuman felt strongly enough about his ideas to give up his practice at the Bar and devote his whole time and money to working boys. What he struggled to achieve single-handed in North London was in the long run overtaken by the State with the gradual development of secondary education and the raising in steps of the school-leaving age. Neuman, an uncompromising autocrat, made few converts in the boys' club movement. That eminent pioneer, Charles Russell, commented that Neuman's ideal club would be:

"... likely rather to repel than to attract the rough lads who most need some civilizing agency to brighten their existence. Compulsion to any kind of brain work acts as the strongest deterrent against the joining of a club by the rank and file, whose typical representative is the boy who is rough, careless, merry, and thoughtless, uncouth in manners, supremely indifferent to his future, and only anxious to become an adept at some form of athletics. The club which is strictly and primarily educational in aim can only appeal to the intellectual aristocracy of our working-class youth."

Between Russell and Neuman and Pelham there were scores of men with their own individual ideas about what was best for the rough boys of the street, each doing things as well as they could using the facilities available. A few Cambridge graduates of the 1890s took over a disused bakers' shop in Hollington Street, west of the Camberwell Road in South London. An ex-Army sergeant and his wife were installed to provide cheap meals for the poor from 5 a.m. until nightfall each day. The boys were consigned to the basement, an unsavoury place which was apt to be filled with sewage when heavy rains and high tide on the river coincided, but it was a place of their own and no more or less uncomfortable than their own crowded homes.

With the provision of cocoa and thick slices of bread and margarine known as "doorsteps," or "dorkers," and the sympathetic presence of the ex-sergeant and his wife, a kind of boys' club came into being. These early members were mostly young costermongers who found that pushing a barrow through the suburbs of South London selling salt and other household items was a good cover for "nicking" anything saleable and portable they happened to come across. They even stole the table games from the club, piece by piece. They were almost, but not quite, unclubbable.

The Cambridge men had a small stable fitted up as a gymnasium, managed to referee football matches which previously always began or ended as a punch-up, encouraged the lads to take the occasional bath, and arranged emigration to Canada for some of the more intractable youths.

But in the end they were forced to the conclusion that little could be done with boys bred to street-trading unless they could be induced to take a regular job (which in their eyes, and those of their parents, was mere servitude). So in 1896 being in work, or at least being willing to look for a job, was made a condition of membership of the Hollington Club.

From that point on, the club (which was later adopted by Dulwich College) became respectable, and many of the costers dropped out. Their white chokers were replaced by collars and ties. Jobs were found, and even suits of working clothes. From the unlikely beginning in a noisome cellar beneath the temperance Coffee Shop three years earlier, the club was steering towards the objective marked out by Paul Neuman. By the turn of the twentieth century, boys had to apply for admission soon after their tenth birthdays, and as Sir Wemyss Grant-Wilson, who was involved in the later development of the club, wrote in 1925:

"They thus became accustomed to look to the Club for all their spare-time amusement, the society of their friends, help in time of sickness or trouble and their annual seaside holiday. Then when their fourteenth birthday came and they left school they were ready, rather than forgo all these joys, to go to Evening Classes regularly after a long day's work—and a rule to that effect was presently made. Evening Classes are a loathsome accretion, but attendance at them has advanced the prosperity of the Club's members, and after all one has to get on individually whilst the politicians quarrel as to how it should be done in bulk. The classes prevent the Club from joining any federation of Clubs and engaging in furious contests in boxing in Balham, ping-pong in Putney, swimming in Shoreditch and football in Fulham, but there are substantial consolations in the gain of better jobs and promotions."

The Hollington Club was selective, in the sense that only those who were prepared or had the ability to go to evening classes were accepted. In Lambeth Walk, made famous by the chirpy Cockney song and dance named after it, Frank Briant opened a boys' club in 1884, which over the years developed into a social and educational welfare organization known far and wide as Alford House.

While Briant was Liberal MP for Lambeth he fought successfully to get some of the social welfare methods developed there embodied in national legislation, and when he died in 1934 the old boys of Mill Hill School carried on his lifetime's work. Also in Lambeth was that rarity: a boys' club run by women. Miss Cochrane, who must have been an indomitable Victorian lady, started the Hercules Boys' Club with a railway arch as its headquarters, and until she was joined by other women helpers, ran it single-handed for the benefit of the roughest boys of the district.

Maude Stanley was another of the same breed. In the 1870s she tried to civilize the boys of the Five Dials area of Soho, which was later wiped out by the building of the Charing Cross Road, with night classes and "treats" such as a Christmas supper and an annual excursion and tea in a Kensington garden. She was helped by her maid and "a gentleman who had some previous experience with rough boys" (in this area they were so rough that a constable had to be stationed at the door to prevent trouble). After starting games on Wednesday evenings and a club on Saturday, Miss Stanley wrote: "It is plain that there is a great need for places of harmless recreation for the immense working-boy population of London, and the clergy would find extraordinary opportunities of gaining a hold over their boy-parishioners by using their parish rooms in the manner indicated." She herself eventually moved on to the presumably gentler activity of running girls' clubs, and founded the Soho Club for Girls.

A hundred miles away in Bristol a boys' home started by Mary Carpenter, another ardent female campaigner against poverty, was closed in 1894 (seventeen years after her death). When the Minister of Highbury Chapel in that city of Nonconformists demanded from his pulpit: "Who in this congregation is prepared to devote his energies to founding a Club for the instruction and welfare of boys in St. Phillips?" an accountant named F. Percy Jenkins came forward. He took over the vacant home and opened it in November of that year as the Broad Plain Lads' Club. He was general secretary for forty years, spending all his out of office hours there and on Sundays conducting a Bible class of a hundred members.

Stories like these show how at the end of the nineteenth century the boys' club movement was, like its members, growing fast. And not just in London, but in all the major towns and cities throughout the country. Some of these clubs were very small affairs, meeting on probably no more than one or two nights a week, but as Charles Russell pointed out, wherever a man devoted his evenings to gathering a few lads around him with the desire of being their friend, there was an embryo club. Charles Booth, in his monumental investigation into the state of London life and labour at the end of the nineteenth century, declared that ". . . the value of well-managed boys' clubs and brigades in the formation of character can hardly be over-estimated."

Dean Farrar, in a preface to Pelham's handbook of clubs and institutes, said that London working boys constituted "perhaps the most important and, strange to say, till recent years, the most entirely neglected class of the community . . . and yet it has been pointed out for many years that it is between the ages of fifteen and twenty that the final habits of life are mainly formed and it is exclusively at this period of life that a criminal career is either avoided or begun."

Whatever a modern club leader or social welfare worker may make of that positive assertion by the learned Dean, in retrospect the great folly of the Victorian age can be clearly seen. The State spent millions of pounds educating the young of the lower classes and then turned them loose as soon as they reached their teens without further education, without the means of recreation or amusement, into the working world and the empty desolation of the streets. It was left to philanthropy and good intentions to do something for them.

PART TWO

"Indeed, it is not too much to say that on the Elementary Schools, the Polytechnics and the Boys' Clubs the future of the working classes largely depends."

From the 1890 report of the London
Federation of Working Boys' Clubs.

I

A Public Outcry

THE DEATH OF QUEEN VICTORIA and the accession of her son Edward to the throne coincided almost mystically with the end of one century and the start of another. But needless to say, despite all the purple prose in the special "golden extra" edition produced by the *Daily Mail* to mark the turn of the twentieth century, the social problems of the Victorian age did not vanish overnight. The *Daily Mail* quite properly hailed the astonishing achievements of the age that had passed, the spread of the British Empire north and south, east and west, and at home the building of the railways and industry through steam power, the discoveries of electricity, X-rays, anaesthetics, vaccination, the invention of motor transport, telegraphy and telephones, the penny post, the motor car, the bicycle—the catalogue seemed almost endless. "We have girdled the oceans with our harbours and encircled the world with our cables . . . we have harnessed the forces of nature. . . ."

And yet when the new king ushered in the Edwardian era (or interlude, as it turned out to be) London was still jammed with horse-drawn buses and carts, hansoms and clarences and private carriages. Hundreds of men and boys were employed at near-starvation wages to keep the street crossings clear of the horses' droppings. Most houses and streets were lit by gas because electric lamps were all regarded with suspicion, and were expensive to install. Bathrooms and central heating were almost unheard of. Hip baths and coal fires in every room were the general rule in comfortable middle class

73

homes, keeping armies of housemaids busy staggering upstairs with cans of hot water and scuttles of coal producing more smoke to thicken London's fog.

In a parish of thirteen thousand souls in South London, the only one with a bath of his own was the rector, Canon Horsley. There was still an immense and seemingly unbridgeable gap between the poor and the rich. And some of the rich were very rich indeed. When two men were fined £500 for keeping a gaming house in Belgravia the police found letters which showed that a leader of fashion had lost £1,500 in a single night at the tables. The young Marquis of Anglesey spent £1 million in just three years after inheriting his estates. His overcoat cost £1,000 and he was accompanied on his travels by his personal hairdresser, a secretary, two valets—and a poet. The Duke of Sutherland used to pin £1,000 banknotes to his wife's pillow while she slept.

To grasp the enormity of this extravagance it is necessary to point out that a "Brownie" box camera cost at that time a mere 5s., six shirts cost 30s., a dozen bottles of champagne 48s., while beer was 2d. a pint. It was possible to furnish a house quite comfortably for £100 and yet the annual household expenditure at Knowsley Hall, the stately home of the Earl of Derby, was £50,000. When the King came to dinner on Grand National night, there were three servants in the house for each of the forty guests. While the King's game larder at Sandringham had room for six thousand pheasants and grouse, many working class families had to subsist on a diet consisting mostly of potatoes and stew made from "three penn'orth of pieces," bread and margarine and "specks"—half-rotten apples and pears. The Salvation Army in Pentonville Road provided breakfast—consisting of a cup of tea and a large slice of bread and jam—for a farthing.

It was officially computed that a family of the "respectable poor" with three children could survive on £1 a week. Unlike the professional and business classes who had begun to cut down the size of their families in the 1890s under the pressure of heavy public school fees, the working classes continued to produce more children than they could possibly afford to feed and house. It was by no means uncommon for the children to sleep six to a bed, head to toe, three at the top and three at the bottom. There was no dole: a long period of unemployment could mean the workhouse, a nineteenth century institution which survived well into the twentieth.

A one-night census of the homeless in central London taken in 1904 recorded no fewer than 1,800 people tramping the streets, and among them fifty children. Those who had homes usually had to share them with one or more other families and there could be up to five or six houses sharing one water tap and one outside lavatory. Not surprisingly, in spite of vaccinations, towns were still ravaged by typhoid and scarlet fever.

Again, not surprisingly, drunkenness was rife. In the East End women were in the habit of giving infants gin and beer "to make them sleep," and at one coroner's inquest the jury returned a verdict that a child of nine had died from alcohol poisoning. A verdict of "natural death" at another London inquest on a seven-year-old who had died of starvation led Hamilton Fyfe to write in the newly-born *Daily Mirror*:

"In the capital of the greatest Empire in the world death from starvation is natural death. If this is natural, let us give up talking about the benefits of civilization, the Devil's mockery of progress, the hell upon earth created for hundreds of thousands by social conditions such as those which prevail in England today. Is there no leading man in Britain who will come forward as the champion of the poor? Is there no one who can point a way and induce the nation to follow, no way of saving the next generation from the same plight? If there be such a man, in God's name let him come forward."

There were in fact many such men in the boys' clubs, who were angry with a society in which the direst poverty contrasted with what Hamilton Fyfe described as "the butterfly-dance" of the wealthy making their annual rounds of Cowes, Ascot, Henley and the shooting-boxes in Scotland and entertaining lavishly during the London season. Concern about the wilful neglect of working boys poured out from 1904 onwards in a cataract of books, articles (not only in the *Daily Mirror* but in the intellectual periodicals), pamphlets and social studies. Sadly enough, relatively little attention was paid to the plight of working *girls*, immured in their basements and attics as overworked little skivvies or savagely exploited as sweated labour both inside and outside their own homes.

Only a year or two earlier Charles Booth had published his minute investigation into *Life and Labour* in London and Seebohm Rowntree published a similar investigation into poverty in York, so at least a systematic effort was being made to gather information on the subject. A generation had grown up under universal compulsory education, yet still in the early 1900s the children of working class families had little choice when they left elementary school at twelve, thirteen or fourteen but to go into a factory earning a "few pence per hundred" on piece-work. If they preferred an outdoor life, they could work just as long hours for just as little money getting up at dawn to deliver milk and going out after dark delivering beer, between times selling newspapers in the street.

In 1899 the school-leaving age was fixed at twelve and in the following year it could be raised to fourteen "where School Boards so decided." It was not until 1918 that school attendance was made compulsory for all children up to the end of the term in which their fourteenth birthday fell.

In Lancashire at the turn of the twentieth century children were employed half-time in the mills before their twelfth birthdays at 3s. a week, and as soon as they were twelve and could leave school they went wholetime for 6s. a week. Boys started work at 5.30 a.m., half an hour before the men, in order to clean and oil the machines. They worked a twelve-hour day.

One of them was James Butterworth, the eldest of a family of five who was forced to work ten hours a day in a vile-smelling dye works when he was just twelve because of the death of his father. In the evening, after working all day in the mill, he sold newspapers in the cheerless streets of

Accrington or served in a cheap eating-house to make a little extra money. He had been one of the brightest pupils at school. He bitterly resented having to leave and envied boys older than himself who were wearing grammar school caps. When his sisters were old enough to go out to work, he did manage to go to night school and at seventeen he was locally famed as "the boy preacher." Later in life, as a Methodist minister in Walworth, south-east London, he was able to provide at Clubland the kind of place that he had so badly needed and missed in his own early adolescence, somewhere to go in the evenings for friendship, recreation and education.

In the circumstances of the early 1900s the majority of girls left home at thirteen or fourteen and went into domestic service. Only the fortunate few boys managed to get jobs in service as hall-boys, or in the hotels as bell-boys and page-boys, hoping for generous tips. Fewer still were dressed up in livery uniforms and top hats with cockades, to ride in the barouches which had yet to be replaced by Daimlers and Rolls-Royces.

Artisans such as engineers, printers, joiners, shipwrights and coach-builders could command 10d. an hour, as much as an unskilled labourer could earn for twelve hours' toil on the railways. These skilled aristocrats of the working class, like the aristocracy proper, preferred their sons to follow their footsteps. Where such nepotism held sway, it was difficult, if not impossible, for a boy from outside to get an apprenticeship and learn a trade. Almost his only hope of getting out of his town ghetto was to run away to sea in a merchant ship or wait until he was seventeen or eighteen and old enough to emigrate or "take the King's shilling." The Army had been given a new lease of popularity by the Boer War, which bridged the old and the new centuries. In their elementary school classes the children had learned to sing patriotic songs about "Bobs" (Lord Roberts, the Commander-in-Chief of British forces in South Africa) and his brave battalions. As Kipling observed in his poem "Tommy":

"It's Tommy this and Tommy that, an' 'Chuck 'im out, the brute!'
But it's 'saviour of 'is country' when the guns begin to shoot."

Even with the war over, there was still a vast Empire to keep in check and jingoism died hard. Colonel Younghusband was marching to Lhasa to remind the Tibetans that they must show respect to the British Raj; in the hinterland of Aden, Captain Lloyd-Jones and sixty men were surrounded by a thousand tribesmen; a desert force was trying to pin down the Mullah in Somaliland and fighting was going on in Nigeria. Thousands of youths from Kennington and Limehouse, Liverpool and Leeds, found themselves sweating it out in Imperial India in khaki shorts and pith helmets. They were paid only 8d. or 9d. a day. But at least like their sisters in service, they had guaranteed food and lodging, a security which few working people in England could boast.

To a respectable Edwardian youth, however, the army was a low calling, and he hankered after employment in an office or a shop. Office boys and messengers could earn 8s. a week, but the hours for shop assistants were longer and the wages lower, sometimes as little as 2d. an hour.

Shop assistants were kept virtually chained to their counters for anything from seventy to ninety hours a week and T. Spencer Jones, editor of *The Shop Assistant*, wrote in 1909:

"Most of the small shops in every trade are overcrowded hutches in which the gas is burning the best part of the day. I have seen young men and women at work in these places at 10 and 11 o'clock at night, and the only rest they have is a half-holiday once a fortnight, starting at 2, 3, or 4 o'clock. They learn nothing, they see nothing of the glories of London. They might as well be in the Australian bush as in the greatest city in the world for what is added to their life."

Many of these assistants were forced to live in as a condition of their employment and were housed in dismal barracks in the back-streets. Account was taken in the meagre wages of the equally meagre meals and lodging they received. They were hemmed in by rules covering every aspect of their daily lives, with fines for any infringement, and they were not allowed to have girl-friends. Until 1910, the only law limiting hours of labour in shops was that of 1892, which provided that no one under eighteen should work for more than seventy-four hours in a week, including mealtimes. Even this was persistently ignored by employers.

Nor were boys employed in co-operative stores, an off-shoot of the Labour movement, significantly better off. Wage rates agreed with their union ranged from 6s. a week at fourteen to 15s. at eighteen.

In *Kipps*, H. G. Wells wrote from personal experience of a youth spent behind a drapery counter, a dismal prospect summed up by the senior apprentice who says: "I tell you we're in a blessed drainpipe, and we've got to crawl along it till we die."

These pallid youths, often deemed by their employer to be "too old at 21," knew that their labour was too cheap a commodity to be presumed upon. In the streets, waiting to take their jobs, was a vast army of out-of-works, graphically described by Chiozza Money in *Riches and Poverty* in 1905:

"As I write there are thousands, if not tens of thousands, of clerks, writers, warehousemen, shop assistants, travellers, canvassers, agents, and others out of work and undergoing terrible sufferings in the endeavour to keep afloat. I have heard of several cases lately in which advertisements offering berths of small account have been hungrily applied for by hundreds of applicants."

The problems of the working boy, however, were analysed, discussed and agonized over. The initiative to do so came from that cradle of the Welfare State in the East End, Toynbee Hall. The Toynbee Trust commissioned and published in 1904 *Studies of Boy Life in our Cities*, a selection of essays on family life, work and other aspects of the problem by men who all had first-hand knowledge of the boys' club movement. It even included a chapter by Lily Montague, a stalwart of the girls' club movement, on "The Girl in the Background", who, she hinted, wouldn't be occupying that position much longer.

At the time there were only about fifty regular and well-managed boys' clubs in London with a total membership of not more than ten thousand. About fifteen thousand other boys were members of parish clubs, which often seemed to have little purpose other than to bribe boys to attend church or Bible classes.

E. J. Urwick, an eminent academic who edited the Toynbee Trust Studies, did not believe that more clubs would be a remedy for hooliganism in the streets, which had existed even in the eighteenth century with gangs of blue-bloods calling themselves Yahoos and Mohawks: "Today the gang is the same in all essentials; only its members are less violent and less daring, and they are not outcasts from decent society, because they have never been in it." Hooligans would only visit clubs as long as it suited them and would inevitably turn them into shambles. For decent boys, their own families and evening school were probably a better influence than the clubs. But between the two groups, he said, was a class of about 120,000 boys for whom clubs would be an enormous benefit. Yet such was the apathy of the middle class, and economic circumstances had changed to such an extent that fewer gentlemen of means were available to give all their time free of charge to the movement, and he doubted whether it would be possible to do more than double the number of existing clubs to cater for the needs of perhaps 20,000 boys. This tentative target was not, as it turned out, achieved until much later.

Sir Robert Morant, Permanent Secretary of the Board of Education, who launched State secondary education in 1904, the same year that the Toynbee Trust studies were published, believed in the creation of "an aristocracy of brains." Some of the Toynbee Hall men thought that either the school leaving age must be raised or evening classes must be made compulsory. Public opinion was not ready for either measure. It had not yet realized that the voluntary system of boys' club and brigades was failing to catch those who most needed to continue their education after fourteen.

Evening school was one way to shorten the shamefully long hours which young boys were required to work. The new buildings handed over by the school boards to the new local education authorities were available for evening classes and recreation but only one in ten of the children who had been educated in the elementary schools were taking advantage of them. There was little of the "old school tie" spirit among the working classes, whose boys valued their independence and could hardly wait to escape from the tyranny of the classroom and the cane.

Teachers in London who organized at their own expense out of school cricket and football clubs had made a start in building up the corporate spirit, but on the whole working boys had more sense of belonging to the buildings or street where they lived, or their club, than they did to their school.

The clubs of the Victorian age were set up to help "rough boys" from the poorest of homes. However, in time most of these clubs tended to become respectable, and unruly urchins with no homes worthy of the name found themselves exluded. If there could be a continual process of starting up new clubs for the roughest boys, which in turn became respectable, a social revolution might be brought about. But resources of enthusiasm, goodwill and money were finite.

Studies of Boy Life concluded:

"If there is one thing the town-child needs—and hates—it is discipline, and yet more discipline, of body, mind and character. The club can catch him, but cannot discipline him; the Boys' Brigades can discipline him to a small extent, but cannot catch or keep him when he most needs it; the voluntary evening school can do neither. Nothing short of a compulsory system, in which both the physical and mental training are combined, can hope to do both successfully."

In their own individual ways Paul Neuman in North London and the Hollington Club south of the river, both started in the previous century, were in the early 1900s trying to do just that.

At least the working boy was now recognized as a social problem and was not being ignored and neglected as he had been according to Dean Farrar twenty years earlier. Most of the writers of a flood of books on boy labour were connected with boys' clubs and settlements, a few were dons, many were Labour thinkers.

The impetus for social change came from these unpaid workers with boys, a movement epitomized by Alexander Paterson, one of the young Oxford graduates who gathered around "The Doctor"—John Stansfeld—at the mission in Bermondsey. His human account of the work in *Across the Bridges*, published in 1911, was a best-seller, not least among the boys of Eton. Like many of his contemporaries he had lived in one of the waterfront buildings and taught in an elementary school. More than any other book of the period, it illustrates the tragedy of bright and hopeful boys of fourteen being turned into coarse and ignorant adults by the ceaseless round of casual work alternating with unemployment and overcrowding, malnutrition and bad health.

This tide of protest led to a public outcry and a spate of official inquiries and reports. Their subjects ranged from the employment of boys out of school hours and at night, to health and medical inspection, school meals, juvenile employment exchanges and street-trading. Very often such reports are put on the shelf and forgotten, but in this period of a reforming Liberal Government—in which David Lloyd George, as Chancellor of the Exchequer, was setting up the foundation of the Welfare State with insurance and old age pensions—a flurry of legislation followed. Acts were passed restricting the employment of children still of school age and the hours of those who had left school, juvenile employment committees were set up at the new labour exchanges and new rules were laid down for the probation of juvenile criminals. Having discovered the juvenile world at long last, the state appeared to be trying to take it over.

How much effect all this had on the life of the town boy is open to question. This boy was bred to the rough environment surrounding him from birth, which killed off in infancy most of his weaker brethren. It goes without saying that he had powers of survival, but he was not much given to pondering the justice or injustice of his lot. He took his pleasures as and when he found them. As to overwork and injury, bad food and disease, he could take what would finish more genteely brought-up individuals: and this was proved beyond doubt in the two great wars of the next half century, in the mud of Flanders and Normandy, in the sands of the Western Desert and in the jungles of Burma.

The public school caste took it for granted that they and they alone, could show working class boys the best way to lead their lives. After a few years in the East End or south of the Thames "getting to know the local conditions of life from personal observation . . . helping where help is needed," as Dr. Picht—the German academic who wrote a book on the Settlements—phrased it, most of them went into the Civil Service and ended up at senior level with a knighthood or some lesser honour.

One of them ended up as Prime Minister. Clement (later Lord) Attlee went to Stepney in the East End on a foggy evening in 1905 to have a look at a boys' club organized there by his public school, Haileybury. In a speech at a boys' club dinner forty years later he said: ". . . leaving Stepney station that night and walking up through the fog in Limehouse were the steps that first led me to my present position."* He continued to go to Stepney to the point where he was working there almost every night in the week, until the First World War interrupted his activities. He recalled a small club which used to run from eight to ten o'clock in the evening:

"The boys used to come from their work. I was comparatively unemployed, being a briefless barrister, I had time on my hands, and I wanted to do something for the very young boys in the streets around, so I started a small boys' club, but had not any people to run it. I appealed to the boys of my own club and they came home from work, snatched a very hasty tea and came out and worked unselfishly for the small boys and ran that club. I remember a number of boys who themselves started or helped in forming, clubs because they realized what they got from it . . . I was fortunate in serving through an apprenticeship under a great club man, a man of very fine character, a man of great unselfishness, and I had a number of good colleagues, most of who fell in the First World War."

This was the strictly amateur approach, impelled by the best of religious motives. In the first decade of the twentieth century it was already beginning to wither and die. Organized religion was losing its grip even on the middle classes, and the poor, instead of hoping for a better life in the next world, were looking to the State for one here and now.

* That position was at the head of the first Labour Government with a working majority, elected in a landslide victory immediately following the Second World War.

2

Be Prepared

SCOUTING FOR BOYS was an Edwardian invention; something which sprang directly from some of the more humiliating aspects of the Boer War. Despite all the flag-waving and the jingoistic fervour of the music hall songs and sketches of the period, the start of the war had shown that the new breed of British manhood, bred in the smoky towns, was low in both health and morale. That a handful of Dutch farmers, bred with Bible and shotgun on the open veldt of South Africa, could out-manoeuvre and out-shoot the soldiers of the Queen of England came as a shocking blow to the easy confidence of the ruling classes in England. Almost as much of a shock were the unwashed thousands who poured forth from their ghettoes, where previously they had been not only unheard but unseen as well, to revel wildly in the streets of the West End (which was reserved, of course, for carriage folk and their servants) when the relief of Mafeking was announced.

The hero of Mafeking Night among the rude celebrating crowds was Colonel Robert Baden-Powell, who had held out under siege in that small town far to the north of the Cape Colony against overwhelming odds until relief forces arrived. Baden-Powell was a professional soldier in his early forties, but the uniform and military manner concealed a very unorthodox character. More than any other senior officer fighting in South Africa he had measured up the terrain and the nature of the enemy, the simple yet cunning Boer farmer. He produced a manual called *Aids to Scouting* for the benefit of the British "townies" who had been hastily thrust into a uniform and put aboard troopships for Cape Town. He later said: "My idea of training boys for scouting dates from 1897, when I applied it to young soldiers ... Even the Scout Badge was that which I used for the scouts in the 5th Dragoon Guards."

The military manual, with its flavour of cowboys and Indians, found an unexpected readership among small boys at home in England who were lucky enough to lay hands on a copy. Boys wrote to Baden-Powell asking for his autograph and his advice. He replied to one letter from a boys' club: "You should not be content with sitting down to defend yourself against evil habits, but you should be active in doing good.... Make up your mind to do at least one 'good turn' to somebody every day ... no matter how small ... the great thing is to do something."

So the seeds of what grew into a great world-wide youth movement were sown; the Good Deed a Day, the Promise, the Law and the Badge Tests of scouting. Even the motto, "Be Prepared" (linking up in such an orderly manner with the founder's own initials), was born in the Boer War when he was writing home to warn Britain of the need to be better prepared for war in the future to avoid a repetition of the humiliation it was then suffering in South Africa.

Back in England, at that time the youngest major-general in the British Army at the age of forty-three, Baden-Powell was invited by William Smith, now knighted, to a mass rally of more than seven thousand members of his boys' brigades. It was, said B-P, the finest muster of lads he had ever seen, but he couldn't resist adding that Sir William would have ten times that number if only he gave more variety and attraction to the training offered. In reply, the Boys' Brigade leader (who was only three years his senior) urged him to rewrite his manual for soldiers for the benefit of boys. Baden-Powell took the advice seriously and the result, *Scouting for Boys,* was first published in fortnightly parts in the spring of 1908 and issued in a complete edition in May. Backed by a Fleet Street mass-circulation periodical publisher, Arthur Pearson, it was an enormous and instant success, reprinted eight times within the year. By 1940 it had sold nearly 600,000 copies and was still in demand.

Baden-Powell and William Smith also differed radically in their approach to religion. The creed of the Boys' Brigade was avowedly evangelical: "The advancement of Christ's Kingdom among boys..." while the Scout's Promise, made on joining, was more simply: "To do my duty to God." B-P, in his characteristically orders-of-the-day style, pointed out: "Note that it does not say 'To be loyal to God', since this would merely be a state of mind, but to *do* something, which is the positive, active attitude." Hence the good-deed-a-day rule.

He had no wish to tie his boy scouts to any particular church. In *Scouting and Youth Movements,* published twenty years later, he wrote:

"It seems to me very probable that there is as much religious feeling as there ever was, if not more, lying close below the surface in the nation, though it may not express itself in church-going. ... By God's Kingdom I mean the prevalence of love in the world in place of dominance of selfish interest and rivalry such as at present exists."

Intentionally or not, the scout movement caught the spirit of the Edwardian interlude when there was a rebirth of idealism without the solid core of religious belief of the Victorian age. One of the greatest problems of the time, as we saw in the previous chapter, was what to do with the great mass of working class youngsters trapped in the streets of towns. It was not easy in those days to reach country that lay perhaps just beyond walking distance. Train and bus fares were beyond the reach of most youngsters' pockets, and so were bicycles. Scouting appealed particularly to younger town boys as an alternative to street games of "cowboys and Indians" or "cops and robbers," or the ubiquitous "Black Hand Gangs." As Eagar says in *Making Men*:

"Boy-scouting, by familiarizing boys with 'woodcraft' and encouraging independent adventure, made a practical outlet for interest aroused in the schools by Nature Study, which became part of the curriculum in the 90s, though as late as 1910 there were London boys who had no idea that any flowers were 'wild' or that timber came from growing trees."

He goes on to recall the reaction of one of his Bermondsey Boys' Club lads, Bill Tate, when at fourteen he saw the sea for the first time at camp near Lowestoft: "Gor lumme! Fancy the LCC [London County Council] putting all that sand dahn *'ere!*" A member of the Hollington Club, writing about seaside camps, talked of "the contrast between the clamour and smells and filthy simmering pavements of mean streets and the summer camp."

As a boy at Charterhouse, Baden-Powell used to skip compulsory games to watch birds and to track animals in the out-of-bounds woodlands in the surrounding Surrey countryside at Godalming. He believed that the worst little town-bred hooligan, thief and liar had a spark of goodness in him that could be aroused by contact with natural environment. He instinctively took to boys with a touch of the devil in them. His biographer, E. E. Reynolds, observes: "He preferred Kim to Peter Pan; he knew that the one thing most boys desire is to grow up and be men, and his whole object was to enable them to become sound men in body, mind and spirit."

Scouting grew from its inception at an astonishing pace. *Scouting for Boys* was published in the same year as Russell's *Working Lads' Clubs* and had already by that time enrolled tens of thousands of boys. Russell, apparently not as willing as Sir William Smith to countenance a rival organization, confined himself in his book to this somewhat terse comment: "General Baden-Powell's Boy Scout Scheme, very unpractical as a whole, gives many useful hints as to how the time of young boys may be occupied in camp."

The Rev. H. S. Pelham commented in *The Training of a Working Boy* in 1914, that scouting was unattractive to boys of the poorest classes and pointed to "a grave danger that men, with merely some knowledge of Scoutcraft and not attested as fit to undertake the moral and religious education of boys, were indiscriminately allowed to start Troops."

It may be true that scouting, like the boys' brigades, tended to attract boys who were, as Eagar puts it, "in the comity of the nation, who attended church or chapel, had decent and orderly homes and, as a rule, accepted the usages of society." Boys' clubs, on the other hand, catered for working boys deprived of opportunities by poverty. They were self-supporting rather than dependent adolescents, neglected because they did not attend church and were members of what would now be called "problem families." If they were not already in conflict with society at large, there was a danger that they soon would be if nobody gave them a helping hand.

The strictures of Russell and the Rev. Pelham on Baden-Powell's new youth movement look remarkably like sour grapes. His "unpractical scheme" soon proved its value, apart from giving hints on camping (which boys' clubs and brigades had pioneered much earlier in any case). Many boys' clubs, particularly in towns like Liverpool and Nottingham, incorporated scouts and brigades. Scouting was perhaps mainly for younger boys, but it attracted large numbers of adolescents too.

Baden-Powell was not, however, a simple soldier or an unpractical dreamer. He was a brilliant man of many parts—an actor, writer, artist and humorist, a sailor and horseman, and above all an educationist with a great understanding of the needs of boyhood and youth. He saw that the new education intent, as Trevelyan says, "on producing not peasants but clerks," inculcated ambition to win prizes and secure pay and position instead of the old-fashioned public school values of commonsense, manners, guts and, above all, service for others. To him, in the 1920s, it came as no surprise that the country was divided against itself with self-seeking individuals, cliques, political parties, religious sects and social classes. Like most upper class men of his time he was intensely patriotic and he aimed to strengthen national unity by bringing up boys who were efficient morally and physically, with the idea of using that efficiency in the service of the community as a whole. He saw more clearly than most that the great towns in which most of the nation lived had robbed boys of their heritage of field and hedgerow, green valley and hill, woods and streams. By giving that heritage back to succeeding generations of boys, he ensured that his name would live when boys had forgotten who was the hero of Mafeking.

3

Backward Birmingham

AT THE SAME TIME that General Baden-Powell was formulating his ideas for *Scouting for Boys*, the great city of Birmingham awoke from the sleep of the past century and suddenly became aware of the disgraceful plight of the pool of child labour which had helped to earn it the title of "the workshop of England." This awakening was stirred by the launching from Cathedral House of the Birmingham Street Boys' Union in 1905. It was founded, as its handbook said, to "deal with one great social problem in a definite way; this problem is the boys and girls who spend their childhood in the street subject to influences of degrading character. It is estimated that there are at least twenty thousand of such children in this city, and it is from their numbers that the loafers, criminals and unemployables are chiefly recruited."

This view was more than justified by the inquiry undertaken in the following decade at the request of Birmingham Education Committee by Arnold Freeman. His report, entitled *Boy Life and Labour*, was published in 1914, and showed that Birmingham had been indeed singularly backward in regulating child labour. Thousands of children still came home after school to work in sweatshops sewing buttons, hooks and eyes from the factories on to cards to be sold. This was a hangover from the Victorian age of small workshops in the Black Country, where very small children were used to blow the bellows to keep the fire hot, were taught to make the easiest kind of nails at seven or eight years of age, and at ten or twelve were expected to turn out a thousand nails a day. In the middle of the nineteenth century nails, chains, nuts, bolts, files, buckles and stirrups were still being manufactured under the old domestic system in the villages of South Staffordshire and Worcestershire, but women and children were also being drafted into the factories in the Birmingham district for heavy work such as the stamping of buttons and brass nails and notching the heads of screws. As late as 1887 a deputation from the Cradley Heath nail and chain makers had waited on the Home Secretary to argue against proposals in a new Factory Bill for restricting their employment on humanitarian grounds.

Clearly the traditions fostered in the shadow of that forest of smoking chimneys had been carried into the twentieth century. Freeman found boys working anything up to forty hours a week out of school hours in barber's shops, lathering chins for shaving, and others who sold papers in the streets or hung about the railway stations hoping to cadge a copper or two.

Once they left school their chances of becoming skilled tradesmen were negligible. They were hired in their thousands by small Birmingham factories and workshops at 7s. a week and discarded as soon as they reached sixteen or seventeen, the age when they became insurable, wanting higher wages as well. There was always a plentiful supply of fourteen-year-olds waiting to take their place to work long hours for low wages. A sample taken by Freeman comprised: 6 boys apparently destined for skilled work, against 44 for unskilled work and 21 probable unemployables. As the Rev. H. S. Pelham remarked in *The Training of the Working Boy*, published in the same year as Freeman's report, "generation after generation of healthy youngsters grow up to be seedy louts."

Both these exposés of civic indifference to youth arrived after the great public outcry which had already brought about legislation in Parliament to improve the working life of adolescents. It remains a mystery why Birmingham, which under Joseph Chamberlain in the 1870s set the pace for other industrial cities in developing municipal amenities, lagged behind in this important respect. Apart from the few Catholic boys' clubs which were started up when Chamberlain was mayor, voluntary efforts to provide leisure and recreation seemed either lacking or doomed to failure from want of enthusiasm. It might have been because of a general demoralization of the working classes brought about by the inhuman conditions in which they lived and worked, but people in Liverpool, Manchester and Bristol, not to mention London, endured conditions just as bad as in Birmingham. Certainly the working men of Birmingham did not set their sons any example of corporate life. Repeated attempts to start mechanics' institutes and working men's clubs ended in failure. Against this background the setting up of the Birmingham Kyrle Society in 1880 must have been a considerable act of faith, since its object was: "To increase the stock of pure and innocent pleasures open to the hard-working poor, thus leading them to seek and find enjoyment in something higher than the gin-palace and more refined music-hall."

The society started separate evening classes for boys and girls, out of which grew separate clubs at the end of the 1880s. Within a year or two the boys' club had become a lively self-governing organization with a highly successful football team and a band. Unusually, for that time, the boys held dances with the girls' club in a newly built hall in Sheep Street. But Midland factory girls had a tradition of mixing on more or less equal terms with their menfolk. In the early years of Victoria's reign the Children's Employment Commission had noted that young girls from the forges "often enter the beer shops, call for their pints, and smoke their pipes like men." It is not difficult to imagine their grand-daughters howling with derision at the Kyrle Society's offer of "pure and innocent pleasures." Yet that society had at least managed to breathe life into two clubs for young people. The Birmingham Young Men's Christian Association, founded in 1849, waited for the twentieth century to arrive before it opened up a part of its premises to young boys.

As we have seen, Rugby School started up a boys' club in Birmingham towards the end of the nineteenth century and various other public schools followed, but again they were all trailing in the wake of the great social movements which had started in other parts of the country.

The impetus to the boys' club movement which came from the founding of the Birmingham Street Boys' Union was provided by Canon Carnegie. He looked to Oxford University for men who were prepared to do what had been done in London at Toynbee Hall and other places, to come and live among the working people in Birmingham and share their problems.

One of those who came was Norman Chamberlain, a cousin of Neville and a nephew of Joseph Chamberlain, the man who "parked, paved, assized, marketed, gas-and-watered, and improved" Birmingham before moving on to Westminster and affairs of State. Norman Chamberlain had distinguished himself at Eton and Magdalen College, Oxford; he had travelled abroad, and in 1907 he and three other Oxford men settled into a small house in Edgbaston and began an intensive study of the urchins who lounged about the railway stations and sold newspapers. Most of them came from bad homes or had no homes at all, like the waifs Dr. Barnardo had discovered in London several decades earlier. They had been callously thrown on to the streets after being employed for a couple of years after leaving school in dead-end factory jobs. They were a pest to magistrates, police and public alike, but Chamberlain discovered, perhaps to his own surprise, that he liked them. Many of them had sharp intelligence as well as courage, and were able to keep a sense of humour even in their hopeless situation.

Chamberlain opened a club for them and arranged for some of them to seek a new life in Canada. They repaid him if and when they made good. A large number did make good, and when he went to visit them in three successive summers he found them living a life with families of their own which was as far removed from the streets of Birmingham as another planet. After several changes of home, Chamberlain eventually moved his rough boys—too rough even for membership of other clubs started up in the city centre by Canon Carnegie's Street Boys' Union—into the basement of the building occupied by the recently created Juvenile Employment Exchange. When they got into trouble with the police and were hauled up before the magistrates, he spoke up for them.

In the city where his uncle, having made a great deal of money from the manufacture of screws, had provided all the outward signs of municipal pomp and pride, Norman Chamberlain immersed himself in the lower stratum of society which had been overlooked. Quite simply, it had been forgotten that adolescent boys and girls, even more than grown men and women, needed something more than unremitting toil in their lives. Norman Chamberlain was personally striving to provide what was missing, but being a Chamberlain in Birmingham was not in itself enough.

He and his friend from Oxford, Edward Birchall, collected evidence for official enquiries, including those of the Poor Law Commission. Chamberlain became a city councillor at about the same time as his cousin Neville, who was destined to become Prime Minister and go down in history as the appeaser of Hitler. A highly controversial measure of National Insurance was introduced by Lloyd George in 1912, but universal unemployment benefit was still to come. However, the heady spirit of social reform induced the local authorities in Birmingham to adopt a scheme worked out by Norman Chamberlain, as chairman of the advisory committee to the newly formed Labour Exchange, in which the city's education department and the local representatives of the Ministry of Labour would work together on all aspects of juvenile welfare.

Meanwhile voluntary workers had formed thirty-four clubs in what was now renamed as the Street Children's Union because it had become obvious that young girls as much as boys, if not more so, were the victims of the street.* The clubs accepted boys at the early age of nine but it was soon found that youths in their teens would not have anything to do with clubs run for children, so they were organized separately as junior clubs for boys between ten and fourteen and senior clubs for those from fourteen to eighteen. In 1911 they took over the boys' and girls' clubs in Kyrle Hall, which then became the headquarters of the Street Children's Union.

In the new Edwardian age of enlightenment even some of the factories started forming clubs for their boy employees, although the majority of lads looked on such projects with the deepest suspicion. The first in the field in 1900 was the Bourneville Youths' Club for the boy labour at Cadbury's cocoa and chocolate works, and it attracted four hundred members. Among those who followed suit and started works boys' clubs of their own were Guest, Keen & Nettlefold and ICI metals.

In the Birmingham of the early 1900s all the streams of effort which went into the making of the boys' club movement as a whole can be seen merging. The pastoral work of the church brought about the Street Children's Union, while Norman Chamberlain was working among the very roughest of them in the manner of a Dr. Barnardo or a General Gordon; the paternalism of Victorian millowners flowered again in the factories, whilst the hand of twentieth century State paternalism created the Juvenile Employment Exchange; Oxford Blues and public school men were at the same time trying to civilize Birmingham youth, just as they had civilized Whitechapel and Bermondsey.

* After the First World War it had yet another change of name and became the Boys' and Girls' Union.

4

Many Mansions

IN THE FIRST TWENTY YEARS OF THE TWENTIETH CENTURY, boys' clubs in in the industrial towns of England were beginning to develop a recognizable pattern, although there was still plenty of room for individual identity. The movement's house had many mansions, even if some of them were in a tumbledown state.

But some of the leaders keenly felt the lack of a national headquarters and policy. In *Working Lads' Clubs*, Charles Russell argued forcefully for "a central office for all the lads' clubs in the kingdom":

"At the present time it is most rare for a lads' club manager in one part of the country to have the smallest knowledge as to what other clubs exist elsewhere.... There are probably many people who would like to found boys' clubs if only they knew how to set about it, just as there are many who do start them on very vague principles, and stumble along in the dark in their search for a workable and efficient scheme of operations. Given a central office to which letters of inquiry might be addressed, the best information would always be available. To it, also, men desirous of devoting some of their leisure time to the interest of boys, but not already in touch with anybody connected with a club, might apply.... In this way the office might form a very useful 'labour bureau'...."

Russell goes on to suggest that a central office could publish a national journal and perhaps give loans to struggling young clubs. He also felt that such an office would help to bring together the many individual organizations throughout the country into a nationwide movement. When the clubs of Manchester and district formed themselves into a federation in 1907, the year before the *Lads' Clubs*, with its call for a national office, was published, there was no consultation of any kind with the London federation, which had existed for the past twenty years. Similarly, the Liverpool Union of Boys' Clubs came into being in 1911 with fourteen clubs affiliated but no apparent sense of belonging to a nationwide movement. Russell made it clear in his book that his idea of federation was not "a mere union of those within one city, nor simply a mutual arrangement for inter-club competitions for ... sport and games." His was an altogether wider concept, but, alas, nothing came of it in his lifetime. Like other club managers and leaders he had to rely, in his days at Heyrod Street, Ancoats (Manchester) on his own initiative and resourcefulness. Before the Manchester and Salford Playing Fields Society was formed in 1907, he advertised in the evening papers that any working boys' football team who were unable to find a ground should get in touch with him. The captains and secretaries of street football teams lined up at Heyrod Street and within a couple of weeks no fewer than sixty teams who could produce evidence of a dozen members and the possession of a real football were on his list. Russell arranged the matches, collected a few shillings from each captain in advance of £1 rent for a season, and sent out his club officers to map out pitches and put up goal-posts on thirty acres of open land not far from the city centre.

When he was organizing the rebuilding of the Heyrod Street club in the early 1900s he could find nothing in written form to help him select the best lay-out and design, and it was this lack of advice which led him to write the first practical text-book of boys' club management, *Working Lads' Clubs*. It gives a vivid picture of the typical Edwardian boys' club in the midst of mean streets, a few minutes' walk from the box-like little houses where the boys lived and the factories where they worked.

Russell gives many practical hints for the outfitting of such clubs:

"The windows should be of frosted glass up to a man's height, or—and this is far more homely—should be fitted with blinds or curtains. For this purpose there is perhaps nothing better than crimson holland blinds with spring rollers. . . . Except to meet cases of emergency, such as fire, there should be only one means of entrance and exit. A club which members can enter or leave by two different doors is full of possibilities for all kinds of mischief. . . . The upper halves of all doors in the club should be glazed, the better to secure proper supervision. . . . Some boys, particularly untamed new members, are always on the *qui vive* to outwit their officers, and three or four lads often find great pleasure in 'sporting their oak', which means that gambling and other unauthorized proceedings may be taking place behind a closed door."

He does not elaborate on what other kinds of "unauthorized proceedings" might go on behind doors made entirely of wood, but he does warn that the removal of keys and bolts is no solution because boys have other ways of fastening doors, like placing a chair with the top of its back rail under the door handle.

Russel goes on to recommend a glazed brick dado, or skirting, up to 5 feet, with the ordinary brickwork painted or distempered, as the best kind of wall in all clubrooms, since "boys always lounge against the walls." He says that photographs of harriers or of football, cricket, gymnastic or swimming teams which had gained honours for the club should be placed in prominent positions, and that:

"The entrance hall must contain an effective well-kept notice-board and an honours board, upon which will be painted a list of the distinctions won by the club in sports and games. Attention to small details such as these will do much to foster a good spirit and to remind the members continually that the place is not merely a playground, but, in the best sense of the word, a club."

One of the leading clubs of the early 1900s was the Shaftesbury Club at

Birkenhead. In 1903, having outgrown its rooms in Chester Street, it was installed in new quarters in the converted Ebenezer Baptist Chapel, a substantial stone building in Jackson Street between the main railway line and the gasworks. The total cost of the project was £1,800, raised by public appeal. The chapel hall had been converted into a games room, and a large room underneath was turned into a gymnasium, basket-ball court and "romping-room" for the juniors. There was coke-fired central heating as well as open coal fires. But, almost unbelievable to the six hundred boys who turned up on 15th October to view their new club, it had indoor lavatories. William Norrish, the Club's founder, wrote later a brief note in his annual report which tells us more about contemporary standards of sanitation: "The lavatory, unique in simplicity, and effective in utility, is made good use of. The boys are becoming cleaner year by year, although there are still some startling exceptions. Soap, water and clean towels now rank among the popular features of the Club."

Birkenhead was changing with the times. Electric tramcars were replacing horse-drawn ones. The Argyle was becoming one of the most famous music halls in the north. Saturday afternoon "at the match" had become an established tradition among shipyard workers who crowded Prenton Park to watch Tranmere Rovers play. But there were still hundreds of boys, members of the Shaftesbury Club, who wore boots only on Sundays. Their everyday garb was woollen jerseys and corduroy shorts, and bare feet, but they had cloth caps, special suits and boots to wear to church on Sundays. Their most prized possessions were the metal tallies for which they paid 1d. each and which were their passports to the club in Jackson Street. An anonymous contributor to the *Birkenhead Advertiser* wrote in 1910 of one such lad:

"It was that jolly time between afternoon school and tea time, when right-minded boys are revelling in the freedom of 'school let out'. It was pleasant October weather, and he was still in summer attire, brown legs and feet, uncovered head, and some scanty but tidy clothes. Holding a tiny packet of tea, he was making a beeline up the street when a yellow bill was thrust into his hand, announcing in bold type 'all sorts of things for boys' for a penny a year. Very earnestly he read the list of attractions enumerated, and then carefully folded the paper and hid it among his garments, resolving that Thursday night should find him at the Shaftesbury Club for Street Boys and Working Lads. . . . Thursday evening arrived, and with a few others he was very early hurrying in the direction of the Haymarket and Jackson Street, but soon found they were part of a great throng all bound one way. Before they were near enough to see the Shaftesbury flag flying he found a still greater throng waiting for opening time. . . . He was by no means the only one not wearing shoes and stockings, and there were boys with far poorer clothes than his, but nobody stared at them. He had never seen so many boys together in his life. He was a little awe-struck at first with the shipyard and other big lads, but soon found that little chaps, big chaps, and officers all alike were delighted to see each other. . . . A long string of good things to be done was announced, and when the new Shaftesbury boy was asleep that night in a crowded, stuffy room he had visions of glorious winter evenings and of sleeping in a tent on summer nights, of picking wild flowers and swimming in the sea, and seeing picture-book mountains and running brooks, all real."

By the end of the Edwardian decade "The Shaftes," as it became known, had over a thousand members, their ages ranging from nine to nineteen. Despite the appearance of complete integration given by that contemporary report in the *Advertiser* no club could satisfy the interest and needs of such a range at one and the same time. Older boys and younger boys simply do not mix. In 1911 a new brick building, lit by electricity, was built on the land adjoining the former Baptist Chapel as a club for senior boys aged from fourteen and a half upwards. The building went up in the unbelievably short time between May and October (a good bricklayer in those days laid a thousand bricks a day) and it cost £2,700. Once again the money was raised by public appeal to local businessmen, including William Hesketh Lever of Sunlight Soap fame, and to Andrew Carnegie, the great American philanthropist of the age. Once again "Old Nor," as he was now known to his boys, took to his bicycle in search of benefactors around the district. It was not until 1912, after twenty-five years of completely voluntary service at his own expense, that he agreed to accept an *honorarium* of £72 a year guaranteed by a number of private individuals and not included in the club's accounts. Five years later he became full-time secretary at a salary of £120 a year.

Meanwhile, clubs were springing up in other industrial areas. In the raw new steel town of Middlesbrough, where straight, flat, slate-grey streets spread out from Albert Square and the gothic-style Town Hall, Joe Walton, a lawyer, had started a club in 1906 immediately after being called to the Bar. From the heights of the Cleveland Hills just a few miles away, the iron landscape—dominated by the dockland cranes, the blast furnaces, the factory chimneys and the new Transporter Bridge soaring 275 feet above the River Tees—was no more than a smudge of smoke on the horizon. But the children of the town were trapped in soot-blackened streets like Newport Road and Cannon Street. Walton, despite delicate health, gave all his spare time, energy and money to his club, where boys learned to box and play football (the great sporting passion of the town) and were given the occasional chance to escape to the moors and the beautiful sands beside the sea between Redcar and Saltburn. Joe Walton died young in 1913 but the Joe Walton Boy's Club, as it was named after his death, lived on to produce many notable boxers and footballers.

There is no doubt that many of the best-run boys' clubs were in some of the most depressed areas, and that to many thousands of town boys the club was the only bright thing in their lives. Yet financing the activities which made the clubs so popular was not an easy task. It was a considerable problem to balance the profits from the canteen and the pence paid by the boys as subscriptions for membership and for billiards, football and cricket, against the bills for heating, lighting, repairs, rent and rates, laundry, postage and printing costs and so on. Most clubs had to be self-supporting and make do with dismal accommodation. Few clubs had more grisly accommodation than the one in Shadwell, in the East London dockland. A former mortuary, it was affectionately referred to by its members as "The Deadhouse." In 1909 a local man suggested to a group of lads who used to congregate in an Italian ice cream shop between games of "banker" or pitch-and-toss in the back alleys that they could form a football team. They liked following professional football, but they had never actually played before. The team which they formed was called Albion United, in honour of the pub at the corner of the street. As their numbers grew they felt the need for a place of their own, and found it in the former mortuary, an outhouse at the back of the Wesleyan Mission in Cable Street. It was anything but a "deadhouse" when forty high-spirited Cockney lads filled it. One of the original members described it: "The walls of the place trickled with water, and to get to it you passed along the old cemetery wall for 100 yards, arriving with luck, after a journey on a wet night, through small puddles not less than ankle deep. This was the home of our Club for three years."

Albion United became well known in the district, and to Saturday football the club added penny games of draughts, ludo and snakes-and-ladders and, later on, harriers. There was, needless to say, no open country near at hand, but street running was considered to be a reasonable way of keeping fit. It took some courage, however, to go running with the harriers along the Ratcliffe Highway, where prostitutes lounged in every window and doorway or promenaded with seamen from every maritime nation in the world. Other small boys who gambled away their hard-earned pennies at street corners or in gangs on Sunday morning at the old Fish Market jeered at the harriers and pelted them with mud as they ran through the dark, dirty streets in mid-winter, but more and more of them secretly dreamed of some day being members of "The Albion" themselves.

In 1914 the Albion, now affiliated to the London Federation of Working Boys' Clubs, and meeting four nights a week, used the schoolroom of the Wesleyan Chapel as a gymnasium and borrowed a room at Toynbee Hall for meetings on Saturday night, the most important night of the week for East-Enders, spent mostly in the pubs and music halls.

So many new members were joining that the club had to find a new home, and the Wesleyan Mission turned over to them one of its halls in High Street, Shadwell, which was known as Paddy's Goose. It had kept that curious name from its former occupation as a beer-house and dance-hall kept by an Irishman and known to the licensing authorities as The Swan. Paddy, however, when he was playing host to seafaring men and their painted ladies, was in the habit of calling the stone bird hanging over the door his "goose."

It was twenty years since Paddy lost his licence, but it was still Paddy's Goose to the eager youngsters who swarmed in and by their own labour turned the old bar into a billiard room and canteen and the dancing hall into a gymnasium. The old beer cellars were transformed into a chapel and a dressing room with three shower baths. From this romantic beginning in the early 1900s sprang a whole group of boys' clubs known as the Highway Clubs, after the Ratcliffe Highway, but a long way from the old song which ran:

> You jovial sailors one and all
> When you in the port of London call
> Mind Ratcliffe Highway and damsels loose
> The William, The Bear and Paddy's Goose.

The boys who frequented these clubs lived in a grim little world of narrow horizons, enlivened only by the music hall and silent films, so unlifelike and jerky that they were sometimes called "the shakies." Opportunities to escape the confines of the cities were few and to adventure-minded lads the urge to travel was strong. The Wright brothers had built the first aeroplane and a Frenchman called Bleriot had made headlines by flying across the Channel, but the only way of leaving the shores of England was still by steamship. The dream of many a small boy in the East End was to be a train driver or to "run away to sea" in one of the merchant ships he could see tied up bow to stern at the wharves in the Thames, their flags and the foreign tongues of their crews suggesting far-off ports like Rio and Bombay.

Throughout Victorian and Edwardian times emigration was an ambition of many town-bred boys who had heard of higher wages and better living in the colonies than could be hoped for by a working class lad in England. Some of the early boys' club men helped them to achieve that ambition. Oliver Hind, with his 400-acre Dakeyne Farm near Windsor in Nova Scotia, and Norman Chamberlain paying the passage money to Canada for Birmingham street boys, have been mentioned earlier. Another was Donald Hankey, of the Oxford and Bermondsey group, who sent South London lads to Wales for experience of farm life before paying their passages to Australia. In 1913 he went to Australia himself to look them up and make a study of conditions there for emigrant boys.

A former manager of the Victoria Club in London who emigrated to Montreal in the early 1900s made it his business to meet new arrivals from the old country and hired a room where those who stayed in and around the city could meet once a week. In 1908 there were forty-seven old boys of the club in Canada, keeping in touch with one another and writing home to the club at least once a month. In New York several more banded together to form a British-American Club for lads who, like themselves, had just arrived from England.

Charles Russell saw the organization of help for emigrating boys on their arrival in a new country as another reason for the formation of a federation of lads' clubs in Britain. He was spurred on in his campaign by the success abroad of the YMCA, founded in the 1840s, which had by this time built up a world-wide network of seven thousand branches. When a member emigrated he at once found a club and friends, was supplied with introductions and helped to find a job. Russell wrote:

"Such highly developed organization is a reproach to the lads' clubs, whose members ought to be in a similarly happy position. Large numbers of club members emigrate to Canada in particular, and one of the first results of a general federation would, it might be hoped, be the establishment in Montreal or Toronto of a receiving bureau to which lads could go on arrival."

Not many lads were able to emigrate, if indeed they wanted to, and for thousands of them the local club must have represented an escape, perhaps the only escape, from an inadequate home. Sleeping four or six in a bed could be endured, so could dampness and draughtiness and meagre meals, provided the family was held together by bonds of mutual affection and respect. Where these were absent and there was drunkenness of the father or mother, or both, cruelty to the children, constant wrangling, recriminations and abuse, the eldest son would be glad to escape to the warm bright atmosphere and the friendliness of the club. In some homes his presence at home in the evenings was neither encouraged nor wanted, and the only interest shown was in the size of the pay packet he brought home from work every week.

Russell was at pains to defend the clubs against accusations that they tended to break up family life. He had little patience with middle class critics who thought that boys' clubs should cater only for the very roughest classes. "Do these people ever send their own sons to boarding school?" he asked, inferring that character training should not be reserved only for the sons of the well-to-do. He suggested that if a boy attended the club every night of the week, some inquiries should be made at his home; similarly if a boy was not coming regularly checks were made—it could be that he was giving the impression at home that he was off to the club when he was spending his leisure elsewhere. Occasional "parents' nights" and tea parties for younger brothers and sisters were other ways of keeping a link between the club and the family.

Russell had noticed the extraordinary family responsibility shown by working class youths, especially at camp: "It is rarely a big brother will allow a younger one to sleep in any tent but his own, and on a country walk it is very noticeable how he looks round to see where 'our kid' is."

There was a danger, too, that a club with educational as well as sporting and leisure activities would improve a lad to the extent that he started looking down on his parents, who were often virtually illiterate. In any case he was considerably more fortunate than his sisters, who usually had to drudge at the sink and about the house when they came home from school or work, while he simply had his tea and went out for the evening.

5

Sex and the Edwardian Boys' Club

ALTHOUGH BOYS' CLUBS fostered Victorian public school notions of male chivalry towards the weaker sex (which was all very well in a house full of servants), working class relations between the sexes were very well defined. Woman was firmly chained to the kitchen sink, while man went to pub or club. R. Seebohm Rowntree's study of poverty in York at the turn of the twentieth century quoted one housewife: 'If there's anything extra to buy, such as a pair of boots for one of the children, me and the children goes without dinner—or mebbe only' as a cup o' tea and a bit o' bread, but Jim 'ollers takes his dinner to work, and I never tell 'im.''

There was no co-education and women at work outside the home were carefully segregated from the men. Although there is no evidence of sex in Edwardian boys' clubs (like their fathers in their working men's clubs they preferred to keep the females out) it is reasonable to assume that they talked about it among themselves. But Russell's manual didn't even mention the subject of sex instruction.* He was clearly one of the school who believed that cold baths and plenty of exercise took care of a boy's interest in the opposite sex, although he admitted: "Seeing that the great majority of boys in any club will certainly marry long before they are thirty years of age, it is strange that so little thought or attention is given to their relation to girls and women."

He then went on to say that as a practical question it did not greatly concern clubs which closed their doors to lads over seventeen or eighteen years of age, an indication of the then current failure to recognize the true age of puberty. According to Russell, girls were of little interest to the

---

* A revised edition by his wife Lilian published in 1932 had simply this to say: "The question whether any definite sex instruction should be given to young people is being considered by a special sub-committee of the Juvenile Organizations Committee ... managers should familiarize themselves with the arguments *pro* and *con*, and with some of the best publications on the subject, that they may not be embarrassed or non-plussed when consulted in confidence." The "best publications" at the time were, it seems, those of the Alliance of Honour and White Cross League, organizations dedicated to keeping the youth of the nation pure, chaste and unsullied. Victorian attitudes to sex died hard.

majority of boys' club members, although he admitted there were some precocious boys whom leaders must be "prepared to warn and counsel."

He was, however, very keen on the idea of chivalry towards the opposite sex, and although he still made the Victorian distinction between *ladies* and *women*, he lamented the lack of chivalry among working boys:

"The same boys who seem totally wanting in reverence for girlhood, and indulge in coarse jests and insolent familiarities, almost universally resent insult to their own sisters, thus proving that they are not without right instincts and a sense of shame. These instincts are susceptible to training, and in a club boys cannot be taught too early to respect all girls as much as they wish other boys to respect those of their own family, to feel that their names and honour must at all costs be kept unsullied, to keep a check on their thoughts, words and deeds where they are concerned, and to practise little habits of politeness as occasion demands. Many boys think it manly to express contempt for girls and women. They should be told that it is the very reverse, and whenever they are heard to speak of them lightly or disparagingly they should be discouraged. Above all, they should be taught to speak respectfully of their mothers, and an officer ought never to allow such expressions as 'the old girl' or 'the old geyser' to pass unchecked. Real affection and esteem for mothers do, however, very commonly exist."

Between the ages of fourteen and sixteen Victorian and Edwardian working class boys and girls drifted noticeably apart. In the freer Edwardian atmosphere there was more recognition of developing sex consciousness in adolescents, but even at seventeen a boy usually had two or three male intimates, whose sisters he would meet regularly at their homes, but no serious girl-friend, unless he was "courting." A visit to tea at a girl's home was a recognized sign of courtship, so that a boy never called on a girl at her home unless his motives were towards marriage. The consequence was that few boys or girls were on friendly terms with a variety of members of the opposite sex.

So there grew up in the towns the practice of groups of boys hanging about for two or three hours at a time at a street corner, ogling and whistling after the girls with a great show of bravado among themselves. If one of the lads was daring enough to "pick up" a girl he was a great hero in his pals' eyes. In Lancashire in the early 1900s it was called "stragging," a phrase borrowed from the pigeon lofts that were a popular working man's pastime. To strag was to send out a tame pigeon which would fly round neighbouring cotes and bring other pigeons back. Every town of any size had its promenade quarter where on Saturday and Sunday evenings groups of sniggering boys and giggling girls would promenade, eyeing one another.

The attraction to youngsters of a seat "in the gods" at some glaring, gaslit music hall, were supplemented in the Edwardian period by the innovation of the moving pictures and a pleasing proximity in the darkness to the girl of the moment. Russell, like the Victorian clergyman mentioned earlier, objected to "vulgar" music hall lyrics like "Then you wink the other eye" and "A little of what you fancy does you good." He admitted that the tunes were catchy: "If any leader is able to write topical words to go with the tune, he will give huge pleasure, and ears will no longer be offended by vulgar words."

Other ways of boy meeting girl were to go to a roller skating rink or a dance hall. Lots of boys and girls met their future wives or husbands by picking-up and there is nothing to suggest that there was anything harmful about it. In an age when servant girls were forbidden by their employers to have "followers" and living-in shop assistants were ordered by the rules of the house to lead celibate lives, it seems surprising in retrospect that the opportunity ever arose for pre-marital sexual experience.

But, whatever the obstacles, servant girls managed to find husbands among the butcher's boys, milkmen and policemen who called at the tradesmen's entrance below-stairs, shop assistants managed to "go on the mash" or have "a little fling" under pain of instant dismissal, and boys' club lads were presumably no different. In the latter case the signs were unmistakable when a boy gave up evening classes, billiards and even his beloved football. His friends would shake their heads sadly and say he was "going down hill" or when caught out in some minor misdemeanour would plead on their own behalf: "Well, at any rate, I'm not dancing mad like Bill." As Russell wisely observes: "It must be remembered that if the customs and conventions of the working-class home do not allow of free association between boys and girls, it is inevitable that by hook or crook they will manage to meet somewhere."

Mixed youth clubs were unknown in that period. There were of course girls' clubs and organisations like the Girls' Friendly Society, the Young Women's Christian Association and the Metropolitan Association for Befriending Young Servants. Like boys' clubs they had developed from the 1850s out of Victorian philanthropy and concern for the lower orders. Maude Stanley, who devoted her life to the movement and wrote *Clubs for Working Girls* in 1890, expressed the then current attitudes: "We have not wished to take our girls out of their class but we have wished to see them ennoble the class to which they belong. The tone will soon become free from vulgar boisterousness if ladies will take part in the evenings of recreation."

That sort of snobbishness was hardly likely to attract girls in the era of the suffragettes, when, as Lily Montague suggested in the studies of working boys referred to earlier, the "girl in the background" had not been educated to stay contentedly in that retiring position. Miss Montague at least had a sense of humour. She told of one girls' club leader who took her flock on a country outing and came back alone because the military camp they passed "offered so many engrossing attractions."

This was the difficulty. Mixed clubs for boys and girls between the ages of fourteen and eighteen had been tried but had failed. Mixed classes in evening schools had failed too because the girls' innate tendency to flirt interrupted serious study. Since women far outnumbered men in Britain, girls were forced to chase after boys if they wanted to get a husband.

Club leaders of both sexes agreed that it would be an excellent idea for their respective members to meet regularly for dances, like those held at the Kyrle Club in Sheep Street, Birmingham, twenty years previously. Birmingham led the way in this respect at least and continued to do so, but elsewhere there was little contact between boys' and girls' clubs, even where they were affiliated. Like the public schools, boys' clubs have maintained their monastic quality into the twentieth century. In an age when co-education is the rule rather than the exception, these schools and clubs still fight to preserve their all-male status.

6

The End
of the Interlude

THERE WAS LITTLE INCREASE in the numbers of men voluntarily engaged in boys' club work in the early 1900s; instead there was an increasing tendency to employ paid managers. As the clubs developed a definite purpose and more businesslike methods of management, running them became a specialised job.

While many of the older clubs—including the Kensington and Cyprus Boys' Clubs—faded out, new and larger ones, much more lavishly equipped, were springing up in London. The Eton Manor Boys' Club, founded in Hackney by a group of wealthy Old Etonians who lived at the almost palatial premises in the style to which they were accustomed, had extensive playing fields and a membership of four hundred.

Of the thirty-one clubs affiliated to the London Federation in 1900 only twelve remained ten years later, but the total number of affiliated clubs rose to thirty-nine in that decade. Most of the new ones kept to the tried and tested formula of "football in Fulham, boxing in Balham and ping-pong in Putney." But they brought the standards of competition and equipment up to a level which kept the rougher boys out. Almost alone, the Oxford and Bermondsey Clubs—Gordon, Canterbury, Decima Street and Dockhead—remained faithful to the boys from the poorest homes, in spite of the fact that they did not win cups and medals at cricket and football.

Up to 1914 the Bermondsey Club's football elevens, travelling to Blackheath on short winter afternoons, would change in a hired room at the tram terminus in Greenwich and carry their goalposts up the hill to the pitch for twenty-five minutes' play each way before it became too dark to see. It was not until after the war that the London County Council provided changing rooms nearer at hand, together with goalposts and properly marked out pitches, and it was not until 1923 that the National Playing Fields Association was founded. Down the Ratcliffe Highway, one of the toughest areas in all Edwardian London, the rough boys had to teach themselves football and start their own club in the Deadhouse and Paddy's Goose, as we have seen.

The Church of England was much less of a force behind the London boys' clubs of the early 1900s than it had been in the previous century. The clubs were not particularly helpful in bolstering up falling church attendances, and the new generation of curates, trained in the theological colleges, were not so keen on games as their predecessors.

It was in the towns of the Midlands and the North that the pioneering phase of the boys' club movement was carried over into the twentieth century. But in London, as Anglican influence waned, other churches discovered a new interest in the movement. The Roman Catholics opened St. Dominic's Boys' Club in Kentish Town and the Fisher and Downside clubs in Bermondsey. The Free Church opened a splendidly equipped club at Fairbairn House in West Ham and raised a serious challenge to Eton Manor in track-running and swimming.

Institutes died out with the development of State education, and most of the boys' clubs which survived in London—unlike those in Manchester and other parts of the North, which laid great stress on evening classes—seemed obsessed with physical fitness alone. The public school men and others of the older generation who had started boys' clubs in Victoria's day were now trying to change society as a whole instead of being prepared to carry on under the existing conditions of blatant inequality. There is no doubt that many of them were moved to action by experiencing for themselves what life was like at its lowest levels.

So the end of the Edwardian interlude with the death of the king was accompanied by an unprecedented flurry of legislation designed to alleviate the sufferings of the working classes and lay the foundations of the Welfare State. Unexpectedly, it was also accompanied by great civil violence, a whole series of strikes and the marching of militant suffragettes demanding votes for women, battling with the police and going on hunger strike in jail.

Against such a background of unrest, the problems of boy life which had excited such a spate of literature and such public indignation faded into the background. Boys continued to be overworked and underpaid, but for many of them an unforeseen and unimaginable change in their mode of life was on its way.

PART THREE

"We should have bred men, thousands and thousands of strong, capable, self-respecting men, instead of a crowd of bewildered, resentful and indifferent idlers who have lost the decent boyhood we gave them only to drift towards a shadowy and shiftless manhood."

J. B. Priestley in *English Journey*, 1933.

I

Never Again!

AT THE ENTRANCE TO A RECREATION GROUND about a mile outside Birkenhead, there is a bronze memorial tablet. Its inscription illustrates the cost of the "War to End Wars" to just one boys' club:

"This Playing Field is a memorial to the 630 past and present members of the Shaftesbury Boys' Club who served in the Great War, 1914–18, of whom 70 laid down their lives."

There are scores of such memorials up and down the country. A whole generation was lost in nearly four years of hopeless struggle to gain a few hundred yards or a mile or two of ground, only to retreat again. The cost in lives was three-quarters of a million from the British Isles alone, and most of them came from that generation which had been promised a brighter future by the elementary schools, polytechnics and boys' clubs. The Victoria Cross, the supreme award for gallantry, was won by two club lads, one from Ardwick Lads' Club and the other from the Meadow Boys' Club, Nottingham. Sir William Smith, the creator of the Boys' Brigade, died three months before the outbreak of the war in which whole companies of his boys, scarcely grown into men, marched to the sound of gunfire and "whizzbangs" instead of bugles and drums. Many of those fortunate enough to survive their first taste of real soldiering suffered for the rest of their lives from a legacy of shrapnel wounds and disfigurement, the after-effects of poison gas and the trauma of years spent amidst carnage in the mud with lice and rats for company.

The sufferings of officers were as bad as those of the private soldier. At one stage the life expectancy of a junior officer sent out to the Western Front was six weeks. Many of the finest products of the public schools and the universities, including some of those who in the pre-war years had devoted themselves to helping boys less fortunate than themselves, perished. Norman Chamberlain fell with a remnant of his company of the Grenadier Guards in 1917. His friend from his Birmingham Street Boys' Union days, Edward Birchall, was killed in the previous year after winning the Distinguished Service Order. Harry Riley, the man who did so much for the poor lads of Burnley, was another whose life ended prematurely in France.

At home there were desperate shortages of food. Civilians were killed in air raids by Zeppelin airships and later by aircraft, although the total of 1,117 dead only equalled the numbers of lives lost in single air raids in the Second World War.

On the north-west coast of England Birkenhead and Liverpool, the port through which flowed supplies of food and war equipment from America and Canada, were well beyond the range of German Zeppelins. Life went on much as usual, but in 1917 there were more obvious signs of a war going on when thousands of American soldiers called "doughboys" and wearing Boy Scout hats arrived to help finish Germany off. Birkenhead, the great shipbuilding town, underwent an increasing boom in industry during the war as Allied shipping losses from U-boat attacks mounted and the gaps in the Navy and Merchant Navy had to be quickly filled. Day and night the town rang to the sound of hammers on steel in the shipyards; unemployment became for the time being a bitter memory of the past.

Leslie Bibby vividly describes how the town was affected by the war. A Tipperary Club was formed where working people could come to write letters to those at the Front, knit comforts for the troops and read about the progress of the war in the newspapers, the only source of news in those pre-radio and television days. Just before war broke out, William Norrish had started recruiting boys of twelve to fourteen as Pioneers, who paraded with dummy rifles and were taught, among other things, the arts of trench-fighting. They were a self-governing off-shoot of the Shaftesbury Club and they elected their own officers (with the exception of the commanding officer), conducted their own meetings and meted out their own punishments. Their commander was "Yazzy" Davies, an old boy of the club, who came from Jackson Street. Norrish was very proud of them, as this extract from one of his war-time reports shows:

"The Pioneer Boys did their best to cover the Club with glory, doing good work on and off parade, under orders and on their own initiative. They have run hundreds of errands mainly to the homes of Soldiers and Sailors, they cleaned windows, filled coal sacks, collected a ton of waste paper for the Mayor's fund, helped the Red Cross depot, and placed a seat for the wounded day by day for a long period. Easter morning found them visiting homes bereaved by the war with tributes of flowers."

The Birkenhead Pioneers clearly owed some of their inspiration to the Boy Scouts who were engaged in similar war work all over the country. But the club had its own heroes in the Old Boys from Thomas Street, Davies Street, Elgin Street, Henry Street, Ivy Street and the rest, who had answered Kitchener's call. Their names and details of service are preserved in *Comrade in Arms,* a printed list which Norrish prepared and mailed to them each Christmas during the war. Eight of them won the Military Medal and three the Distinguished Conduct Medal. Two of the latter, James Baker and John Wilson, received their decorations at the club, and Norrish wrote of the first:

"The Mayor received the Medal by express post, together with an extension of Leave, and the same evening, before an enthusiastic gathering, including the Baker family, radiant with family pride, the Mayoress gracefully decorated the gallant lad, whose soldierly reply was, 'I wish to thank the boys for their welcome. I have only done my duty and hope to do more. It was at the Shaftesbury Club I learned to swim, and to that I owe my ability to perform the act for which I have received the medal. . . .' "

The war had some interesting social side effects, again illustrated by what was happening in Birkenhead. In 1916 the Shaftesbury Club for Street Boys and Working Lads became officially the Shaftesbury Boys' Club. In the days of working class prosperity, the members no longer had to walk the street in bare feet, and they were no longer prepared to be labelled as "street boys." They belonged to tightly-knit little communities where neighbours constantly popped in and out of one another's houses and they were proud of their streets and their clubs in a way that is rare indeed today.

At the same time Mr. Lloyd George, out of concern for production in the munitions factories, introduced some profound changes in the life-style of what Oscar Wilde called "the drinking classes." He restricted the hours during which people could drink on licensed premises and increased the price of a pint of beer to an unheard of 4d. These licensing laws were the death knell for thousands of street-corner beer-shops and gin-palaces and ushered in the era of "Time gentlemen, please" and the off-license where drink could be bought to take home.

Yet another sign of the times in Birkenhead in 1916 was the removal of the gas mantels at the old Baptist chapel in Jackson Street and their replacement with electric lamps. In the following year the War Department made an unsuccessful attempt to commandeer the club as a registration and medical centre. But the club managed to fight off the military with the support of the local Press, by pointing out that it was used by men home on leave and also did valuable work in preventing juvenile crime in the darkened streets.

The streets were darkened as a war-time economy measure to save fuel, but since it was not within German bombing range Birkenhead did not have a full-scale blackout. Elsewhere raids were an entirely new experience. So too, for the British at any rate, was conscription, introduced in 1915 as the supply of volunteers was drying up. All able-bodied males between the ages of eighteen and forty-one were pressed into service.

A member of the Highways Clubs, which sprang from the Deadhouse and Paddy's Goose in the East End, wrote: "As time went on, and our activities increased still further, the need for such work among working boys in these parts became more and more necessary, particularly as the War went on and more fathers and elder brothers left the homes."

Charles Russell, who had been appointed a member of a committee of inquiry into the conduct of Reformatory and Industrial Schools in 1911 came from Manchester to be chief inspector of the schools, and two years later played a leading part in this work on the home front. The repressive Victorian methods of dealing with young delinquents were exposed by a scandal over the ill-treatment of boys in the reformatory ship *Akbar* and Russell had quickly reformed the system, knowing as he did from his experience in lads' clubs that the delinquents were not some kind of sub-species but the victims of broken homes and neglect. The early years of the war, with so many of the men away at the front, added to the problems.

Magistrates, police and the public were alarmed at the serious increase in juvenile crime. Russell suggested to the Home Secretary, Sir Herbert Samuel, that the way to solve the problem was not to open still more reformatories and industrial schools but to put more effort into helping boys' clubs who were suffering from the absence of so many of their leaders.

Sir Herbert, who before the war had shown his practical concern for the welfare of youngsters by reforming the recruitment of very young boys as messengers and telegraph boys by the Post Office, readily responded by calling together representatives of the clubs, scouts and brigades to form in 1916 the Juvenile Organizations Committee, with Russell as chairman. The Girl Guides were represented on the committee too, although the growing problems of delinquency were mainly confined to boys. This was the first official recognition of the voluntary youth organizations.

An investigation carried out by the committee into seven thousand juvenile crimes in five industrial centres showed that the root of delinquency lay in the lack of anything better to do on dark winter evenings and at the weekends. Boys' imaginations were fired by war propaganda—in which comics whipping up popular feeling against the beastly Hun played no little part—and they wanted to do deeds of daring of the sort that they imagined their elders at the war to be engaged in. One constructive alternative was to get them involved in some kind of "war work," as the schools (also suffering from the loss of about half the nation's male teachers to the army) had done. There were war savings groups and work was organized on the land and in allotments. Cadet units satisfying the military impulse of boys too young to be soldiers were boosted by the war to a total membership of 108,000 in 1918.

The organizers of clubs and activities, who were either women or men long past middle age, faced obvious difficulties in handling boisterous youngsters in the mass. The exhortations of the Juvenile Organizations Committee seemed to produce some effect. At least, statistics of juvenile delinquency showed a decline as the war went on, but this may have been due, as some cynics suggested, to a slightly more liberal interpretation by the Home Office and the police as to what constituted crime and what could be excused as boyish high spirits. In any case, the police were undermanned too, and had even—for the first time—admitted women to their ranks for the duration of the war. It would not be fair to over-estimate the importance of scouts, boys' brigades and clubs in reducing juvenile crime, since they attracted only a minority of boys, but they certainly played an important part in keeping life at home somewhere near a resemblance of the normal peacetime patterns of behaviour.

Russell died suddenly in 1917, working at high pressure up to the end. He may not have formed the first boys' club in the land, but as a thinker, writer and a *doer* he had played a significant part in the development of the movement as a whole. More than anyone, he deserved to be known as one of the founding fathers of the boys' club movement in Britain.

He died at a time when, amidst mounting casualty lists and all the grief and disillusionment they caused, people's thoughts were turning to life after the war. Government committees were set to the task of planning what Lloyd George promised, with more political flair than practicality, would be a land fit for heroes (a phrase which no ex-serviceman could possibly forget during the years of depression which followed). Among the plethora of departmental committees set up in the idealistic days of 1916 was one on Juvenile Education in relation to Employment after the War.

It was chaired by Herbert Lewis, one of Lloyd George's friends from Wales, who seemed to share his gift of rhetoric. The report of the committee —the Lewis Report—declared uncompromisingly: "...we have to perfect the civilization for which men have shed their blood."

The report recognized that employment in the industrial centres on the pre-war pattern was a source of discouragement, disappointment and disillusion among young people who left school at fourteen. Only one in five had any kind of further education and still fewer kept at it long enough to derive any real benefit from it. The report continued:

"In a sense there is only one remedy. But it is a pretty thoroughgoing one; nothing less than complete change of temper and outlook on the part of the people of this country as to what they mean, through the forces in industry and society, to make of their boys and girls. Can the age of adolescence be brought out of the purview of economic exploitation and into that of social conscience? Can the conception of the juvenile as primarily a little wage earner be replaced by the conception of the juvenile as primarily the workman and the citizen in training?

Can it be established that the educational purpose is to be the dominating one, without as well as within the school doors, during those formative years between 12 and 18? If not, clearly no remedies at all are possible in the absence of the will by which alone they could be rendered effective."

It had taken a war to bring to governmental attention what had been perfectly obvious to boys' club managers for years: that the drift of young school-leavers into dead-end jobs resulted in unemployment and delinquency in later years. It was so easy to get the first job at fourteen, at the first place where there was a sign "Boys wanted" or the one offering the greatest number of shillings a week.

Too many teachers seemed to regard elementary school boys as mere fodder to employers who treated them as cheaply-bought machines, easily expendable after a couple of years. The majority of parents, lacking any kind of security themselves, believed in living for the present, and letting the future take care of itself. The addition of a few shillings a week to the family budget was enough to make most working class parents eager for their sons and daughters to leave school and start work as soon as possible.

Boys of fourteen are not noted for weighing up the consequences of what they do, or considering future prospects. So boys who would have made excellent craftsmen became errand boys instead, and when they became too old for that occupation, they were turned out to join the ranks of the unemployed. Boys who might have been clerks found themselves doing work they hated in workshops and foundries, while lads who could barely read and had no head whatever for figures became messengers and office boys.

The Lewis Report concluded that further education of adolescents was the only way to stop this appalling waste of national resources. It recommended what the best brains of Toynbee Hall had recommended twelve years earlier: compulsory further education for all beyond the statutory school-leaving age. But the report went even further by recommending that this education, instead of being confined to evening classes after the boy or girls had done a day's work should be compulsory for eight hours a week between 8 a.m. and 7 p.m. In other words employers would have to let boys and girls out to attend school during the normal working week. Only in recent years had apprentices and a certain number of trainees in the Naval dockyards and the Post Office been given time off to attend classes during the working week. Extending this on a national scale to all working boys was nothing short of revolutionary.

The timing of the proposals was just right. The Great War was grinding to a halt in sheer exhaustion on both sides and when the Armistice was signed on 11th November, 1918, it was greeted with bells and maroons and the firm resolve "Never again!" It was in this mood that the recommendations of the Lewis Committee were embodied in the 1918 Education Act, which enforced universal compulsory day-continuation schooling for all boys and girls between the ages of fourteen and eighteen.

"Never again!" summed up the mood for the country and the Parliament which passed the 1918 Act. Never again would education in adolescence be the almost sole preserve of the children of well-off parents; never again would the nation throw away in those crucial years between fourteen and eighteen all that had been built up during childhood at the tax-payers' expense. What Lewis called the "workman and citizen in training" would continue his education after fourteen to build on the knowledge he had acquired in elementary school, instead of letting it wither. He would have the chance to play games and his healthy growth would be checked by regular medical inspection.

This then was the Utopian design, but such grand designs are notoriously difficult to put into operation and this one was no exception. As soon as the Great War was over, Mr. Lloyd George and his Cabinet were gripped by the fear of revolution and imagined that they were all in imminent danger of being shot by the mob. Empires were falling all over Europe in the wake of the Bolshevik coup in Russia. In Ireland the Irish Republican Army was gunning down policemen, while at home the police had been on strike.

By 1920, when the London County Council, administering an area containing 4 million people, was required by law to introduce day-continuation schools, juvenile unemployment was increasing. Moreover, employers who had not yet grasped that they were part of the new Utopia discovered very quickly that the authorities adjacent to the LCC were not yet required by law to send their working youngsters to school on two half-days each week. So they simply got round the Act by recruiting their juvenile labour across the metropolitan county border and angry London parents blamed the LCC or Lloyd George, or both, for the fact that their elder sons and daughters were out of work. At the same time a large section of middle class opinion considered it no more than the Government's duty to restore the supply of young girls into domestic service, which had been severely disrupted by the war.

So the dream of Utopia began to fade within three years of its being conceived in the heady air of idealism at the end of one of the bloodiest struggles in the history of the world. Even the London Labour Party was not prepared to lose votes by fighting for the survival of day-continuation schools. The thirty-five schools which had been opened by January 1921 were closed less than a year later, and the Geddes Axe performed its ruthless but economically necessary work on many other cherished projects of Lloyd George's "land fit for heroes" in the slump of the early 1920s.

Only one local authority in the whole country stood fast to the principle and the reality of adolescent education for all, and that was Rugby, the Midlands town in which Dr. Arnold in the previous century had evolved the prototype public school for the sons of gentlemen. The local authorities, backed, to their everlasting credit, by far-sighted business concerns like British Thomson Houston, English Electric and Lodge Plugs, who saw that youth was too precious a commodity to waste in an increasingly competitive industrial world, continued to compel its 400 school leavers each year to attend day-continuation classes. P. I. Kitchen, who was principal of the Rugby Day Continuation School, told the full story in *From Earning to Learning*, published more than twenty years later in 1944. His school provided compulsory classes including shorthand and typing and physical training for all working boys and girls to the age of sixteen, not eighteen as had been envisaged in the original grand concept, but in the circumstances it was a notable and lasting achievement. The school had eighty acres of playing fields and it was open every evening for voluntary activities. It was also used as a juvenile employment bureau and medical inspection centre.

A few other elements of the Lewis Committee's concept remained in the hard years to come. Of the voluntary day-continuation schools started between 1919 and 1920 in anticipation of the compulsory system, a handful survived to offer mostly technical training and physical education in co-operation with the more enlightened employers. Some Government offices sent their messengers to classes. Valentine Bell, who had been responsible for the further education of Whitehall messengers during the war, was a Cockney-bred educator who had the gift of being able to talk to a duke or a dustman on equal terms. He ran a day-continuation school at Battersea and during the early 1920s when unemployment was at its worst he was commissioned by the Carnegie UK Trust to report on the junior instruction centres set up by the Government.

A single clause in the Education Act of 1918 which somehow escaped the eagle eye of Whitehall and the Geddes Axe empowered local education authorities to provide social and recreational facilities for young people up to the age of eighteen. One or two local authorities seized on this to provide playing fields for youngsters in their areas who had left school but as often as not could find no work.

But the opportunity to provide all adolescents, and not just a few, with education up to the age of eighteen, and to bring to an end once and for all the exploitation of youth by employers, was lost. In the years between the wars life in the industrial towns and the capital of England was not markedly different from the Victorian age, except for greatly improved sanitation, public libraries, parks and swimming pools and "the dole" for those who stood in seemingly endless queues outside the Labour Exchanges. As in the previous century, it was largely left to men of energy and goodwill, without financial reward of any kind and sometimes at considerable cost to themselves, to cater for the needs of the lost youth in these towns. The torch of progress was, in effect, handed back by the State to the boys' club movement.

2

Getting Together

As THE Scout MOVEMENT grew out of the Boer War and the need to "be prepared," so the National Association of Boys' Clubs was forged in the furnace of the Great War of 1914–18. In the trenches men who had been active in the boys' club movement before the war had time to appraise what they had been trying to achieve and how, if they survived, they could make life better for the growing generation. One of these men was Waldo McGillicuddy Eagar. During an idle day in an observation post behind Bailleul in 1917, he thought back over his evenings and weekends in a boys' club in Bermondsey before he, like thousands of others, had become a temporary soldier. Amidst the craters, the barbed wire and the shell-splintered tree trunks, he set down on paper what seemed to him the distinctive methods and objects of boys' clubs.

After the war, when many officers who had been in France were trying to find some sense of purpose and belonging in peacetime England, some found it in working for youth. Among them was a career soldier, Colonel Ronald Campbell, whose job had been to boost morale in behind-the-lines rest camps with his travelling circus of champion boxers, a "doughty exponent of the bayonet" called Sergeant Wilcox, and a fire-and-brimstone padre nicknamed Woodbine Willy. Campbell had helped many shell-shocked soldiers to re-orientate themselves and now, in peacetime, he was trying to find *himself* in almost the same way. On a visit to Eagar in deprived Bermondsey he found what he was looking for and promptly resigned from the army and joined the movement towards trying to form the national association of clubs of which Eagar had become an ardent advocate.

The first step towards an association came in the summer of 1924, when thirty men from towns and cities in England and Scotland met at Coleshill, Birmingham, at the request of twelve signatories. The signatories were: F. N. Cliffe, Burnley Lads' Club; C. E. Clift, Salford Lads' Club; G. B. Code, Birmingham Street Children's Union; J. Harlow, Edgbaston Boys' Club, Birmingham; Oliver Hind, Dakeyne Street Lads' Club, Nottingham; E. J. Humble, Liverpool Union of Boys' Clubs; W. McG. Eagar, Oxford and Bermondsey Boys' Club; W. A. Norrish, Shaftesbury Boys' Club, Birkenhead; Alfred Peters, chairman Boys' Work Committee, British Rotary; Walter Southern, chairman Manchester and Salford Lads' Club Federation; A. E. Thomas, Joe Walton Boys' Club, Middlesbrough; C. A. Wrench, Federation of London Working Boys' Clubs.

They came together somewhat reluctantly and with considerable scepticism and they had been forewarned that the independent tradition of boys' clubs were sacrosanct. As a group they were wary of slogans and glib declarations; they did not want to be labelled, standardized and directed from London like automatons. Apart from the secretaries, the men who attended came from Birmingham, Burnley, Edinburgh, Glasgow, Liverpool, Middlesbrough and Nottingham. A YMCA representative came from Yorkshire and Robert Wood, who later became Permanent Secretary of the Ministry of Education, was there as an official observer. George Devine, brother of the Manchester pioneer Alexander Devine, who was active in the London Federation of Boys' Clubs, had more or less written off the Coleshill conference in advance: "Attempts have been made before with no effect. Personally I am not willing to spend more time on it. People are interested in their local Federations, not in any national move."

He probably reflected the views of many men who knew the needs of boys in their own areas and knew that their clubs were more than just a means of keeping difficult lads "off the streets." They were not prepared to be dictated to by higher authorities. The fact that the Coleshill meeting was held at all was due mainly to the persistence of F. G. D'Aeth, of the Liverpool Council of Social Service, who, according to a friend, was "an arch co-ordinator . . . always brimming over with ideas about co-ordinating everybody and everything."

No one could deny that in those uncertain days after the war, when so many dreams had come to nothing, there was a need for boys' clubs to co-ordinate and distinguish themselves from the Boys' Brigade or the Scouts, both of whom had been invigorated by hundreds of men who wanted to put their military experience to some more fruitful use.

By the late 1920s the Scouts had grown to be the largest youth organization in Britain, something which Charles Russell could hardly have foreseen when he wrote of General Baden-Powell's "unpractical scheme" in 1908. When the Scout movement celebrated its twenty-first birthday in 1929 with a World Jamboree at Arrowe Park, Woodchurch, near Birkenhead, fifty thousand Scouts from all over the world were gathered together in a great canvas city. They came from thirty-one parts of the British Empire and from forty-one other nations, and as B-P said in his message of welcome: "You are taking part in the biggest concourse of boys that has ever come together in the history of the world; not only that, but also it is a concourse of jolly fine boys, the best from every civilized country in the world."

The English summer, unimpressed, poured down torrents of rain and the camping ground was churned into a sea of mud resembling Ypres in 1915. Yet B-P's spirits, like those of his boys, were undampened. He even made a joke of it: "You see, any ass can be a Scout on a fine day, but the thing is to make the best of conditions on a bad day." It was the force of his personality alone which had made the Scout movement not merely a national, but an international, entity.

The pity is that scouting did not reach boys whose parents could not afford to pay for a uniform and camps and whose opportunities for practising woodcraft were severely limited in the crowded alleyways and back streets of industrial towns. The only hope for recreation and occasional escape from their grim environment for the majority of this mass of underprivileged youth still lay in the boys' clubs. Although it was never voiced, it is more than likely that the outstanding success of scouting impressed upon them the need for expansion and national co-ordination of their own efforts. In the absence of any existing national organization, the twelve signatories called the meeting at Coleshill to discuss the situation.

No momentous resolution came from the meeting. Those present merely authorized a few of their number to convene a conference to discuss the idea of a national federation or association. This provisional committee went ahead with arrangements and, as Eagar—who was one of the members—wrote:

"... improperly but wisely exceeded its reference. It co-opted Captain Lionel Ellis of the National Council of Social Service, who became Honorary Secretary, and Colonel Ronald Campbell. It raised some funds, compiled a list of some hundreds of clubs in 160 towns, promised co-operation to the Carnegie Trustees, who needed advice on grants for Boys' Clubs Libraries, gave publicity to the new move in Boys' Club work and prepared papers on starting, managing and maintaining Boys' Clubs."

So when the conference met at Toynbee Hall in October 1925, it found itself virtually committed to forming the National Association of Boys' Clubs. Interest had spread beyond the initial group to Barnsbury, Bradford, Bristol, Chester, Dewsbury, Eastbourne, Exeter, Hereford and York, and the 80 representatives who attended the conference formed the NABC without so much as a murmur of protest against what Eagar later called the "unscrupulous energy" of the provisional committee.

They unanimously turned down an invitation from the National Organization of Girls' Clubs to join forces. They were told by the London delegates that they had been approached two years earlier with an invitation to become one of the bodies affiliated to the London Union of Girls' Clubs, which they had also declined, with compliments. Male chauvinism was obviously under attack fifty years ago as it is today. But then the attitude was courteous, but firm: women had proved themselves capable of doing men's jobs during the war when they had served in munitions factories and on buses and trams, as well as in the more traditional role of nurses and comforters of suffering males, but now the war was over. Let women run clubs for girls—running boys' clubs was a man's job. They overlooked (and presumably the one woman delegate, Mrs. Tuke, of Hereford, did not remind them) that even in Victoria's day a few women had managed to run boys' clubs very successfully.

Federation and co-operation seemed to be the order of the day under the benevolent umbrella of the Juvenile Organizations Committee, Charles

Russell's wartime Home Office creation which had continued into peacetime. A conference in 1923 at International House was attended by Scouts, boys' and girls' life brigades, and other more exotic youth organizations such as the Order of Woodcraft Chivalry, Kibboo Kift, the Guild of Citizens of Tomorrow and the Practical Idealists' Association. "Boys might be citizens of tomorrow and husbands of the future but before they start mating let us make them into men first"; that, in the briefest terms, was the policy of the boys' clubs who came together at Toynbee Hall in 1925. Out of their deliberations came the realisation of Russell's dream at the beginning of the century, "a central office for all lads' club in the kingdom," and much, much more.

After its somewhat difficult and belated birth, the National Association of Boys' Clubs soon proved itself to be a lusty infant and grew rapidly. Any local Federation of Boys' Clubs could join provided it comprised at least four clubs, and membership of the NABC was also open to individual clubs outside those areas, provided they had at least fifteen members and all their members were aged fourteen to eighteen, charged subscriptions and met at least twice a week "under responsible management." Most well-established boys' clubs were open every night, although of course only a small proportion of members attended for more than a couple of nights a week.

Within a year the association had recruited five federations comprising 262 clubs, plus 33 directly affiliated clubs. By 1930 its strength had grown dramatically to 17 federations, more than half of which had sprung into being as a result of the NABC's formation, and represented 837 clubs. The numbers of directly affiliated clubs had grown to more than 100.

The movement, which up till then had been concentrated in England, was penetrating other parts of the United Kingdom. Scotland, hitherto regarded as boys' brigade territory, formed an association of 50 boys' clubs with 5,000 members and was affiliated to the NABC. Nowhere was the aim of the association—"to promote the mental, physical and social well-being of boys in poor circumstances"—more needed than in South Wales, then in the grip of severe economic hardship after years of industrial unrest among the miners and the collapse of the General Strike. In 1928 the South Wales Federation of Miners' Boys' Clubs was launched with six large clubs as a nucleus.

Older established federations had also benefited from the coming together. The Liverpool Union of Boys' Clubs, now calling itself an association, had 100 affiliated clubs, including some companies of Boys' Brigades, Scout troops and small church and chapel clubs. It had set up a training centre for leaders and helpers and some 130 boys could be found each day at the Dinner-Hour Club where they could buy refreshments (or bring and eat their own) and enjoy indoor games. The Birmingham and District Federation brought together clubs attended by four thousand of the city's total boy population of 60,000. There were close links between the clubs and the

Education Committee's after-care department. Rowntree's Boys' Gymnasium at York was also running a Dinner-Hour Club, at which 75 members paid 1d a week.

The enthusiasm of the NABC pioneers in the face of so much scepticism was thus more than vindicated in the first five years of its existence. The Duke of Gloucester became an active president and the Prince of Wales (later King Edward VIII), whose interest in the distressed areas was well known, donated £1,000 to a public appeal for funds in 1929. The official organ of the movement was *The Boy*, two versions of which had been published after the war by undergraduates at Oxford and Cambridge, one of whom was Charles Hill, who became during the next war "The Radio Doctor" and later Lord Hill, chairman of the British Broadcasting Corporation. The NABC took the magazine over from the undergraduates and made it a controversial quarterly journal devoted to the welfare of the working boy as well as to publicizing its own function as a central office promoting and co-ordinating boys' clubs all over the country, acting as a link with government departments, and raising funds.

The latter concern was, of course, a constant headache. On a local level boys' clubs managed to meet the inevitable gap between their members' subscriptions and running costs with the help of wealthy businessmen and other benefactors. Many of them made do with any premises they could find —from old sheds to abandoned houses and shops—and in the admirable spirit of "make not take" it was left to the boys themselves to paint, scrub and patch. The NABC on the other hand had to have a national headquarters big enough to house conferences and committees, a pattern of local organizations and a staff of paid workers to handle the ever-growing volume of correspondence, publicity, the training of leaders and a hundred other activities. In short, it needed money.

The Carnegie United Kingdom Trust helped to get this organization started and it found its base in a few rooms provided by the National Council of Social Service at 17 Bedford Square, in the heart of Bloomsbury.

Statistically and in other ways the NABC had already justified itself by 1930 but it still lacked a doctrine in the way that Scouts had their law and their promise and the Boys' Brigade their creed of "Christian manliness." The need was remedied by a document entitled *Principles and Aims of the Boys' Club Movement* which was adopted by the NABC as its bible at the annual conference at Oxford. It had been hammered out by a committee of four, including Colonel Campbell, Lionel Ellis and Basil Henriques, a London magistrate who as an undergraduate had launched boys clubs in the East End for members of his own Jewish faith and among whose many books was *Club Leadership*, published in 1933. But the document owed its origin to the fourth member of the committee, Waldo McGillycuddy Eagar, and the notes which he had scribbled in a pad in the observation post at Bailleul thirteen years earlier. Looking back in the 1950s, he wrote:

"The acceptance of *Principles and Aims* by the Boys' Club Movement as a whole was deeply significant. For the first time the unity of purpose which had inspired countless personal, individualistic undertakings was recognized. Formulation gave the NABC its place in the nation's life as a distinctive welfare organisation with a positive national objective."

The document is a long one and not easily summarized but the following extract gives an idea of the clear thinking which went into producing a compelling and logical argument when, like the off-spring of so many committees, it could so easily have been "a camel with three humps":

"The profound changes of puberty coincide in a working-boy's life with an abrupt change of circumstances. He passes at one bound from the protective, encouraging world of school to the rigours and discouragements of competitive employment. The Boys' Club is the only educational social agency which can reach a great many boys who are denied the opportunities and inspirations offered to the small minority who continue education through adolescence.* For half the working boys in our land the street-gang is the one possible club and the street-corner the one practical continuation school. The Club is a constructive alternative to the street-corner; by directing the spirit of the gang to a socially useful end it can in a natural way make it an important social force . . . ."

In 1930 this statement came to the club leaders at the annual conference as a revelation in the mist of national bewilderment and disenchantment. But in the prosaic way of conferences, this one spent a great deal of time discussing whether or not the movement should adopt a slogan. Eagar was all for adopting as a slogan ("sloggan" he pronounced it) the one word: "Fitness." The word to him, as an Oxford scholar, meant fitness of body, mind and spirit which, to quote Aristotle, "consists of living the best life our powers command in the best way our circumstances permit." But all this was rather high-flown for the majority of delegates to whom the slogan suggested merely physical fitness and could be interpreted as meaning that boys' clubs were interested in gymnastics and games and nothing else.

So although the Scouts had "Be Prepared" and the Boys' Brigade had "Sure and Steadfast" and "Remember Now Thy Creator in the Days of Thy Youth," boys' clubs remained (and continue to remain to this day) motto-less. But, much more important, they now had a firm statement of policy on which the future could be based.

In the next decade new clubs sprang into being in towns all over the land where there had been none before. In the milltowns of the West Riding of Yorkshire new clubs took over an old warehouse at Pontefract, an old school at Rotherham and a former pub at Barnsley. Two disused police stations housed new clubs on Tyneside, one at Newcastle and the other at

---

* In 1914 only one child in forty won a free place in a grammar school, and although by 1929 the proportion had risen to one in thirteen, such an education was still reserved for an *élite* of bright children. Even those who won scholarships could not always afford books and uniforms.

Walker. In Preston a boys' club was born in an old factory. The Joe Walton Club in Middlesbrough moved into new red brick premises towering above its squalid surroundings in Feversham Street, boasting a canteen, library, arts room and a football ground on the roof. At Bristol a Saxon watch-tower, one of a ring built around the ancient city, became the home of the Kingsdown Boys' Club. Its stone walls, 6 to 9 feet thick, had over the centuries housed a brewery, a hat factory and most recently the wares of a local sweet factory. Where Kutberth, the Watcher of the Tower, had stood guard in the fifth century, boys now turned somersaults and vaulted the wooden horse. Swings, trapezes and climbing ropes hung from monstrous beams of solid oak.

No less out of the ordinary was the Chung Hwa Club opened in 1933 above a Chinese restaurant in the West India Dock Road, a part of London's dockland with a large population of Chinese. It was started by Miss T. I. Ho for the benefit of Chinese boys in Limehouse, who expressed interest not only in the ping-pong table but in starting up their own cricket team.

Rotary Clubs, Toc H, the YMCA all played their part in building up the boys' club movement between the wars. So, too, did the police and probation officers in many towns, including Rochester, Canterbury, Scarborough, Brighton, Huddersfield, Winchester, Hereford and Hyde. At Norwich almost the whole of the police force turned out to transform a derelict building owned by the Corporation into a boys' club which recruited in the early 1920s more than a thousand members. The chairman was the Chief Constable of Norwich, Mr. Dain, who said later in a lecture to senior police officers from many parts of the British Empire:

"When the lads of a town find themselves associated with the police in their recreational activities and excitement in this wholly natural and unmedicated way, it is inevitable that it should create a new atmosphere. . . . I consider that this kind of understanding in place of the old sense of suspicion and hostility is a factor of greatest importance in making for good citizenship. . . . And, on the other hand, it is all to the good for the police themselves. For it is, of course, a purely voluntary work."

The idea of preventing juvenile crime through personal contact with young lads from poor districts appealed to the policemen of Swansea who set up a boys' club committee in 1932 with, according to the Chief Constable, Mr. May, who was their chairman, "half a crown and plenty of faith." The club started at the old mission in the Strand, where a high proportion of the members were ragged boys who sold the *Evening Post* in the streets, and progressed to an old printing works in Rutland Street and finally a splendidly equipped new building on Town Hill overlooking the whole of Swansea and the Channel beyond.

Nor was it just in the towns and the great industrial centres that boys' clubs sprang into life between the wars. Although, like most social welfare movements, they began in the towns, a need was soon recognized to do something for village lads too.

In a survey of 250 villages in Hampshire in the mid-1930s it was found that fewer than fifty offered any leisure activities for young wage-earners. Neville Goodridge, a former schoolmaster who had taken up a full-time post as secretary of the newly formed Hampshire Association of Boys' Clubs, appealed in an article in *The Boy* in the winter of 1938 for more to be done for lads outside the big towns:

". . . In four out of five villages the lads are leaning over the village bridge idling their spare time away because they have nothing better to do. . . . Consider the life of the village boy. His home conditions *may* be healthier than those of his brothers in the town, but *only* because he is closer to the health-giving influences of nature. Housing conditions in the country are frequently far worse than in the town; overcrowding is no rare occurrence, and the growing boy finds the bridge his only refuge when his work is done."

He described how in one village consisting of one street with a total population of 1,100 and an hourly bus service to the nearest town eight miles away, the friendly proprietress of the village shop had started a club almost by accident. The lads had gathered on an upholstered bench in the shop on evenings when it was too cold to hang about under the oil lamp by the bridge. When their company became too boisterous she loaned them an old mud-and-chalk cottage; they cleaned and painted the place, acquired a couple of dart boards and a billiards table and elected officers and a committee.

Goodridge was involved in another development which took boys' clubs literally to the far corners of the globe—the starting of clubs on ocean-going ships. A young crew member formed a club in the Royal Mail Ship *Alcantara* in 1935 on the South America run. It was allocated a compartment about 20 feet by 15 feet, one wall made up by the sloping side of the ship with three port-holes, and fitted out with a ping-pong table, a gramophone, a library shelf and some comfortable chairs. The club programme included daily physical jerks on deck. Altough the *Alcantara* had only thirty boys in her crew, many of the trans-Atlantic lines operating from Southampton had as many as eighty, mostly stewards, laundry boys and the like, and when the *Queen Mary* emerged from the shipyard she carried nearly a hundred boys. They lived in cramped quarters very different from the spacious staterooms of the passengers. The idea of boys' clubs spread to a number of ships, particularly in the Union Castle Line, and was helped by a Board of Trade ruling which cut the hours of duty from the time-honoured four-watch system.

Clubs everywhere, whether in a village or a town, in a factory, an office or on board a ship, needed men who were prepared to give their time to boys. Somehow the supply of voluntary leaders never seemed to fail.

In October 1934 Reginald Goodwin gave up a career as a tea merchant in the city to join the NABC as assistant secretary. Forty years later, as leader of the Greater London Council controlling an annual budget larger than that of some entire countries, Sir Reginald described in an interview with the author how he first became involved in the boys' club movement in 1929:

"I happened to see in the coat lapel of one of the office boys at Mincing Lane a badge with the words *Fratres* on it and I asked him what it was all about. He said 'That's my club badge.' I had never heard of boys' clubs and he said I had better come and have a look. So that evening I went with him across Tower Bridge into Bermondsey and the Canterbury Club, one of the group of Oxford and Bermondsey clubs started by John Stansfeld. *Fratres* was their motto. I found there a spirit of friendliness which lived up to that motto. It was unique at that time in history when we were in the midst of an economic depression, when there was a lot of unemployment, distress and social upheaval, and people were questioning, very much as they are again today, the standards of society."

As he had no university background, and knew nothing of the origins of the Oxford Medical Mission in Bermondsey, young Goodwin was at first rather over-awed by people like "The Doctor," Alec Paterson, Hubert Secretan (who was also closely connected with Tubby Clayton in the founding of Toc H), Barclay Baron and Basil Henriques. But the Canterbury Club was managed entirely on a voluntary basis by young Bermondsey men who had grown up in the club and he threw in his lot with them, moving into a dockland pub called the Jolly Waterman in Rotherhithe Street and joining the Labour Party. It was a remarkable step for someone from his suburban middle-class background.

Most such men would echo the words of a doctor who gave much of his spare time to a club in South London: "Whatever I've done for *them* is nothing compared with what they've done for *me*." Clement Attlee, who became Prime Minister after the Second World War, said much the same thing in recalling his years as a briefless barrister:

"In helping to run a boys' club I learned more practical economics and more practical sociology than I ever learned through any books.... It is a two-way traffic which benefits not only the boys but the club manager. I always feel I learnt as much from the boys as they learnt from me and I still remember how much I learnt of the spirit of self-sacrifice that exists in poor districts like ours, which made one often ashamed that one did not do more oneself."

3
Boys at Work

THERE WERE OVER A MILLION BOYS in Britain between the ages of fourteen and seventeen whom the club movement could try to catch at this formative age. To the Ministry of Labour they, and a slightly smaller number of girls, were "juveniles available for employment." Once a boy had put on his long trousers and left school at fourteen he was technically a man. James Butterworth, who started Clubland in Walworth, described this type of boy in 1932:

"Only a month ago he was the leader of the 'Black Hand Devils' or 'The Sign of the Blue Dagger', but he now cuts himself off completely from 'kids', for be it known to all that 'he goes to business' and has two kippers for his tea instead of one. It is quite irrelevant that his business may be packing bird seed, scraping labels off bottles or tins, or acting as van-boy. It is enough that he is a wage-earner. He may get into a good job, with chances of office or warehouse promotion, but the blind-alley jobs are numerous, the desire to earn money so great, that he generally takes the first vacancy offered. It is rather tragic that thousands of lads are discharged every year for no other crime than growing up to be insurable at age 16. . . . If he is one of the world's unwanted as too old at 16, his life so far will have had four acts; age 12 'fags', aged 14 'long-uns', age 15 'birding', age 16 'dole'. . . ."

At that time the number of Scouts in London was nearly twice that of the boys' brigades and boys' clubs together. The Scouts averaged 57 per 1,000 of the boy population compared with the brigades' and clubs' 16 per 1,000 each. But it was the boys' club alone which catered for the lad described by Butterworth. In poverty-stricken inner London areas like Walworth the membership average rose to 33 per 1,000. Scouting's proportion of membership was higher, on the other hand, in the better-off suburbs.

A high proportion of brigade and club boys were engaged in some form of unskilled manual labour. The journal of the National Association of Boys' Clubs, *The Boy*, was in no doubt that they were being exploited by employers. In October 1936 it quoted the report of the Chief Inspector of Factories showing that youngsters of fourteen and fifteen were in some areas working from 8 a.m. to 8 p.m. and up to 4 p.m. on Saturdays and commented: "There is no industrial necessity for this misuse of juvenile labour in any occupation."

In the following year a Home Office committee appointed by Sir John Simon to survey hours of employment of young people reported that something like 600,000 boys and girls (mostly boys) had been left outside existing regulations limiting hours of work. Van boys, for example, not only worked excessive hours but did so to such an irregular pattern that it was virtually impossible for them to attend clubs or evening classes. Messengers, porters, errand boys, warehouse boys, hotel page boys and lift boys suffered from the same abuse, often having to work at night.

The Scottish Juvenile Voluntary Organization reported to the committee the case of a hotel boy, aged fifteen, whose hours were:

Weekdays   7 a.m.–12 noon
              12.30 p.m.–4 p.m.
              6 p.m.–11 p.m. except Fridays, when he finished at 6 p.m.
              (presumably from 12.30 p.m.)
Sundays   8 a.m.–11 a.m. or 8 a.m.–10 p.m., alternate Sundays

The Boy snorted: "Ninety-two actual working hours in a week with a long Sunday (only 81 in a short week!) with a spread-over normal weekday of 16 hours. That's the way to breed young Britons!" The Home Office Committee was of the opinion that even a week of forty-eight hours, exclusive of mealtimes, was too long to give the necessary opportunities for continued education and recreation.

The Factories Act of 1937 brought a number of hitherto unregulated occupations within the scope of a new law limiting the working hours of young people under eighteen to forty-eight a week, forty-four for those under sixteen, restricting the amount of overtime they could be made to work and making holidays compulsory on Christmas Day, Good Friday and every Bank Holiday. Boys and girls employed in collecting and delivering goods, carrying messages or running errands for factories and workshops and working in docks and warehouses benefited from the new regulations. But hotel page boys and lift boys, messenger boys for Fleet Street newspapers who did a lot of night work, cinema boys and boys working at fairs remained outside legislation. So, by some curious anomaly, did boys who worked for carriers like Pickfords and Carter Paterson, because they were not in factories!

But they were not as badly off as boys of their age employed underground in the heat, dust and darkness of the mines. Nor were they as likely to be maimed for the rest of their lives. Following the death by accident of a young boy in 1938 on his first day down the pit, Captain Radcliffe, secretary of the Durham Association of Boys' Clubs, wrote to *The Times* that the colliery companies could, if they started a proper system of training and apprenticeship, "end the industrial evil of employing boys of 14 and 15 underground to the acknowledged detriment of their health and the danger of their lives. Some few colliery companies have set the example, but it is not being followed, and the time has surely come when the State must intervene to forbid a practice already illegal in most European countries and against both conscience and common sense." The Census of 1931 showed 5,944 boys of fourteen and fifteen employed as hewers and getters at the coalface in mines in England and Wales: this may have been a tiny proportion of the total force of 438,664 men employed in those jobs, but it was nonetheless a scandal that any should have been employed as the twentieth century entered its third decade. Another 11,687 lads under sixteen were employed underground filling tubs and conveying the coal to the shaft.

The first job a lad had down the pit was usually as a "trapper," opening and shutting the doors which controlled ventilation. He might then become a pony driver, performing marvellous but usually forbidden feats of acrobatic skill in the confined space and cursing and loving his pit pony at the same time. Although the number of ponies in the pits was declining year by year, they were still widely used in the 1930s. The highest position he could reach as a lad under eighteen was as a putter, a hewer or a getter, at which stage he felt himself to be a man indeed. It was desperately hard work over long hours for a growing boy. The advantages to the colliery owners were obvious—lads were cheap to employ and learned their jobs quickly—but the dangers were appalling and accidents to boys frequent. Every village had its limping or one-armed casualties.

It was that very danger which attracted boys down the pit, as the Labour MP Jack Lawson described his own experience in *A Man's Life*: "The mystery called and drew me like a magnet and I was thrilled when, at last with some forty others, I found myself sliding slowly and steadily down the deep shaft." But Danny, the pit boy hero in A. L. Boden's *Miner,* experienced this reaction after witnessing a fatal accident: "Not while he lived would he forget the blackened, contorted face he had seen in the light of the flickering oil lamp."

The 1931 Census showed that there were more boys under sixteen down the mines than there were in offices (fewer than fourteen thousand of the latter). More than a hundred thousand were employed in transport and communications as errand boys, messengers, porters and so on, blind alley jobs leading to no definite trade, and just over thirty thousand worked in shops: all of them were boys of an age at which today they would still be at school. Ever-increasing mechanization of industry brought into being work which could be easily done by a fourteen- to fifteen-year-old boy or girl, and which ended abruptly when they became sixteen.

The machine age was resting heavily on young shoulders and some employers at least had a bad conscience about it. As one of them explained to a Rotary Conference in the Midlands in 1938:

"My product depends entirely on juvenile labour. I am in competition with a cheap product imported from Japan. I *have* to discharge my employees as they become adults, because the work can easily be done by youngsters and I couldn't afford to do it with adult labour. So it is a real blind alley occupation. What am I to do about it? I am conscious that I am not doing any good to those whom I employ, because the work doesn't fit them for anything when I have to sack them."

Even in relatively prosperous London, where in the mid 1930s there were hundreds of vacancies waiting to be filled, there were juvenile employment problems. Valentine Bell, who ran a junior instruction centre in Battersea, wrote of a boy who had eight jobs between leaving school and his eighteenth birthday. His first job, at an engineering works, lasted six months. He was mainly engaged in sweeping up the shop and he was sacked for "larking about." Skilled trades or those that were organized under powerful trade unions strictly regulated the entry of juveniles and where apprenticeships were available at £1 a week or less entry was usually deferred until fifteen and a half or sixteen years of age. Of the 120 lads who were ordered to attend a course of instruction at his centre in the last four months of 1936, the majority were over sixteen. Some had been earning £2 to £3 a week at unskilled jobs and Bell commented:

"They have a false idea of their own value and have been spoilt. They expect to find a job which pays just as well, and refuse offers of employment at a less wage. George is one of these. He had been getting over £2 a week sorting out waste paper. He has refused job after job, he was disqualified for benefit and now has a grievance or, at least, thinks he has. He cannot realize that the only job where he is likely to get a wage of £2 is 'waste paper sorting.' . . ."

A few boys at the centre came from bad homes and were dirty, ragged and perhaps verminous. Their main ambition seemed to be to hang around stalls, sell programmes at the dog tracks or gamble in the streets. Some were work-shy. Others had problems in getting on with their workmates or "rotten bosses." But a large proportion were genuinely unlucky and seemed to be continually losing jobs through no fault of their own.

The only sure way of giving these boys a better chance in life seemed to be to raise the school leaving age. The manifesto of Stanley Baldwin's Government, issued on the eve of the general election of 1935, promised among other things to raise the leaving age to fifteen, with *exemptions for beneficial employment*. What did that mean exactly? According to a leader in *The Boy* it meant that in London, where there was a shortage of four-teen-year-olds for employment, exemptions would be given as a matter of course to nearly every boy and girl. In the depressed areas, the brightest, strongest and most employable boys would be allowed to leave at fourteen, while the rest would be kept in school until they were fifteen. The editorial continued:

"Will the givers of exemptions regard blind-alley jobs in the unregulated occu-pations as beneficial employment? No job, in fact, is beneficial to a youngster unless it trains him, develops him, continues his education, gives him a chance of permanent occupation and leaves him time, while he is still a boy, to be some-thing more than an employee."

No man made a greater contribution to informing the debate about the evils of boy labour than Sir Hubert Llewellyn Smith, who was chairman of the National Association of Boys' Clubs throughout the latter half of the 1930s. He was a distinguished civil servant with an Oxford background. He had lived at Toynbee Hall in the East End in Canon Barnett's day and played a leading part in implementing Lloyd George's social reforms. Llewellyn Smith's Rose and Ring Club developed into the Stepney Craft

School and his concern for the welfare of boys was happily taken up by his two sons, who helped to run the Crown and Manor clubs in Hoxton, a very poor area of London.

Sir Hubert had contributed to *Life and Labour of the People in London,* Charles Booth's massive survey of the late nineteenth century capital, and between the wars he was chairman of the less voluminous but equally weighty *New Survey of London and Labour* (the former publication ran to seventeen volumes, the latter, nine). In the forty years between the two surveys there had been, as we have seen, a great expansion in the number of clubs for boys. The new survey discovered close on eighty thousand boys between the ages of eight and twenty-one in one or other of the juvenile movements in London. Boys' clubs, it concluded, had succeeded in attracting many of the poorest and roughest boys between the ages of fourteen and sixteen who were not amenable to other movements, adding:

"Yet it must be confessed that in the past the criticism that club influence was too negative was frequently justifiable, and it is today not without some force. Every club faces what is really a dilemma. It must either aim high, and see many of the boys who need it most drop by the wayside, or it must try to be a home for the poorest boys and rest content with rather lower standards. There are many practical difficulties too. It is not easy for a club which meets no more than twice a week to arrange a programme which will really satisfy the movement's aim—especially if it is limited to a single room."

Another practical difficulty was that long hours of work left boys little time for recreation, a difficulty apparently not recognized by the British Broadcasting Corporation when in the autumn of 1935 it announced a new series of talks in the "Young Ideas" series on "My Job." The speakers were to include a girl working in a nursery school, one of the youngest reporters in Fleet Street, a stage electrician and a boy training to be a hotel manager. Club leaders were quick to point out that the hour chosen for the broadcasts, 7.30 on Friday evenings, was precisely the time when they were busy with the first rush of the evening opening and too early for many boys who could not get to the wireless at the club before eight o'clock (few had one at home), after getting home from work.

It needed pointing out to the middle classes, as indeed it was by F. W. Lestrange in his book *Wasted Lives,* published in 1936, that "the children of the working classes have brains and hearts and souls as well as bellies. . . . The millions of youngsters whom the State (and that means you) is misusing are practically indistinguishable—except that far too many of them are undernourished—from your own sons and daughters, brothers and sisters."

Under a montage of photographs of errand boys, van boys and page boys the author wrote the caption: "Over school age—why?" Yet nothing came of Mr. Baldwin's promise to raise the school leaving age. Boys continued to be employed at a time when further education would have been more beneficial to them than a blind-alley job, while thousands of older youths remained out of work.

4

Out of Work

IN THE EARLY 1930s the dole for a married couple with three children was 29s. 3d. a week. The BBC broadcast interviews with unemployed men and their families who had to struggle just for enough to eat with nothing to spare for papers, the pictures, or sports. One man from the Rhondda talked about his gratitude for the kindliness and comradeship of the Welsh valleys and then went on:

"The second thing I am glad about is that I haven't a son. It must be heartbreaking business to watch your boy grow to manhood and then see him deteriorate because there is no work for him to do. And yet there are scores of young men in the Valley who have never worked since the age of sixteen. You see, at sixteen they become insurable and employers sack them rather than face the extra expense."

In 1934 the first Government grants were made to boys' clubs in these areas of high unemployment through the Special Areas Commissioner and it was here that the movement came into its own as "a constructive alternative to the street corner, directing the spirit of the gang to a socially useful end." The club was also an escape from often drab and disheartening conditions at home, for, as Captain Glynn-Jones* of the South Wales Miners' Boys' Clubs told an audience of social workers:

"The boys' associations with a home are linked with a tired mother, an absent father, and a host of children fighting for existence; with such ideas as minding the baby, clearing out to make room for others, and generally 'getting out of the way', with innumerable childbirths, illnesses, washdays, bath-tubs, and funerals, with rough, hasty words and the use of the strap as a short-cut to discipline; and with a general feeling that he is just there as the next item of contribution to the meagre family resources. In most cases there is not, and cannot be, under present housing conditions, any real home life; everything is dull, drab and cramped, and there is beauty in very little of what the boy experiences."

Nowhere was the tragic waste of opportunity provided during the war to break down the class barriers more apparent than in the mining districts of South Wales. After the war the class struggle intensified and flared into open conflict in the General Strike of 1926, leaving a legacy of bitterness in the harsh years of unemployment and deprivation which followed. As early as 1922 the Ocean Coal Company had recognized through its network of

* Now Senior Vice-President of the NABC.

miners' welfare committees the crying need for leisure facilities for adolescents working in the pits, as well as the need for institutes, recreation grounds and pithead baths for their older brothers and fathers. In that year a boys' club was started in the old colliery offices at Treharris, with an annexe in an ex-army hut. The salary of its full-time leader was paid by voluntary contributions from the local miners.

Two years later a commodious club building was erected at Nantymoel, thirty miles away, on a colliery rubbish tip—the only site available. It was planned as the local war memorial with a donation of £3,000 from the Miners' Welfare Fund. That same year of 1924 had been designated as Boys' Year in the coalfields and there was a concentrated effort to open more clubs and also to establish a permanent seaside holiday camp at St. Athan, one of the first of its kind in the country. It preceded by a few years the commercial holiday camps launched by Billy Butlin in the 1930s.

Boys from Treorchy in the Rhondda who attended the camp at St. Athan in 1926 started a movement for their own club (their neighbours at Ton-Pentre had opened one in the previous year). Sadly, the industrial troubles of that year brought miners' welfare grants for club buildings to an abrupt end, but 150 boys went ahead with their scheme using very cramped quarters in a local sports pavilion.

In August 1928 a weekend conference of boys' club leaders, secretaries and members at the St. Athan camp formed the South Wales Federation of Miners' Boys' Clubs. The development of clubs was helped by the Pilgrim Trustees who gave a grant of £5,000 and the Miners' Welfare Joint Committee who gave a further £10,000. By 1936 some £20,000 had been collected and allocated and the federation numbered thirty-four clubs with 3,300 members. Yet still more money was needed. Only eighteen of the clubs had permanent premises of their own. Furthermore, miners who were earning low wages for back-breaking work in the dark and wet below ground tended to be reluctant to contribute to the wages of a full-time boys' club leader who appeared to have a soft job with lots of spare time. Yet a strong case can be made that without these clubs boys in areas like South Wales would have had nothing to hope for or to believe in.

After the Wall Street crash of 1929 and the shock waves it sent around the world, unemployment in Britain rose from just over a million to almost 3 million in two years, while the value of exports was halved. The hardest hit areas were those of the traditional Victorian industries of coal, iron shipbuilding and cotton. The internal combustion engine and abundant electricity should have meant the good life for everyone; state education and welfare and the right to vote should have led to a fair chance for all. But that was not how it turned out. Instead there were contrasts almost as stark as anything which Disraeli inveighed against in Victorian England.

As the cost of living fell in the 1930s those who were fortunate enough to have a job were able to spend more on food, clothes, wireless sets, gramophone records, and so on. The number of cars on the roads went up from 1,100,000 to 1,800,000. In the south-east, an area of gleaming new factories it was, according to J. B. Priestley: "Everything given away for cigarette coupons." Yet on Tyneside, only 274 miles to the north, children were still running about in the streets without any shoes on their feet and once respectable artisans were reduced to picking up cigarette ends from the gutters. In one club in Newcastle 100 per cent of the boys' fathers had been out of work for three years or more.

Depressed areas (DAs, for short) were places where in some cases a whole community was out of work, in others the figure was 70 or 80 per cent. Young people migrated south in search of work, or stayed where they were and grew apathetic. The Bishop of Durham in a letter to *The Times* in 1932 stated that adolescent lads affected by the massive unemployment in his diocese were in most cases underfed. The National Association of Boys' Clubs sent its officials on tours of the distressed areas and one reported from Jarrow:

"The depression here has lasted for twelve years and the town is completely dead. The majority of shops are to let, there is no traffic or movement except the quite aimless crawl up and down the streets of hundreds of workless men, women, boys and girls. There is a ghastly silence hanging over the place. . . . Here is, in fact, a town where hundreds of boys are sinking into demoralization daily, where there really is no money but the dole. It is up to us to establish a club here above all places. It is a miracle that the boys are not all hardened criminals by now."

The name of Jarrow became synonymous with the Hungry Thirties. Three years later, when unemployment had fallen from its 3 million peak of 1933 to 1,670,000, that dismal town's unemployed marched in sheer desperation 274 miles to the Houses of Parliament to demand work. With three-quarters of the population unemployed, even the pawnshops were giving up the struggle and closing down. In the meantime boys' club leaders from London had visited Jarrow and reported back to their members about the need for a club there. Collections were started, raising £81, little enough, but a start. A total of £781 was found, enough to begin a club. Jarrow Boys' Club was opened on Monday, 23rd September, 1935. It was housed in a former police court, brightly painted and fitted out with a gymnasium, reading room, hall, handicrafts room, changing room and a bathroom in what had once been a police cell. It shone like a beacon in a sea of misery. Soon there were other beacons throughout the rest of Durham, a county of large, straggling mining villages, each of two or three thousand people dependent for their very existence on the local pit.

Without the Depression there might have been no boys' clubs in Durham. By 1937 there were forty-two affiliated to the county association, where three years before there had been only eight and, six years previously, none at all. There were boys' clubs of all sorts and sizes, big and small, town clubs and village clubs, some with full-time leaders and some run by volunteers, two-nights-a-week clubs and others open five nights a week, occupying all manners of premises.

As in South Wales, the Pilgrim Trust donated £5,000 in 1931 to start boys' clubs in Durham and before the county association was formed Toc H started four key clubs at Durham, Consett, Chester-le-Street and South Church, the latter being a hopelessly distressed mining village on the out-skirts of Bishop Auckland, where the pits were idle and the local people had had no work for years. In another mining village, Herrington Burn, where at least the pit was working, the YMCA started an active club for both men and boys in a collection of huts. At Silksworth the local colliery manager started a club which caught the imagination of the whole village. The relatively prosperous Home Counties and individual towns in the south-east of England contributed to the running costs of such clubs. Rotary Clubs, local community and social service councils and finally the King George V Jubilee Trust also gave much needed support.

Captain Radcliffe, secretary of the county association, wrote in 1937:

"The Durham miner, as it well known, is a conservative person; he is not used to the idea of anything being done specially for 14-18 boys, certainly not to the conception that their recreation is more important than his own, and the idea has to be introduced slowly. But it has taken firm root already in many villages and, given time and understanding, the Durham miners will be as proud of their village boys' clubs and as ready to help them, with both money and work, as are the Welsh miners in the villages of the Rhondda Valley to-day."

Great as were the needs of mining villages, the needs of the Tyneside towns, dying around the locked gates of the silent shipyards, were perhaps even greater. The pit village boy could at least escape into the surrounding countryside which, in spite of all that man had done to spoil it, still retained some of its wild beauty. The boys of the shipyard were locked in their grim environment. With so many pubs and shops shuttered and empty for lack of trade, premises were all too plentiful, but potential leaders, like the two medical students who started a boys' club in a disused pub in a poor part of Newcastle, were hard to find.

Felling, on the south bank of the Tyne, had the only premises in Durham designed and built as a boys' club. South Shields, on the other hand, began in two rooms, back and front, of a small shop in one of the poorest streets of the town. The club at Hebburn was housed in a wooden hut, specially extended, decorated and fitted with central heating and electric light by unemployed members of the local Community Service Centre.

In Sunderland, another shipyard town in the north-east, a home for St. Cuthbert's Boys' Club was constructed free of charge by the men of the Church Institute from a condemned house and an old garage door. A small club at Whitburn, a suburb of the town, raised money by selling their own handicrafts, and transformed a paved school-yard into a garden with a lawn, flower beds and a fish pond.

17. *Above*. The Hitler Youth.

18. *Below*. Army Cadets of the Crown and Manor Boys' Club, Hoxton, learning map-reading from an NCO in November 1944.

Opposite page: 19. *Top.* The canteen of the Crown and Manor Boys' Club, Hoxton, during the Second World War. 20. *Bottom.* The Chelsea Boys' Club during the Second World War.

This page: 21. *Right.* Boxing training at the Crown and Manor Boys' Club, Hoxton. 22. *Below.* Physical training on an NABC training course.

23. *Above*. The NABC football team, winners of the Junior Championship of Great Britain at Wembley in 1950.

24. *Below*. Tenements in the Hulme district of Manchester. From the *Picture Post* of 26th January, 1954.

When the Duke of Gloucester visited the north-east boys' clubs in 1935, the year of the Jarrow Hunger March, he found many clubs with their own gymnasia, complete with mats and vaulting boxes, and shower baths. Yet in the poorest districts boys had to be bought kit out of the funds before they could make use of these facilities. Perhaps the most striking example of self-help was at South Hylton where, as part of a complete village social service scheme, they were constructing a football ground and a swimming pool as well as a gymnasium.

Premises alone, however, were not enough, for there was no guarantee that a club would take root. Frank Sendall reported in 1935 from a town at the mouth of the Tyne where at least 10 per cent of boys between the ages of fourteen and eighteen were unemployed:

"The main occupations of the town have had to do with the sea and ships, and so the comparatively long water-front and its immediate hinterland is 'tough'. The boys and lads are dressed as is rarely seen in London now, that is to say, in ragged trousers or shorts broken out at the seat. Small boys are often really filthy and run about bare-footed. Clean hands and faces are rare; organizations are few and cover less than one in every ten boys. And it must be remembered that of the lads in work by no means all are in good and progressive employment.... There is one Boys' Club right in the centre of the area. It has no regular leader, and when no one turns up then the lads, if they get in, have a good riot. Boy officers attempting any restraint or reporting trouble are dealt with later. The local authority which tried to run this Club gave it up at last as a bad job. What a pity! The premises are sound and roomy. The area all round is condemned slum property and will be razed in the course of years. The boy population is going hooligan."

Juvenile unemployment was rife in nearly all the industrial centres of the north. The most tragic aspect of the problem was that of boys who left school at fourteen either to go straight into the ranks of the unemployed, or to find themselves sacked shortly after they had begun their working life. Between September and December 1934, nearly half a million boys under sixteen were handed their unemployment books—among them more than 150,000 in the distributive trades, 38,000 in engineering and 33,000 in coal mining. In Liverpool the problem was so serious in the mid-1930s that a committee of inquiry was set up by the local education, employment and social service authorities. In October 1934, there were over 13,200 young people between fourteen and twenty-one registered at the employment exchanges and juvenile employment bureaux in the city. The committee reported:

"Many of the young unemployed have been without work for several years; some have never worked since leaving school. Others have had no more than casual or intermittent employment, while not a few, after two or three years in fairly regular but definitely unprogressive employment, have been thrown out to make room for younger workers.... The best years of their lives have thus, in more cases than it is possible to enumerate, been wasted altogether, and they have reached, or are rapidly reaching, an age beyond which the opportunities of acquiring skill in industry do not exist for them."

But the remedies suggested by the committee—raising the school leaving age, setting up day-continuation schools, junior instruction centres, and the rest—were depressingly familiar and had not shown themselves to be particularly effective. The raising of the school leaving age from fourteen had become a political time-bomb and most politicians seemed to feel that the parents themselves would not vote for it. The opportunity to set up day-continuation schools had been lost, as we have already seen, after the war. By 1934 more than a million young people had passed through the junior instruction centres (or JICs) which were set up immediately after the war to provide practical work and physical education for the out of work adolescent. The idea of these centres was to prevent demoralization and to get boys and girls back into employment as soon as possible, but critics considered that they merely trifled with the problem under a portentous name and others, more bluntly, regarded them as no more than waiting rooms for cheap labour.

Boys' clubs played their part in providing activities for the unemployed. The Shaftesbury Club at Birkenhead, for instance, stayed open during the day so that members and ex-members could come in to a warm fire and mend boots worn out by tramping the streets in search of work. Daytime classes were held in conjunction with the local juvenile employment bureau, education department, YMCA and police court mission. A working party of unemployed boys repaired and repainted the club building and removed 12 lb of pigeon guano—which was duly sold—from the steeple of the Jackson Street Chapel. Together with the sale of baskets, this raised almost £6 for club funds. Half a dozen unemployed old boys of the club were employed at 9d. an hour hedging and ditching at the newly acquired playing field at Prenton Park and getting it ready for the winter football season.

Efforts like these were better than mere charity and voluntary attendance at a club was better for the morale than enforced attendance at a junior instruction centre. The have-nots had become increasingly resentful and wary of being patronized by those who had no real idea what it meant to be out of work and to go hungry; the story was told of Lord Carson visiting an army bath-house during the war, and observing to his aide-de-camp: "I had no idea the lower orders had such white skins." The growing generation between the wars expected more from life than their fathers who had fought in the war, but in most cases they were disappointed. As the Education Committee of Kent County Council expressed it in a report in 1936, boys and girls leaving school "have in their hands, heads and eyes, the keys by which they hope to unlock the gate to a new world. . . . The gate does not open upon a land of promise. Before them lie desolation and disillusion."

In the deprived areas of the North and South Wales, where thousands of boys grew into men without any prospect of any kind of job, London beckoned. Hitching lifts in lorries, sleeping in hedges, begging a crust and a drink here and there, teen-aged boys made their way there expecting to find the streets paved with gold. They were the fodder of the hotel kitchens, a constantly moving and self-renewing source of cheap labour. They were lost in the antheap of the great metropolis which had lured them and used them but had no real need of them, because it, too, had a considerable pool of unemployed. All too often they ended up back in the dole queue, or hung about the automatic machines in the amusement arcades and drifted into petty crime. Others swelled the ranks of the down-and-outs sleeping under a covering of newspapers on the Embankment or in a Salvation Army hostel. Some, terrified by the endless streets of London, headed for the open road beyond and became tramps.

The call of the open road, like the lure of London, worked powerfully on the imagination of youth but led only to disillusion. Rescuing lads from the road was the mission of a number of small voluntary groups, one of which was Waterside House at Willesborough, in Kent. It had started in a rented, tumbledown, eight-roomed house in a Maidstone slum before it moved to a house in $4\frac{1}{2}$ acres where twenty-five lads could be housed at one time. One of its committee helpers explained: "Half the battle of rescuing boys off the road is to accustom them to work again. During their wanderings they have lost so many things—not only their job, but independence, self-respect, friends, hopes, initiative, and the power to work—and all these things have to be recovered before they are fit to keep a job. . . ."

But once a boy had become a tramp it was no easy task to get him back into regular work. Out of 226 young vagrants aged between fourteen and twenty-one who were accepted into Gray House at Bicester only twenty-one remained in the jobs that were found for them. The rest were either dismissed or absconded to return to vagrancy or crime. This noble experiment lasted for only three years and Mr. Frank Gray, who launched it, died in the knowledge that it had been a failure. Like Dr. Barnardo in the previous century, he had the courage to tackle a seemingly impossible task, and when this twentieth century effort collapsed the joint vagrancy committe of the counties of Berkshire, Buckinghamshire and Oxfordshire commented pompously: "So long as legislation, casual wards and indiscriminate private charity enable and encourage youths to take to the road there will never be a lack of habitual vagrants and criminals."

When that statement was made, in 1935, the workhouse was supposed to be dead, but the attitudes of an institution which had lasted a hundred years were not so easily disposed of. Boy tramps were a particularly scandalous feature of the Depression and the voluntary efforts to rescue them concentrated on those who were physically and mentally fit—the rest were left in the casual wards amidst the other outcasts of society.

Despite juvenile courts, an improved probation service and a network of approved schools and Borstal institutions, teen-aged boys were still imprisoned among grown men. In 1934 alone, eight hundred boys were sent by London magistrates to Wormwood Scrubs Prison. Basil Henriques appealed to his friends in the boys' club movement to take an interest in these boys when they came out of prison:

"On his discharge the outlook of the young prisoner is a pretty hopeless one. Many of them have committed their offences because, having quarrelled with their home or having no home, they have found themselves stranded and destitute. Many through a lack of guidance and discipline after leaving school at fourteen have learnt no trade. A distressingly large number of quite young boys have 'had to get married', with a child either on its way or already arrived. Difficult though they are, no one would dare to call these boys irreclaimable, and yet the Discharged Prisoners' Aid Society is called upon to rehabilitate them when they are sent out of prison with no home, with no trade, and with no money of their own, with no friends, with no character, and with no fear of imprisonment as a deterrent of future crime. It is not surprising that a very large number return to prison after a very short period of release."

Enlightened magistrates like Henriques dreamed of the day when young offenders between seventeen and twenty-one would be sent to Borstal or put on probation instead of being sent to gaol. The Home Office report on the work of its Children's Branch in 1938 shows that some approved schools were moving with the times and allowing their boys out hiking in khaki shorts and shirts in which they looked rather like ordinary Boy Scouts. The headmaster of the approved school at Tiffield made a habit of knocking before he entered his senior boys' club room and nearly every boy was on a committee of some kind.

But by contrast, in other homes, orphanages and approved schools, the Home Office inspectors found repressive Victorian-style discipline still enforced where boys sprang to attention when they were spoken to and looked pasty and cowed. In one such institution the boys slept in hammocks; in another they were marched a distance of 200 yards to the cricket field and then "fallen out" to play, still wearing the rough tweeds in which they worked in the fields.

Some of the older established boys' clubs were linked with homes for boys. Many of the newer clubs were ready to make links with Borstal institutions, mainly through cricket and football games. During the years of unemployment the possibility of a boy ending up in one or other of these institutions himself was increased.

To get adolescent lads out of the dole queue and away from the temptation to crime or vagrancy, the government attempted through the Ministry of Labour to transfer juvenile labour *en masse* from areas like Durham and South Wales to the Midlands and London. The Ministry made up the meagre wages of these boys so that their landladies would be paid 16s. a week and the boy himself would have 4s. or 5s. a week for clothes, fares and spending money.

But the scheme was strongly criticized by some club leaders on the grounds that it was being used by anti-social employers as a means of getting cheap labour which they made no attempt to train for skilled or permanent employment, and that both they and the local offices of the Ministry were careless about the conditions youngsters between fourteen and sixteen were set to work in.

Edward Harrison of the Roadmender Club in Northampton, a flourishing town where there was relatively little unemployment, claimed in an article in *The Boy* in the winter of 1935 that these boys were working long hours, and in some cases illegal overtime, for as little as 8s. 5d. to 17s. 3d. a week at the barest possible piece-work rates. This was made up to £1 a week by the local employment exchange and even if a boy had been sacked for dishonesty he could still draw £1 a week from the exchange while they found him a new job. Boys and girls were missing family life at a crucial stage of their lives, without the benefit of the four months a year at home which adolescent pupils at public schools had, and in some cases they were living in poor lodgings with landladies who took little or no interest in their welfare.

Mr. Harrison's strictures added fuel to the controversy over the whole scheme. Valentine Bell, who was chairman of the Battersea Juvenile Advisory Committee which had fifty youngsters from the depressed areas on its books, retorted that they were not being pushed into dead-end jobs or being underpaid or made to work long hours in unsatisfactory conditions. Landladies in general were taking a great interest in the welfare of their young lodgers, who were usually treated as part of the family. Firms were reluctant to move their factories to the depressed areas, so it was essential that juveniles in particular should move to areas where there was work because "No lad should be allowed to lead a maimed life."

Whatever the merits or demerits of the scheme, the fact was that there was a *voluntary* mass exodus of whole families from Durham and South Wales to Birmingham and London between the wars. Emigration was still seen by many others as the only hope of a better life. Although the worldwide depression reduced the numbers leaving the Old Country for the dominions and colonies, the National Association of Boys' Clubs ran its own Colonization Scheme, as it was called, to speed the passage of likely lads. John D. Player, the Nottingham cigarette and tobacco magnate, promised an annual donation of £400 for three years to the scheme because he was "convinced that Club Boys would rather live hard in the Dominions than rest or rot in idleness at home." Considering how many working boys polluted their lungs with "tabs" or "fags," Mr. Player's donation might not have been considered over-generous. As far as the rising generation was concerned, it was in many respects the Age of Neglect. Only today, when the physical and educational welfare of youth is seen as one of the first priorities of the state, is the work of boys' clubs in that period—continuing the tradition established in the Victorian and Edwardian periods—seen in its true perspective.

5

Somewhere to Go, Something to Do

BY 1931 only one in five British people lived in the country, while the rest lived in the great urban sprawls of Manchester, the Black Country of the Midlands, the West Riding of Yorkshire, Tyneside and Glasgow, and above all in London and its ever-spreading suburbia. A start had been made on clearing the slums left over from the Victorian age, and thousands of families found themselves transplanted in great new redbrick estates like Becontree, covering four square miles and built in the 1920s by the London County Council in the flat wilderness beside the Thames to the east of the capital, leapfrogging the belt of genteel suburbia which lay between the open fields of Essex and the ghettoes of the East End. Birmingham Corporation built fifty thousand houses. South of Manchester the vast Wythenshawe estate of municipal housing rose in the 1920s and early 1930s. Twenty to thirty thousand people were set down in a new housing estate just outside Slough in Buckinghamshire to house workers in new light engineering factories springing up along the Great West Road.

These "homes fit for heroes to live in" offered amenities undreamt of by earlier generations of working people: indoor lavatories, bathrooms and some kind of garden, however small. There were, of course, those who felt instinctively that improvements in housing would not make the working classes behave like civilized people. Apocryphal stories were told at the bridge and tennis parties in the better-off suburbs of council house tenants who used the bath as the most convenient place to store the coal.

John Betjeman called for "lovely bombs to fall on Slough," and certainly the overall appearance of the council estates was one of depressing uniformity. A common complaint among the new inhabitants was that they missed the close-knit community life of the ghetto they had left, the social orbit of pub and club. This applied as much, if not more so, to adolescents as to their parents. Furthermore, many of the new estates lacked adequate transport. Long journeys made morning and night to and from work left little time, money or energy for leisure activities.

At the end of the war Dagenham was merely a village in Essex, supplying market garden produce to London, twelve miles away. By the early 1930s, with the development of the Becontree estate largely within its boundaries, Dagenham had become the largest working class suburb in the capital and the home of the Ford Motor Company in England. Nine out of ten boys in the schools hoped to become motor engineers, but sadly there were local jobs for only two out of ten. The rest were compelled to travel into London every day to work. Dagenham's population had grown to 100,000 but it was essentially a dormitory town, as Leslie Hutchinson, assistant director of education for Barking, pointed out in *The Boy* in December 1932:

"Ford's works to the east and Barking's factories to the west provide the only local chance for work, and neither can absorb all the lads leaving school. A boy worth his salt has to join the army of workers in central London and use his home as a dormitory when the day's work is done. The distance, cost, and wear and tear of travel add greatly to the strain of an eight-hour day and, when a boy works longer hours or constant overtime, he leaves his home before seven and fails to return home until the same hour at night. As travel facilities are neither adequate nor within the means of residents, hundreds of men bicycle to work in east London at all hours of the day and night so that the main roads at sundown are a constant stream of oil lamps bobbing back home to a good night's rest."

There was no doubt that for boys who were still at school the Becontree estate offered a far better environment than the stagnant yards and acrid alleys which they had left behind. The new cottages were built in rows of four, six or eight, each set in their own gardens and containing at least one big sitting room, a scullery, three bedrooms and a bathroom. The new schools had playing fields, laboratories and workshops, and beyond the school were tempting open acres covered with ragwort and thistle and dotted with water-filled gravel pits, where boys could fish or launch home-made rafts. Within bicycling distance were Hainault and Epping forests.

Many of the residents of the new council estates were newly married couples with young children, but even in the early years of new towns like Becontree it was realized that sooner or later the need for clubs for adolescents would have to be met. At Dagenham a one-storey brick building was built by London parochial charities to cater for both boys and girls, with their own entrances and rooms at separate ends and a large gymnasium hall in the centre for joint use. The boys' side contained a library, changing room, canteen, games room and hobbies room, and the girls' side much the same, except that the hobbies room was replaced by a kitchen (still at that time regarded as the only proper place for a female).

Another example of attempts to create a sense of community in the new estates was the Slough Social Centre. One of three large buildings was given over to a boys' club and a girls' club.

The rash of council estates built in the 1930s was accompanied by a boom in speculative private house building, encouraged by low interest rates, and so the face of England was changed between the wars. The new Americanized face of arterial and by-pass roads, filling stations, cinemas and dance halls, dog-racing and dirt tracks, Woolworth's and cocktail bars was most apparent in the over-crowded south-east corner of the land. J. B. Priestley wrote somewhat disapprovingly in 1933 of driving into London past

"... miles of semi-detached bungalows, all with their little garages, their wireless sets, their periodicals about film stars, their costumes and tennis rackets and dancing shoes."

The young citizens of the suburbs and the brand new council estates were continuing the process of making England more and more middle class. Boys developed early the skills of home-making with their fretwork and construction of simple wind-up gramophones to play records like "I want to cling to Ivy," the hit of 1933. The Scout Shop "imperial headquarters" in Buckingham Palace Road proclaimed itself paramount for "tents, ruc-sacs, blankets, groundsheets, sleeping bags, knives, axes, cooking utensils, text books, and everything for camping, hiking and the great outdoors." Bicycles were being produced very cheaply and could be bought on the hire-purchase system (or, as it was quickly dubbed, the "never-never").

The Becontree boy was only twelve miles away in distance from the ghettos of Whitechapel or the Elephant and Castle, south of the river, but he already belonged to a different world. The Duke of York, after visiting the latter area, described it as "a wilderness of desolation with miles of ugly, vulgar, shoddy stuff without one scrap of beauty or brightness, one touch of imagination, one message of history." Within a half mile radius of the Elephant and Castle were crammed eighty thousand people, a bigger population than the city of Lincoln. It was here in Walworth in the 1920s that a Methodist minister called James Butterworth started a club for boys in "The Dug-outs" beneath a dilapidated chapel, a gloomy gaslit place with a huge pulpit and massive, wheezing organ pipes.

Butterworth, who was so small and slightly built that he was sometimes mistaken for a boy himself, had trained for the ministry after serving as a private in the Bantam Battalion of Lancashire Fusiliers during the war. He was sent to Walworth to save the moribund chapel, built more than a hundred years previously about the time Napoleon was retreating from Moscow and when the area was populated by prosperous and respectable merchants and their families, all of whom had migrated to Sydenham and Penge and other outer suburbs as Walworth steadily descended the social scale. In the 1920s they still returned on Sundays, led by *pater* in top hat and frock coat, to worship at the old chapel. They must have wrinkled up their noses at the large, brilliantly-lit pub next door, the wide terraces of fine houses with pillared porticoes now turned into slum tenements, the smoky little factories, railway arches and coal sidings despoiling what had been gardens, and the trams clanking down Walworth Road.

But the new minister at Walworth soon made it obvious that he was more interested in helping boys in the mean streets around the chapel than in leading his respectable congregation in Sunday prayers. Indeed, he told them that there were Methodist churches in the suburbs where they lived, so let them worship there. From his own experience as a child sent out to work at the age of twelve in a Lancashire mill town he knew that life for him and thousands like him could have been very different if church and chapel had been open other than on Sundays and special occasions. They could have given boys from the dyeworks and spinning mills an alternative to the cheap music hall, parading the streets and the dinner-hour pastime of pitch-and-toss.

At Didsbury College ex-Private Butterworth had noticed that within a few short years after the war parsons seemed to be drifting back again to a class apart. He was still at Manchester when he met Patrick, a lad who had been reared in the shadows of the derelict old Methodist chapel in Walworth, and whose "generosity, as lavish as his thefts, produced the heights of good-naturedness and the depths of some pretty despicable roguery." Patrick was a member of a reformatory school football team which came to play the Manchester boys. When Butterworth later visited the place where he lived in Walworth he was offered a seat on a sugar box, trying hard not to be sick in a foul-smelling basement room while making conversation with parents who appeared to be permanently drunk. The only place where Butterworth could talk in relatively privacy with Patrick was at the cinema, and, as he recalls in his book *Clubland*:

"During the 'big picture' Patrick whispered, 'I can't stick it, sir—tonight I shall commit another crime so that I can be sent back to the school. I shall have a bed there, clean sheets and plenty of air; I shall hear the birds sing and see the meadows too.' He did commit another crime. But he was not sent back to the school. Society sent him somewhere else for the crime of never having had a decent chance."

Butterworth's book became a best-seller in the early 1930s. It was dedicated to one of his club members, George Moody, a page boy at the Savoy Hotel who died at the age of sixteen. It even attracted the attention of the House of Lords when Lord Rochester, the Paymaster General, told them in February 1933 how the original "Dug-outs" had developed into fully-fledged clubs for both girls and boys and the building of the first Clubland Church:

"The entire premises have cost £34,000, every penny of which has been raised by voluntary contributions, and now the young people themselves, some 500 in number, ranging in ages from ten to twenty-five years, are contributing no less than £1,000 a year in weekly sums and varied efforts for upkeep. It is open every night, and I invite your Lordships to see the place for yourselves, for, as an example of what can be done by voluntary effort, it will well repay a visit."

Butterworth, who was by this time known throughout his teeming parish as "the wee parson," gives an intimate insight into the life of the place in the years between the wars. There was not a single patch of grass where the twenty thousand children of the area could play. The streets, however, were crammed with entertainment and variety: costers with their donkeys, ice cream vendors, hot potato merchants, punch-and-judy men, organ-grinders. At every window and barrack-like doorway families sat to enjoy the noise of this long since vanished sub-culture of the London streets. Second-hand clothes and rags-bottles-and-bones men trooped round with their barrows calling people from their homes to sell or buy according to their economic circumstances. Strolling acrobats, dancers and street fiddlers performed outside the pubs (and the cinemas which were offering a new kind of entertainment).

The Cockney boy took pains over his appearance outside working hours. His hair, clipped close around the ears, was sleeked down with brilliantine, and he acquired a vast wardrobe of coloured socks and ties, although his one good suit would be "pay as you wear." The trousers had to be kept sharply creased by being kept under the mattress at night and folded in brown paper during the day. At the street corner on a Saturday night he and his pals would stand around eating fish and chips from greasy newspaper, telling dirty stories, talking about film stars, cup chances, goal scores, racing tips, and whistling after the girls. If anyone dropped out of the gang it was understood that he had "gone birding" or that he had a "tart" or a "peach." He might be back in the ranks within a week full of boasts about his conquest, or he might become involved in serious courting and end up "getting spliced."

Sunday markets in the poorer areas of the big towns and cities, of which Petticoat Lane was (and still is) the most renowned, made the Sabbath the happiest day of the week as well as the one day which was free from uncongenial toil. Vendors of pets and patent medicines, clothes and furniture, books and bedsteads, fish, fruit and fowl had to shout their wares in competition with hucksters, tipsters, comedians, distributors of religious tracts and soap-box orators of every description. While the silence of the tomb reigned in the suburbs and the country towns, Sunday in the ghettoes resounded to the mad melodies of the fairground organ, the street cries and the noise of the crowded pub.

The working class attitude to religion was summarized by Butterworth:

"Dad says that religion is a sort of hobby some folk go in for like Sam takes to dog-racing. The Scotsman upstairs says there are two pastimes in Scotland, drinking whisky and going to Kirk, and it's all a matter of taste. The coster down the street, looking out on crowded courts and spacious rectories, said he couldn't see any connection between parsons and the Christ they preach about. He thinks they go off to Brighton on Monday with the Sunday's takings, and though everybody in the street believes they 'make something' out of religion, it isn't worth arguing about as nobody has any intention of ever going to church. . . ."

Reg Goodwin, assistant secretary of the National Association of Boys' Clubs, told boys' club leaders in Newcastle in 1936 that the man-in-the-street had no time for the church or parsons:

"He regards the former as the meeting place of sanctimonious and 'pappy' sort of men or of cattily-minded, unfriendly women, and the latter he regards with half humorous contempt as belonging to an age out of touch with a world in which machines have become not the slaves but the masters, in which money appears to be of more importance than goodness, and poison gas and aeroplanes, tanks and torpedoes the deciding factor in any international argument. . . . We all know of empty churches by the dozen in densely populated districts, or at best of churches whose congregations consist almost entirely of elderly women. I do not know a single church, where the normal services have been maintained, which has a reasonable representation of youth in its membership...."

Goodwin was speaking as someone who was closely involved with boys' clubs which had a very definitely religious foundation. In the Bermondsey clubs, as in many others, the evening always ended with ten or fifteen minutes of prayer led by the boy leaders. At Easter the seventeen- to eighteen-year-olds, together with the club managers, went to a permanent camp at Hall's Green near Sevenoaks for what they called a Retreat: a time for meditation, discussion and prayer which played an important part in the whole life of the clubs. Young men like Reg Goodwin whose own lives were examples of Christianity, giving help to those who most needed it, were impatient with a church that seemed remote from people's everyday lives, more concerned with rituals and robes than current political, social and economic realities. There was something unreal about expecting a crowd of Bermondsey boys to sing, without sniggering: "Your harps, ye trembling saints, pluck down from off the willow tree."

The waning influence of the church on the young was accompanied by the weakening of home influences and the breaking up of family life, encouraged by a tremendous boom in facilities for amusement and entertainment, with syndicated cinemas and dance halls, skating rinks, billiard halls, dog-tracks and dirt-tracks for motor-cycle racing springing up everywhere. Now that every town and every suburb had its Palais de Danse and its Regal Cinema, the family was no longer the centre of an adolescent's life. "Going to the pictures" became more than merely a craze with the introduction of the "talkies" in 1929; it became a way of life for the young. Apart from the fact that the fantasies of Hollywood provided a welcome escape from the drabness of an English winter during the Depression, the cosy darkness of the back row was an infinitely better place to go courting than some draughty doorway in a back alley. Holding hands in the "sixpenny dark" or the "ninepenny light"—cinema and music hall respectively—was the usual road to romance.

Many club leaders disapproved, but they had to admit that there were few boys who did not go to the "flicks" at least once a week, and there were some in the big towns who went three or four times a week. Youngsters on theft charges were apt to claim that they stole to buy some tabs and go to the pictures.

But the dance halls, which transformed dancing from a polite social exercise of the middle classes to a mass entertainment where it was no longer regarded as bad form to dance with the same young lady more than three times in one evening, were seen as an even more hostile force by club leaders. One of them, Valentine Bell, aired their feelings in an article in *The Boy* in June 1932:

"Among my unemployed lads (3,000 have passed through my hands during the past two years) there are a number whom I call the 'dance-hall type' and I frankly do not like them. They are flashily dressed and pose as being very sophisticated in sex matters. I came up against them, in the first place, because they objected to work in the Gym, as the exercise bagged the knees of their trousers. I came right up against them the second time, when I discovered them exhibiting certain contraceptives in order to impress the other lads that they were men of the world and very knowing 'cards'. My inquiries into their methods of spending their leisure time led to the discovery that a great deal too much of it was spent at 'dances' and there was not the slightest doubt that the growing habit was a bad one. Continual dancing with scantily clothed girls is certainly not good for lads who have just become sex-conscious; especially in these days of 'bunny-hugging'. Many a lad has lost his self-control after an exciting night at a dance, and has lived to regret it."

It is easy to laugh now at Mr. Bell's concern for the morals of the rising generation more than forty years ago, but he was expressing the alarm of his generation at the spectacle of the fox-trot and the Charleston and the frenzied rhythms of jazz which seemed to be blaring forth on all sides from wireless sets and gramophones. In 1937 Sir Percy Buck was asked, as musical adviser to the NABC, to visit some clubs and report on his impressions. They were not particularly encouraging. Individual attempts to make music had suffered from the commercialization of entertainment, but there had been a vogue for mouth organs and banjos (the latter popularized by George Formby). Drum and fife bands survived into the age of gramophone and wireless and although Sir Percy found them "dreadful, speaking musically," he admitted that they bred enthusiasm and brought boys together. He was less enthusiastic about the prospects for more singing in the clubs (except for the occasional cheery sing-song) "because the broken voice is almost unmanageable." As for serious music:

"I honestly don't think much, or anything can be done at the moment. The type of boys I know you are (quite rightly) trying to humanize doesn't throw up a percentage to whom Bach and Beethoven can yet mean anything. From many years' experience of boys I know you can't give them good stuff by word of command, you must wait till they want it. And to bring that day nearer I should, if I were head of a Club, have a gramophone and make it play, at all odd times, those records of the limited range of tip-top stuff which the quite unsophisticated can enjoy: e.g. Tannhauser prelude, Unfinished Symphony, Coriolan Overture, and a few more...."

Sir Percy sounds rather a musical snob and like many of the older generation of the 1930s he retained Victorian ideas about what would improve the tastes of the lower orders. Highbrows were scathing about jazz, the movies and the BBC alike. But when a boys' club run by Cheltenham College Mission in a drab part of south-east London put on its own ballet in the summer of 1934 *The Times* thought it worthy of an extended notice and a photograph. Working boys dancing ballet instead of the foxtrot at the local Palais was news. They had worked it up themselves when they were in camp, dancing and miming to music on a gramophone. Boys' clubs in Bermondsey even produced Shakespeare.

A more familiar entertainment got up by boys' clubs in the 1930s were the black and white minstrel troupes with the traditional "Mr. Johnson" and his corner-men, Bones and Tambo, with black faces and wigs and lips made up with carmine grease paint. Twenty boys could be kitted out for a troupe with white tennis shirts, pyjama-striped trousers and bright coloured belts and ties for under £3. The repertoire was traditional and unvarying: cross-talk, jokes, riddles and of course songs like "The Old Folks At Home" and "One More River."

The reading tastes of working boys were similarly unsophisticated. The "penny dreadful" had passed away with the ha'penny daily newspaper but it had been succeeded by the "tuppeny blood" and the fourpenny comic. *Marvel, Magnet, Wizard, Rover* and *Adventure Tales* adorned the windows of small newsagents and corner shops in the side streets together with jars of acid drops, peppermints and toffees. In a serial called "Right Away, Rovers!" Dick Dane scored goals with ease. He started off as a fireman on the railway and ended up inheriting the wealth of a director, having supplanted the director's nephew who was a scoundrel and a bounder. Good always triumphed over evil. The forces of the latter, invariably portrayed with broken noses and cauliflower ears, ended up in prison while the former achieved the wealth and happiness they so richly deserved. The *dénouement* had to be reached by way of a veritable hail of bullets, poison darts, spears or hurtling spanners and phrases like: "The Headmaster was imprisoned behind the door and slowly suffocating. Would the new boy be able to open the door without the combination?" and "There's a guy here I want, 'an 'is name is Snake Budgeon! Keep your hands off your guns, boys, or mebbe the slugs'll start flying." Indian unrest, exploration, the slave trade and the Chinese opium traffic were popular themes. Stories about flying were expected to contain a wealth of technical, if pseudo, data about ailerons, thrust-boxes, injector pumps and so on.

Apart from the comics and pulp fiction, the free public lending libraries which were to be found in any place of any size in the England of the 1930s supplied a wide range of reading matter for the rising generation. Cheap paperback "Penguins" were not launched until 1936. James D. Stewart, chief librarian of Bermondsey's public libraries, where 200,000 books were used by young readers every year, reported in 1934 that the first demand was for books of action and adventure and a strong demand for new ideas rather than those of yesterday. The adventure yarns of authors like Westerman, in which trains, ships, motor cars, aeroplanes and wireless played a prominent part, led many boys on to technical books dealing with these in a practical way—indeed 40 per cent of the non-fiction books issued from Bermondey's junior libraries came within this category. Mr. Stewart commented:

"This is a 'snippet' age, and many people are so accustomed to having their information served in tabloid form that continuous interest has become difficult. But by making a good representative selection of books available, and by endeavouring to interest our boys in using libraries *before they leave school*, much can be done to counteract the sudden cessation of mental activity that so often marks the attainment of the school-leaving age, and the laziness of the spoon-fed mind of later years."

Mr. Stewart noted a distinct reaction against the self-consciously improving books of the Victorians—*Eric, Self-Help* and so on. Next to books of adventure and action came the closely related subjects of travel, history and geography, and after that a lively demand for books on games, amusements and hobbies. How to make things was one of the great crazes of the 1930s boy. The "Hobbies shop" flourished, sending out kits and tools by mail order. In Edinburgh there was a Hobbies Club, a community of over a hundred boys devoted entirely to making model aeroplanes, yachts and battleships, constructing wireless sets and gramophones, developing and printing photographs. A book called *101 Things for a Boy to Make* included model winches, turbine motors, steam boilers, kites, hot air balloons, garden seats, bird boxes and flower stands. It also included instruction in mending electric bells and fuses, hanging wallpaper and french polishing.

Holidays with pay did not come within the scope of the law until the later 1930s, and by then the scope for travel had extended far beyond the boys' club traditional bank holiday under canvas at the seaside. It was unheard of in England (although not, of course, in America) for a youth to own his own car unless he was the son of very wealthy parents. But state schools had begun to organize journeys and tours, and from every town boys set off independently in twos and threes by bicycle, train, bus or even on foot for weekend camping trips. Some club managers viewed the trend with misgivings, like the one who wrote in the summer of 1933:

"Club-tours would be admirable: for instance we might run a walking-tour in the Lake District; but the expense is prohibitive. The cost of a tour must always be greater than that of accommodating them in a camp. But independent camping—there I hesitate. The Club idea is not that boys need merely to be given the chance of being together and being themselves, but of being themselves in the atmosphere of a club and with the guidance and friendship of leaders. One must feel quite confident that the boys who go off on an independent stunt in the Club's name are boys who know and respect the technique of Camping and Country-walking and Cycling too well to bring discredit on themselves and the Club by pigging it or committing serious trespassing or neglecting the elementary rules of health.... Moreover there is a very real danger to morals, which must not be exaggerated, but cannot be ignored ... important though the encouragement of initiative and enterprise is, it would be disastrous if it were discounted by the contraction of Rheumatic Fever from sleeping out.... I am told that the inhabitants of the Canvey Island district have found parties of independent boy campers the most damnable nuisance, and I should hate to think that boys wearing our badge had in any way contributed...."

Nonetheless, independent rambling, hiking and cycling had arrived to stay as boys from every kind of home discovered their own countryside, sleeping under haystacks wrapped in a single blanket or inside a thick hedge and taking a morning bath in the nearest stream. The procession of youngsters in shorts and heavy boots with rucksacks on their backs had become a weekly exodus from the towns. It was the Youth Hostels Association which gave a boost to the new mobility of the younger generation by providing simple accommodation at a standard charge of 1s. a night or 6d. for juveniles. In 1935 there were two hundred youth hostels in various parts of the country, in farms and cottages, barns, mills and castles, including thirteen around Snowdonia in North Wales. By 1939 the numbers had grown to 285 in England and Wales, of which 35 had been opened in a year.

Tours abroad were still largely the prerogative of public school boys. The Public Schools Exploring Society mounted expeditions to the arctic forests of northern Finland and among the brown bears in the unmapped interior of Newfoundland. Surgeon Commander G. Murray Levick, the leader, explained that the object was to teach boys "to find their way about and fend for themselves in those surroundings. It is hoped that this will stimulate the spirit of adventure and provide the nation with a number of pioneers who will serve their country by going to the outskirts of our Empire and not be afraid of the hardships they will find there. . . ."

So the Empire-building tradition was still very much alive in the public schools. In 1933 a party of Wycliffe College Rovers and Scouts travelled 2,500 miles to Algeria and back on a camping expedition for just £8 a head. They "roughed it" by travelling third-class. They had a special return fare to Paris by train and Channel steamer of £2, and a fourth class or *au pont* (on deck) passage between Marseilles and Algiers was a mere 31s return. They found the "proximity of natives" on the voyage most interesting.

In these days of the mass package tour it is difficult to appreciate that even such modest prices as the Wycliffe College boys paid were beyond the reach of most working boys, even if they had been able to take the necessary time off from their jobs. Even so, the Workers' Travel Association managed to arrange Continental tours for clerks and artisans, and by 1938 a party from the Dunstable Pioneer Boys' Club, feeling very bold and adventurous, was stepping ashore at Ostend. For most of the members it was their first glimpse of a foreign country, something which they had planned, saved up for and talked about for twelve months.

They toured Germany, visiting castles which flew the swastika flags of the Nazi regime, viewing the terraced vineyards above the Rhine and steaming past the Lorelei rocks to the accompaniment of a German male voice choir. The cost of the trip was £6 per boy and they each took 30s. spending money. They were starting what they hoped would become a club tradition —an annual visit abroad. It seems that they noticed nothing in Germany in that summer of 1938 to arouse fears about the future, or to suggest that trips up the Rhine would soon be out of the question.

6

Keeping Fit—
for What?

ADOLF HITLER attached enormous importance to the youth movement in Germany: indeed it was the very foundation of his plan for a master-race of tall, blond and beautiful Aryans. The Hitler Youth was formed as early as 1926 for boys between the ages of fourteen and eighteen—in other words, precisely the same age group covered by boys' clubs in England. But there the similarity ended. By the end of 1934, after Hitler had become the *Führer*, or leader, of Nazi Germany, the Hitler Youth had absorbed all other organizations and numbered 6 million boys. All the youth organizations in Britain, including clubs, brigades, scouts and cadets, could not muster half a million at the time.

Boys graduated from the Hitler Youth to six months' compulsory labour service, followed by two years in the army. After that they might join the Storm Troops or the SS, the elite military force. First and foremost, their duty was to obey the *Führer*, and this was demonstrated for all the world to see at camps of six thousand boys grouped with their leaders under the colossal legend: "I was born to die for Germany" and at mass rallies where the close-cropped well-drilled legions of youth stuck their right arms stiffly into the air and chanted: "Heil Hitler!"

Education, broadcasts and writing of all sorts in newspapers, books, theatre and films, even music and art, became vehicles of Nazi propaganda, strictly controlled by censorship, with the Gestapo, or secret police, to back it up. Intellectual activity was sneered at by the Nazis, who made a fetish of physical fitness.

It was this latter aspect of Nazism, epitomized by the Hitler Youth bursting with obvious good health and high spirits and Germany's success in the Olympic Games, which made the deepest impression on the rest of the world. A pamphlet published by the Boys' Clubs of America in 1935, while asserting a belief in individuality as opposed to regimentation, and democracy as opposed to dictatorship, nevertheless confessed a sneaking admiration for some of the more militant forms of youth movement in Europe. In Italy Mussolini—"Il Duce"—had made physical training compulsory, in effect, between the ages of six and eighteen, since at six a little Italian boy became a "Figlio della lupa" (son of the she-wolf), at eight a "Ballila" and at fourteen an "Avanguardista." All these bodies were part of the Opera Nazionale Ballila, a very important department of the Ministry for National Education. After eighteen, physical training was merged with military training. The American pamphlet spoke of "boys' faces lit up with an almost ecstatic expression of devotion to an ideal of an all-dominant Italy from which every citizen gained significance, to which every citizen owed unquestioning loyalty at whatever personal surrender of freedom, property, life itself."

In Moscow, it went on, "you could not for the moment but be stirred by the fanatical devotion of boys as they sang to the glory of their country." Communism, like Fascism, believed in catching them young. The Young Communist International was told in 1935 by Dimitrov: "Your duty, comrades, is to find such ways, forms and methods of work as will help to create a new type of mass organization of youth in capitalist countries, organizations which, without imitating the Communist party, will concern themselves with all the vital interests of toiling youth and train them in the spirit of the class struggle."

In Russia, boys and girls' organizations were not segregated as they were in the west. Both sexes were members, in ascending order of age, of the Octoberites, Young Pioneers and Komsomols. By 1937 most big cities boasted a Palace of Pioneers, the first of which, at Kharkov, was a former governor's palace fitted up for the youngsters with model railways and tramways, a power station, an automatic telephone exchange and a radio transmitter, a gymnasium, a library, a puppet theatre, art studios and music rehearsal rooms.

A corner of the Park of Rest and Culture in Mosciw was called Children's City and included all kinds of open air games and apparatus as well as a biological research station and pavilions for model making and painting. It appeared that even on a month's summer camp in the mountains or forests, the Young Pioneer wanted to carry on with the model aeroplane he was making or the story he was writing.

All these manifestations of concern for youth must have looked very worthy to the New York of the depression years, plagued by the gangs of boys roaming the waterfronts and living in the rotting tenements of the East Side. With capitalism's talent for displaying its warts, this was the face of America that was shown to the world in the film *Dead End*.

The Boys' Clubs of America, Inc., having come into being at about the same time that Russell was appealing for some form of national organization in Britain, had spread its influence from coast to coast across the great continent. A superb site of hundreds of acres known as Clear Pool Camp had been presented to the Madison Square Boys' Club to provide an escape from the horrid slums of New York to the woodlands and waters less than forty miles away. It would take another war and another generation of dead in the battlefields before the boys of London came into an estate of their own (at Hindleap Warren in Sussex).

When he launched the King George's Jubilee Trust in 1935 the Prince of Wales said: "I have ascertained that nothing would give the King and Queen so much pleasure as a national thank-offering devoted to the welfare of the rising generation." In a broadcast speech he had said that he believed there were over a million boys and girls between the ages of fourteen and eighteen with no opportunity of enjoying the games and chances of self-development to which they were entitled.

To many people in Britain physical training and drill savoured of militarism at a time when pacifist feeling was at its peak. Yet if the pages of *The Boy* are anything to go by, the National Association of Boys' Clubs was becoming obsessed with physical fitness (idealized portraits of muscular athletes, naked statuary and bronzes, and boys performing "gym and PT" appear in issue after issue). Waldo McGillicuddy Eagar, who was editor of the journal, declared in an article in June 1934:

"The Germans and Italians are giving their boys a concrete ideal, a challenge to be fit for their country's sake. The martial values which they extol, Englishmen deprecate, hoping that if British boys are not warlike there will be no more war. . . . It may be said that we are presenting our boys with a higher ideal than my-country-right-or-wrong-patriotism . . . and that British boys of today can be fired by the highest of collective enthusiasms, the enthusiasm for the world. Well —perhaps they can. None the less, it may be that young Germans and young Italians have now a better chance of saving their souls alive than young Englishmen, simply because they are presented with attainable ideals and called upon for practical loyalty. . . ."

Eagar had devoted his life to the genuinely democratic ideals of the boys' club movement, yet he could not see the true meaning of Nazism, any more than could Neville Chamberlain when he went to Munich to negotiate "peace in our time". Dazzled by the muscular, bronzed battalions of the Hitler *Jugend*, some club leaders in Britain failed to perceive that the *Führer*, with his propaganda machine, his racist theories and his encouragement of the younger generation of Nazis to spy on their parents, was poisoning the wells of youth.

Out of their concern for the allegedly poor physique of English youth, these men were deceived by the showy facade put up by the dictators in Europe. *The Boy* enthusiastically reported the building of thousands of gymnasia and public sports grounds in Italy, the regular medical inspections in the legions of the *Balilla* and the practice of sex education, with the comment: "Italy means her boys to be strong men, and healthy fathers." This was training of youth to the Spartan ideal—not only this, but Il Duce had given Italy the *autostrada* and made the trains run on time.

Not all boys' club men were taken in, however, and a lengthy controversy rumbled on in the correspondence columns of *The Boy* following Eagar's somewhat rash, even though qualified, praise of the dictators' schemes for youth. All seemed agreed that something was wrong with British youth, particularly the section of it which liked nothing better than to hang around the dog-tracks, dance halls, billiard saloons, funfairs, amusement arcades and cinemas, and spent any money it had left on cigarettes and football pools. But there was an equally strong feeling—reinforced by demonstrations of Moseley's "blackshirts" against the Jews in the East End—that putting British boys into coloured shirts was not the answer. In any case Jewish boys' clubs were, and had been for many years, an extremely strong part of the national movement.

In 1938 George Lotringa, the manager of a Jewish boys' club in Bethnal Green, tried the experiment of combining Jewish and Christian boys in one club and found that it worked perfectly well. It had always seemed illogical to him that Jewish and Christian boys had gone to school together and then at fourteen had separated and joined different clubs. The experiment showed that differences in religion were no barrier to the boys mixing freely among themselves.

Rex Regis, a club leader in Hammersmith, summed up the feelings of the ordinary voluntary worker in the boys' club movement when he wrote in the summer of 1938: "Do we want a Chamberlain Youth or a Moseley Youth or some quite Red movement? Of course we don't. We want our lads to be individual, to be each one of them different. And that is the fundamental difference between Englishmen and men who are not English."

Regis believed, as did many of his countrymen, in the innate superiority of their nation over all others, a nation that still presided over a vast empire on which the sun never set, a force of enlightenment to the peoples of the outer darkness that began on the other side of the English Channel. To them Il Duce was simply "Musso the Wop," Hitler merely Corporal Schickelgrüber. Richmal Crompton in one of her *William* books which were avidly read by thousands of youngsters had her juvenile hero talking about "The Nasties" and making a joke of their Jew-baiting.

It was hardly a joke that Italian and German boys were once again the victims of jingoistic patriotism. Captain Radcliffe wrote from the depths of depressed Durham in 1935: "The spectacle of millions of youths, aflame with high ideals of service and self-sacrifice is, I admit, a dazzling one, and it tempts us too. We are apt to get weary at times of trying to instil high ideals into the minds of boys who have been deceived from childhood with the false gods of the cinema and the cheap press." But he wisely observed that there was little hope of getting the working boy to love his country "until his country has given him a good deal more concrete proof of its love for him."

In Cumberland, Tyneside and Durham malnutrition was so rife that doctors considered it unwise for many boys to take part in physical training. When Reg Goodwin joined the staff of the National Association of Boys' Clubs in 1934, one of his main jobs was to help develop clubs in depressed areas. Visiting Tyneside for the first time he was shocked to see hordes of boys in the streets without shoes or stockings on their feet—and this in the age of motor cars, aeroplanes and a journey from London to Newcastle at a hundred miles per hour by train.

The turning point came two years later, with the Physical Training and Recreation Act. As Sir Reg recalled in an interview with the author:

"This act was of great significance. Under its provisions government funds for the first time became and have remained a major source of strength to youth organizations. Until then they had no government support at all—in contrast with what was happening in Germany and other continental countries, who were devoting a lot of time to training their youth. From 1936 onwards we were able with government aid to employ staff to concentrate on physical recreation and training. At the same time there were grants towards the cost of building new club premises. By July 1939 offers amounting to £127,000 had been made for 100 Boys' Club schemes costing £266,000. But the war intervened and very few were ever built."

From 1934 onwards the NABC gave every year a substantial part of its income to the clubs, federations and county associations. Starting with Yorkshire in 1931, associations for thirteen counties were established in eight years. Staff were appointed for field work, leader training, drama, handicrafts, art and physical recreation. And since club members were mostly working adolescents, the NABC took a close interest in such matters as juvenile unemployment, health, excessive hours of work and night shifts, and holidays with pay, acting as a lobby for improvements in the welfare of boys by collecting evidence and submitting papers to the government about the abuse of labour.

All-embracing, all-controlling movements directed entirely by the State were not the British way of doing things. Nor were shirts of whatever uniform colour. Delegates to the Boys' Conference at Rubery, Birmingham, in 1935 concluded their deliberations with the singing of "Auld lang syne" around the NABC flag. They had expressed unanimous feeling against mixed clubs, although they were on the whole in favour of mixed cycling and rambling and social evenings, where girls and club members over sixteen could mix. It was admitted that there was some form of gambling in most clubs but the craze of dog-racing at new tracks up and down the country had little serious effect on club life. These conferences of boys in camp had started in 1932 and were the first attempt to take club members into the leadership's confidence.

The British way of fostering the youth movement was in fact a haphazard mixture of philanthropy, government aid, self-help and voluntary enthusiasm. In 1935 the NABC had acquired its own headquarters, still at 17 Bedford Square, and had taken on two more assistant field secretaries. Royal patronage played a significant part in the promotion of the movement. As we have seen, an active part was taken by the Duke of Gloucester and the Prince of Wales, whose reign as King Edward VIII ended abruptly with the abdication crisis. His younger brother, who succeeded him as king, had also shown an interest in the boys' movement by starting the Duke of York's Camp, where public school boys, boys from suburbia, boys from council estates and boys from slums came together. Four hundred boys at a time attended these camps and met in the first instance as total strangers to one another at the Royal Mews at Buckingham Palace. They then travelled by train to the camp. One of the boys wrote:

"Mixing is such an integral part of Camp that it occurs automatically and without hitch or incident. Before attending one's first Camp, one thinks about mixing and determines to make an effort to do so. Once having got into Camp, or even into Buckingham Palace Mews, all such thoughts are immediately overwhelmed by the fact that there is no need to mix; the mode and manner of the meeting make an oil and water effect impossible."

By 1938 a total of seven thousand boys had passed through the Duke of York's Camp. Its effectiveness in breaking down class barriers only anticipated what was to happen on a far, far wider scale during the impending war when young conscripts from all walks of life had to live together, not just for a week, but month in and month out. As far as the King was concerned, he was quite ready to join in singing with appropriate actions "Underneath the Spreading Chestnut Tree" around the bonfire on the last night of camp. Perhaps for the first time, the people were allowed to see their monarch on the newsreel at the local cinema as a warm-hearted human being mixing freely with his subjects.

In 1938 King George VI attended the London boys' club boxing championships at the Albert Hall and climbed into the ring afterwards to present the cups to boys who had hastily changed from their shorts and vests into Sunday-best suits. Here was the complete contrast to the *Führer* hysterically haranguing his regimented ranks of youngsters.

The Hitler Youth was portrayed in the open air, brown as berries, shunning nicotine and alcohol, tramping the mountains and forests or plunging *en masse* into some crystal-like lake. But the glare of publicity in Britain focused on the boy in the boxing ring at the Albert Hall. The Prince of Wales was there in 1929 to watch boys from the clubs in the London Federation beat boys from the Army, Navy, Royal Marines and Royal Air Force. The heaviest of them weighed in at a mere 9st. 9lb.

Yet a survey carried out at the time (and published in *The Lancet* in December 1931) showed that telegraph boys and other messengers employed by the Post Office in London were on average 16 lb. heavier and $1\frac{1}{2}$ in. taller than their predecessors of the early 1900s. In a group of two hundred boys examined for service in the Post Office in the years 1905–08 only three weighed 11 st. or over. A similar group between 1929–31 included twenty-two who weighed 11 st. or over.

The conclusion drawn from this evidence was that better housing, better food and medical inspection in schools had brought about a great improvement in the physique of young men. They were also getting more exercise and fresh air. Of 150 London telegraph boys interviewed in 1934 only 8 said they had no outdoor hobby, 72 were regular cyclists into the country at weekends, 63 played football and cricket and 41 were regular walkers.

Although only 25 belonged to any club or scout troop, 59 were regular campers in groups of two or three.

There was, however, little room for complacency about the health of working boys between the ages of fourteen and sixteen, and until the gap was closed towards the end of the 1930s they were completely ignored by the National Health Insurance Scheme. Regular medical inspections came to an end when the boys left school. Tuberculosis was the most serious menace to their health, but the few doctors who gave their services voluntarily to boys' clubs found that the greatest number of defects were found in teeth, tonsils and vision. Examination carried out at the Oxford and St. George's Club in Whitechapel in 1933 showed only 47 boys out of 313 to be free from defect and at Shrewsbury House Club in Liverpool only 6 out of 86 boys.

In the absence of any national statistics, it is impossible to say how far these two clubs represented the state of health of the working boy population as a whole, but there was certainly a great deal of concern about hollow-chested, spindly-legged English youth. The obsession with physical training travelled across the English Channel from Germany and Italy and led in 1937 to the founding of the National Fitness Council. The craze for "physical jerks" swept through the boys' clubs, and at the same time outdoor activities like canoeing and mountain climbing were being developed, although on a very small scale.

Kurt Hahn, the founder of Gordonstoun School in Scotland, where the future Duke of Edinburgh was a pupil, introduced in 1938 the idea of fitness badges for boys' clubs as well as public schools. Hahn had developed his educational theories—based on a strong sense of self-discipline, outdoor activity and service to the community—at Salem in Germany but he came to Britain after Hitler's rise to power. His "Moray Badge" was awarded not only for prowess in jumping, running, throwing and swimming, but included expedition tests in walking, climbing, animal watching, exploring, sailing and riding. The general idea was to stretch a boy's horizons as well as making him physically fit.

Fitness—the word was on everyone's lips—but keeping fit for what? The Germans and the Italians seemed to know, but in Britain the debate continued with desperate uncertainty. According to a schoolmaster, Harold Stovin, in *Totem*, published in 1935, the pursuit of the fitness cult was merely an expression of moral bankruptcy. Boys' clubs were a poor substitute for a radical improvement in the education system and *esprit de corps* was nothing more than an expression of the herd impulse which made war and its need for discipline possible.

Fifteen district leaders of the Hitler *Jugend* came to England in the summer of 1938. They went to Clubland in Walworth and the Webbe Institute in the East End and they watched a swimming gala. They smiled, said thank you politely in English and went away. Between them they were responsible for about the same number of boys as the total membership of the National Association of Boys' Clubs, even though it had doubled during the 1930s to 160,000 boys in 1,670 clubs.

In the following summer Sir Hubert Llewellyn Smith told 220 club leaders (including three women) who gathered at Oxford for their annual conference that the association had now emerged from adolescence and stood on the threshold of manhood: "For to-day we meet for the last time as a purely voluntary assemblage; tomorrow we are privileged to enter on the fuller life of an organization, still voluntary in its principles and leadership, but incorporated by Royal Charter with all the added prestige and responsibilities attaching to that exceptional mark of national recognition."

Two months later Britain was plunged into the Second World War and the National Fitness Council sank into oblivion, as did so many of the blueprints for splendid new boys' clubs. Again, as in 1914, the boys' clubs provided thousands of fine recruits for the armed forces. But this time they were being matched against the products of a very different youth movement, controlled and conditioned by a dictatorial State and primed for war.

7

War Again

THERE WERE FEW, if any, cheers when the Prime Minister Neville Chamberlain told the British people over the wireless on the morning of 3rd September, 1939, that they were at war with Germany again. It was not like 1914. No one wanted this war but it had been seen as inevitable for some time and the public mood was to get on with it, entertaining no doubt as to who would win.

Having hoped for peace, Britain was ill-prepared for war. Unlike Germany and Italy it had not trained its youth to be soldiers. At the end of the 1914-18 war more than 100,000 boys were enrolled in cadet units, but by 1930 they had dwindled to less than a third of that number and the decline was hastened still further by the withdrawal of government aid. The cadet movement was kept going on a voluntary basis by a few members of the House of Lords who formed the British National Cadet Association, which soldiered bravely on until 1945. But in 1939 it numbered only 180 units with 22,000 boys, of whom 18,000 were aged between fourteen and eighteen.

Considering that Britain was the world's leading maritime nation, there was a similarly surprising lack of strength in the Sea Cadet Corps—in 1938 it totalled a mere 5,500 members. Perhaps the reason was an innate British distaste for the sight of boys in military uniforms, or perhaps in the case of the naval cadets, the bulldog breed and hearts-of-oak tradition no longer appealed to boys. However, when the Air League of the British Empire formed a cadet corps in 1938 it caught their imagination immediately. The Air Defence Cadet Corps had 42 squadrons within six months, 173 by the end of the following year and over 200 when in February 1941 it was taken over by the Air Ministry and reformed as the Air Training Corps (ATC) with the expressed purpose of giving pre-training for the RAF to boys of good quality.

By then, in hundreds of draughty church halls, Scout huts and drill halls up and down the country, boys were in uniform, training for war or defence. At the outbreak of the war at least 244 boys' clubs had their premises commandeered by the authorities, or could not open because they had no black-out arrangements to comply with air raid precautions, or no air raid shelters. In some cases the club leader or secretary, or even both, were called up. But more than 1,000 clubs stayed open.

In anticipation of previously unheard of destruction and devastation by enemy bombs, wholesale evacuation of the major towns and cities was ordered. Parties of children, labelled and carrying their gas masks in little cardboard boxes, were packed off to unknown destinations in the country. Schools in urban areas were closed down and private houses and youth club premises were used as part-time classrooms for children who had not been evacuated. In the reception areas new clubs were opened for evacuees and local boys.

In the winter of 1939 virtually the whole population, men, women and children, seemed to be on the move. Everything was in a state of flux. Yet society soon settled into a new pattern of life in which the black-out, air raid sirens, rationing and the rest played a prominent part. Of $1\frac{1}{2}$ million mothers and children evacuated from London in September 1939, nearly $1\frac{1}{4}$ million quickly returned home. Schools, cinemas and theatres reopened.

Within a few months Arthur Tyrer, the veteran leader of Brighton Boys' Club, was writing:

"Actually one finds that running a boys' club in wartime differs little from the normal life of a club. True, the first three or four weeks—where the 'black-out' was something of a novelty—were rather hectic. Boys seemed to be more 'worked up' and expressed this in noisy fashion inside. But now they have settled down. One other feature is that the shelf in the canteen where 'boyish valuables' are deposited is now filled by all kinds of ingenious torches. There are fewer cycles brought to the club and the attendance of boys who live in the distant housing estates has been affected by the darker nights. We have opened the club an hour earlier in the evenings and close half an hour earlier. Several older men have come in to help us, in place of members away in the Forces and others who are working late on Government jobs. There has been an interesting revived interest in old-fashioned table games which one imagined would never 'go' in a boys' club. 'Happy Families', 'Snap', 'Lexicon' and even 'Ludo' have provided groups of boys with quite genuine fun...."

Brighton, although only sixty miles from London on the south coast and directly facing "E-boat Alley," was a reception centre for evacuees from the capital and, like market towns and hitherto sleepy villages throughout the Home Counties, had felt the impact of lively boys from Bermondsey and Battersea. Not all evacuees were youngsters who had never seen a bathroom, didn't know that milk came from a cow and to whom the only *real food* was fish and chips. One of the new arrivals at the Brighton club was a secondary school boy whom the others described as "very posh."

All over the country, boys' clubs were organizing schemes by which their members could contribute to the war effort or "do their bit" as it was called. The syllabus of training issued by the Pontypridd and Treforest Boys' Civil Defence Corps included signalling, map reading, first aid and fire fighting. Liverpool Boys' Association formed a civil defence cadet corps to train boys in similar skills, plus anti-gas measures and the effects of high explosives. Boys over sixteen would be sent to act as messengers, "gossip-quellers" and helpers at ARP posts and auxiliary fire and ambulance stations.

Llay Boys' Club in North Wales enrolled thirty-two of its members as a cycle patrol in conjunction with the local Home Guard. The boys' club at the de Havilland aircraft factory were concentrating on collecting envelopes for reuse to save paper, growing medical herbs and making splints as well as stirrup-pumps for fire-fighting. The Webbe Club in Bethnal Green provided volunteer stretcher bearers for the Children's Hospital and telephonists for the Chest Hospital. Boys' club premises at Wallsend were turned into a rest centre for people bombed out of their homes and thirty of the senior boys were registered as rescue workers.

Whatever the peacetime apathy of British boys towards the cadet forces, in wartime there was a great impulse to get into battledress well before the age at which they could be conscripted as soldiers, sailors or airmen. By 1943 the ATC and the Army cadets had a strength of 200,000 each and there were said to be six applications for every place in the Sea Cadets. At seventeen a boy could join the Home Guard and be a real soldier alongside his father.

Immediately after the Battle of Britain it was the ambition of almost every boy to be a pilot in the RAF, to be one of those young men the new Prime Minister Winston Churchill had movingly described as "The Few." They were idealized in the comics, with characters like "Rockfist Rogan." Local squadrons of the air cadets, who were supplied with old aero engines and airframes for instruction purposes and were allowed to visit squadrons at airfields like Biggin Hill, acted as a magnet. Boys could join at fifteen and some who had left school at fourteen hastily resumed their education in subjects like mathematics in the hope of getting accepted for training as a pilot. Despite the heavy loss of life in the air and the urgent need for replacements, only the very brightest and fittest boys were able to get through the training. One was Leslie Tolchard, captain of Sunderland Christ Church Boys' Club, who became a Bomber Command Pathfinder and won the DFC and bar as a flight lieutenant. Others went as navigators, wireless operators and, most hazardous of all, as air gunners in those exposed perspex turrets at the tail end of Lancaster bombers. The chances of their returning uninjured from a bombing raid over Germany, or indeed of returning at all, were not high.

The RAF made the strongest appeal to the imagination of adolescent boys because the war in the air was something that was taking place in the blue summer skies of 1940 above their very heads, not something merely to read about in the *Daily Mirror*. The wreckage of Dornier and Heinkel bombers shot down by the Spitfires and Hurricanes could be seen on the ground, and fragments collected, along with shrapnel from shells and bombs, as "trophies."

For the majority of club boys, the standards of mental agility and physical fitness required for aircrew were too high. They were, as in the previous war, conscripted into what they mockingly referred to as the PBI—the "Poor Bloody Infantry." An American journalist who accompanied the German Army on its advance across Europe to the English Channel wrote in *Atlantic Monthly* about his first sight of young Englishmen who had been taken as prisoners of war:

"What impressed me most about them was their physique. They were hollow-chested and skinny and round-shouldered. About a third of them had bad eyes and wore glasses. Typical, I concluded, of the youth that England neglected so criminally in the twenty-two post-war years when Germany, despite its defeat and inflation and six million unemployed, was raising *its* youth in the open air and the sun. I asked the boys where they were from and what they did at home. About half were from offices in Liverpool; the rest from London offices. Their military training had begun nine months before, they said, when the war started.

"But it had not, you could see, made up for the bad diet, the lack of fresh air and sun and physical training of the post-war years. Thirty yards away German infantry were marching up the road towards the front. I could not help comparing them with these British lads. The Germans bronzed, clean-cut physically, healthy-looking as lions, chests developed and all. It was part of the unequal fight."

This was a subjective impression, rather than an objective report, and appears coloured by the fact that the Germans were plainly winning and the English were being driven into the sea. But the reporter's unfavourable comparison of the physique of the British conscripts and that of the Germans rings true. Between the wars when they were growing up, the former had been neglected not only materially and physically, but educationally and spiritually as well. The fact that boys of good physique, good morale and good intelligence were given a crash course in secondary school subjects by the ATC to bring them up to the standards required by the RAF for trainee pilots, and that many of them emerged as sergeant pilots to give sterling service, was in itself an indictment of pre-war neglect and waste of youth. Had it not been for the demands of war, most of these youths who had left school at fourteen would have attained nothing more glorious than a job as an assistant warehouseman or behind the counter in the Co-operative stores, or in the stock room at Woolworths.

Captain Radcliffe's work as welfare officer at an infantry training centre in the north-west of England brought him into contact with many hundreds of raw recruits and he wrote at the time that most came with the idea of making the best of a bad job that had to be done, and only about 10 per cent actively disliked army life and were unhappy. Most recruits rapidly put on weight and improved in fitness although they all complained about the size and heaviness of army boots after lightweight pointed shoes, and of course about the food. Compulsory dental treatment was also highly unpopular.

He found that the public school boy adapted much more easily to army standards of cleanliness and discipline than the lad from the back streets, but he added: "None of them show any sign of class hatred, or dislike of officers because they belong to a different class. From the day they join they accept the orders of both the NCOs and the officers in good spirit and I have not seen a surly face. Their friendly eagerness to salute in the first few days is almost as noticeable as their ignorance of how!"

"Going to the pictures" was a drug to most of these youngsters and they went to the cinema on every occasion they could get out of barracks. No more than 10 per cent were church-goers, 80 per cent were interested in sport and games, only a small proportion were drinkers. Although at least 60 per cent read books regularly, very few read anything other than adventure and crime stories. Captain Radcliffe found that their language was less lurid than that of the 1914–18 Tommy and that they behaved courteously to the ATS girls at dances—"Only a small proportion are deliberately immoral; many, perhaps, hope more or less vaguely that an opportunity to be so will occur, but are content to leave the provision of the opportunity to the opposite sex." He felt that many recruits were ignorant of sex matters and should be given instruction before they joined the army.

He found their cheerfulness also somewhat disturbing:

"These young men . . . laugh and smile far more here than they do in civil life. Can it be because they found in the army life in wartime so many of the things which they have wanted often perhaps in peacetime, and which our civilization has failed to give them? Things like a common cause to work for, good comradeship, a shared loyalty, adventure, good health and security of employment?"

These, of course, were the very things that boys' clubs had tried to provide and one of the boys in uniform from a Bermondsey club confirmed in a letter to *The Boy* in the spring of 1940 that the British Expeditionary Force was in good heart. Their biggest grouse was the inadequacy of Army pay, as they received only 10s. a week: "Few of the men in my battalion eat the army supper at half-past six, so the greater part of their pay goes for sausage and mash in the canteen at a shilling a time. Add cleaning material and cigarettes and what's left out of ten bob?"

These BEF troops needed all their reserves of spirit and irrepressible humour when they found themselves herded on to the beaches at Dunkirk, strafed by enemy guns and dive-bombers as they waited for the armada of little boats to carry them across the channel to England. A few soldiers of one regiment, who were former members of the same club, formed a football team and challenged all comers for two days while they were waiting for a boat! Many of them were hardly out of boyhood; they had scarcely begun to shave every day and the older recruits chaffed them about their adolescent spots and pimples. But at least the minimum age for active service in His Majesty's armed forces was eighteen, whereas the Merchant Navy signed on boys as young as fifteen to serve in convoys which were under attack by marauding packs of U-boats.

E. Hailey Clark, the warden of Talbot House Seafaring Boys' Club in Southampton, told the story of Eric, who joined his first ship at the age of sixteen in July 1939, a couple of months before the war broke out. In September the ship was reported sunk by an enemy submarine and for weeks nothing was heard of the crew—until suddenly it was heard they had landed safely at a port in South America. Eric returned none the worse to Southampton and in December was off to sea again. In January 1940 his second ship was sunk by mines. But he was picked up safely and in February was away at sea in another ship. It is not recorded if Eric survived the war, unlike so many of his youthful shipmates who did not.

The Southampton Club, with some two thousand members scattered across the seven seas, tried to make their time ashore a happy one. With six or eight months or even longer spent at sea, living, eating and spending every off-duty hour in a cramped and over-crowded fo'csle, conditions for the crews in many merchant steamers of the time were no better than slums. Now added to that was the appalling danger of torpedo, mine and attack from the air. The warden at Talbot House wrote:

"Like many other things, ships sirens have been silenced, and we no longer get the familiar sound that used to herald the approach of the big ships. . . . Sometimes early morning or late into the night one looks up from an office desk to find an excited mob of young boys all anxious to know if they can be accommodated, and get any mail that may be awaiting them. Letters! Home! The anxiety for news after weeks at sea. It may be from the eleven thousand miles of ocean from England to Melbourne or again, the six thousand miles of Atlantic from the Cape, or from the incredible spaciousness of the Pacific, or the Western Ocean with its gales and storms. . . ."

But for the majority of boys between fourteen and eighteen, too old for school and too young to be called up, there was work to be done on the land, in the offices and factories, and down the mines. A statement by Ernest Bevin as Minister of Labour and National Service in 1943 that he might be compelled to direct lads between sixteen and eighteen to work in the pits caused considerable indignation, but the fact was that with so many men serving in the armed forces the nation needed the labour of women, girls and boys to keep the industrial war effort going. There were more than thirty thousand boys between fourteen and eighteen working below ground in the pits alongside men who had refrained from military service. They were the unsung army of Bevin Boys.

After an initial *increase* in the numbers of unemployed while Britain adjusted to a war economy, the scourge of idleness virtually disappeared. Everyone was needed and there was concern about the long hours which adolescents were working in the factories, leaving them little time for proper rest or relaxation. Although the Factories Act of 1937 limited the working hours of boys,* exceptions were made by factory inspectors where it was considered necessary to aid the war effort. The YMCA Boys' Work Committee in Leeds discovered that many employers were not bothering to apply for licences before putting their juvenile workers on overtime, not

* See Chapter 3.

only during the week but on Saturday afternoons and Sundays, too. Youth had money in its pockets, but little to spend it on other than the pub and the picture house. Boys straight from school earned about 13s. for a forty-six-hour week in the mills of Lancashire and West Riding, and some worked as many as fifty-two hours in one week. In engineering works around Manchester the average wage for these very young boys was 12s. for a forty-five-hour week, which five hours' overtime could bring up to 14s.

Outside working hours, the blackout and the air raids on all the main industrial centres made it difficult to go anywhere for pleasure. The older boys spent most of their spare time wearing tin hats on fire-watching duty or with the ARP, Home Guard patrols, or the Auxiliary Fire Service. From Christmas 1940, on through spring and summer of the following year, *The Boy* reported many instances of individual bravery during the Blitz. A senior boys' weekend training course at Bristol had to take to the air raid shelter, where they sang "Roll out the Barrel" to drown the sound of the anti-aircraft barrage and bombs falling close by. Later a team of volunteers under a club leader ventured out with a stirrup pump and buckets of earth to smother the incendiaries which were falling all around:

"Two boys climbed over the glass veranda, up the drain pipes, on to the roof of the main hall. Another gang discovered the ladders and hoisted one up to the worst fire on the roof. Buckets of earth were passed up and one incendiary was smothered whilst the fire was put out by buckets of water. At the other end of the building the bomb had not broken through the roof and a boy scraped away the pieces of burning bomb with a broken tile. He calmly covered the remaining mess with earth and then, monkey-like, walked along the guttering to help his colleague deal with the fire. . . . Bombs were still shattering around and the patrols became used to throwing themselves flat every time the scream and whine of a bomb was heard."

When the worst of the bombing was over the boys went out in search parties rescuing people where they could, but leaving the dead or those too seriously trapped in the wreckage of their homes for the attention of the official rescue parties. They carried messages to ARP posts and first-aid stations. The premises of a boy' club in the area were used as a rest centre for the homeless and the boys stayed for two days serving over eight hundred cups of tea.

At the height of the Blitz on Plymouth in the spring of 1941, club members who were AFS messengers promoted themselves to fully-fledged fire-fighters and manned hoses until they fell from sheer exhaustion. One boy worked almost without break for seventy-two hours fighting fires in the docks. Another, who was fire-watching at a church, dashed to save the crucifix and church ornaments when a high-explosive bomb demolished a part of the building. Another bomb came down, seriously injuring him and killing another watcher outright. There were fourteen boys' clubs in Plymouth before the Blitz; there were only four after it.

At about the same time a boy in London wrote:

"Twelve high explosives fell outside the club—all within a few score yards, as well as other bombs on the homes of members. All our doors and windows (or what served as windows) were blown in. . . . Club was in full swing at the time, but once again, and this is the third bombing here, we were amazingly protected and no one in the club was hurt. Unfortunately others were, some of our members being homeless, relatives being injured, and a younger brother is among the dead. On the Saturday, as a result of the bombs outside, the gas mains were fired, flames lighting up the sky for miles as at our last bombing eight weeks ago. Club was quickly evacuated and in three minutes all members were in a local shelter, except such as were giving a helping hand. A little later as rescue work proceeded and it was seen the flames would not reach the club, our premises served for helping some of those hurt and dazed by the explosions, and club blankets came in extremely useful. Our club leader was in charge of the club at the time and he did a splendid bit of work under most appalling conditions."

Sebag Montefiore, a supporter of and worker in boys' clubs, threw open his stately home at Wintershill in Hampshire as a weekend retreat from the war-torn towns, calling it the Montefiore Country Club for Boys. There, amidst the spreading acres of parkland, rose gardens, lawns and yew walks, eighty boys filled the great house with laughter and song each weekend as they revelled in the luxury of hot baths and showers and beds with cool sheets instead of a rough blanket in a damp air raid shelter. They came and went in green-covered lorries, glad to be away for a time from the whistle and crash of bombs and the menacing grumble of the anti-aircraft guns. All they had to pay for were their meals (a total of 4s. 3d. over the whole weekend) and concerts were laid on by ENSA, the combined services entertainment organization.

It was all too rare an opportunity to get away from a war in which civilians were as much in the front line as the troops. In all more than sixty thousand civilians were killed in air raids, almost half of them in the London area. Sam Ansell, leader of the Brady Boys' Club in Whitechapel told his lads:

"I have come to the definite conclusion that the sooner all you young fellows have found an alternative for going to the public shelters night after night, the better. . . . I say quite unhesitatingly that its effect on you physically, mentally and morally is detrimental to your future health and careers. Many of your mothers are away from home, and, as you know, no matter how much notice you may have taken of your mother in the past, no one can take her place to watch you, your feeding, your cleanliness, your appearance and above all your happiness. . . . I find that many of you do not get your underclothing off other than either when you have a bath, or change into clean underclothing or come to the cottage. Quite a number of fellows are living mainly on food bought at cafes and so on. . . . Then again many of you go to these shelters, in many cases quite unwillingly, and with nothing really to do, with the result that one sees quite a fair amount of card playing, perhaps dancing in a corner where there are no bunk beds, and much more which you know. . . ."

Boys needed men to replace fathers who were away at the front, and also mothers who were busy at all hours of day and night in the munitions factories. Even in country towns, the influx of evacuees and troops billeted locally had changed the pattern of life and added temptations to boys who were earning. Where there was one cinema show a week in pre-war days there would be two or even three and the weekly dance would have become bi-weekly.

The few dedicated club leaders who had not been called up did their best to provide counter attractions. Before British Restaurants were set up in church halls and requisitioned cafes, serving nourishing meals for 1od. or 1s., the clubs found that food was a great attraction for boys. Wartime comics portrayed gargantuan feasts of mashed potato, with sausages sticking out like cannons, but boys would readily queue up for a portion of scrambled egg (made from dried eggs) or beans on toast at 4d. a time. A Ministry of Food licence had to be obtained before a club could open a canteen, and returns made to the local officer of that vast bureaucracy. Government inspectors, or "snoopers" as the public preferred to call them, went everywhere to make sure that rationing regulations were not circumvented.

At a time when the entire population was registered and documented, and men and women were being conscripted into the services and "work of national importance," Whitehall kept a close eye on what had become known as the Youth Service, which comprised—apart from boys' clubs—boys' brigades, church lads' brigades, Scouts, the Co-operative youth movement, young farmers' clubs, ambulance brigade cadets and the YMCA as well as the whole range of clubs for girls, Girl Guides, the Girls' Friendly Society and the YWCA. Mixed clubs were becoming popular, if only because of the shortage of premises, and the question of sex education was much discussed by leaders. The official policy of the Board of Education, which had assumed a new responsibility for boys and girls up to twenty, was that the teacher, the youth leader, the employer and the trades union official were all "partners in the training of the young." But according to Dr. A. E. Morgan, who had written a survey for the King George's Jubilee Trust published under the title *The Needs of Youth* just before the outbreak of war: "I have some experience of the club movement, the scouts, girl guides and brigades, and I have no praise too high for them. But so far as impact on adolescents goes they have largely failed."

Whilst it was true that boys' clubs attracted a relatively small proportion of working class youth, their influence on that section was by no means insignificant. The NABC, receiving its first annual grant from the Board of Education in 1942, was able to take on more field officers and research and publicity staff. Although many clubs were bombed, hundreds of new ones came into being, and co-operation with the Army Cadet Force extended the movement still further. To replace the constant drain of leaders into the

25. A group of boys training at Woodrow High House for a visit to Germany in 1950 to show German boys how British boys' clubs were run.

Opposite page: 26. *Top.* Physical recreation at a training camp run by the NABC. 27. *Bottom.* A gymnastics competition held at Nash Court in 1961.

This page: 28. *Right.* Canoeing has become one of the most popular sports with boys' club members. 29. *Below.* Modern club facilities; the Monty Hind Boys' Club, Nottingham, opened in 1965.

30. *Above*. The Duke of
Gloucester, who
succeeded his father as
President of the NABC
in October 1974, opening
the Downside and
Worth Boys' Club in
December 1974.

31. *Left*. Sir Reginald
Goodwin, retiring general
secretary of the NABC,
with Brigadier Davies-
Scourfield, his successor,
in July 1973.

services, a serious effort had to be made to train senior boys in their responsibilities.

In wartime boys grew up fast and more of them were finding in themselves the ability to organize their own leisure time with their contemporaries. James Cox, who had been a member of Clubland in Walworth and the St. Bride's Institute in Blackfriars, describes in *The Boy* (winter 1939-40) a club started under a railway arch in Brixton:

"It contained two table-tennis tables, and a piano with a very tired tone. I shall never forget that ancient piano; it resented every tune knocked out of it, it seemed to protest with every note that its days were finished.... Our total membership was never above 25. We were a mixed community, and between both sexes existed a marvellous comradeship. We never made profits—more often we ran at a loss. We called ourselves the Ravensbourne Table Tennis Club, and sported a plum red shirt with a very impressive golden badge. Club nights every evening—including Sunday (usually all day). If only people when building and forming clubs would realize that the boy does not want palatial buildings and scores of activities. Give him a few—I stress *few* (no more than 25)—other members of about his own age, a couple of large rooms and a sense of freedom, and he'll form his own activities and be perfectly happy."

Lees Street Lads' Club was formed in Manchester in the summer of 1942 by a man and ten boys with the help of £2 15s. 6d., enough to buy one football, a draughts set, a ring board, a table tennis set and a membership book. The room they met in measured only 15 ft. by 10 ft. and the membership grew to thirty boys within three months. A new home was found in a hall attached to the Lees Street Congregational Church—a tenancy conditional on the boys attending Sunday morning service. This was in the old tradition of pioneers of the boys' club movement, a tradition which neither Hitler's bombs nor the grey blanket of State regimentation and control could stifle. The movement was still growing and throwing up new shoots. In 1940 the first Boys' Club Travelling Theatre took to the road from South Wales, the same area in which the first boys' holiday village had been set up at St. Athan during the Depression. Among the company of boys who were introduced to Emlyn Williams and Dame Sybil Thorndyke during the interval of *The Corn is Green* at the Piccadilly Theatre were Donald Houston, an unemployed milk-roundsman's boy from Llwynpia Boys' Club, and Dick Davies, a pit boy from Blaen Boys' Club. For both of these boys their clubs were to prove the gateway to an acting career. For thousands of unknown boys growing up in wartime Britain the clubs were a gateway to a wider life beyond the blacked-out streets.

In the early 1940s, after years of struggling on behalf of the boy of fourteen to eighteen, the clubs found themselves surrounded by others who were suddenly aware of his existence. Youth committees, youth squads and youth centres of all descriptions sprang into being and the "youth problem" was elevated, in the spring of 1943, to the status of meriting a debate in the House of Lords. Their lordships, ranging from Lord Southwood, the founder of the Odhams newspaper and magazine empire which included the left-wing *Daily Herald*, to the Archbishop of York, spoke unanimously in favour of raising the school leaving age, reducing the working hours of adolescents, improvements in housing and medical services, and encouraging the voluntary youth organizations with more State aid.

The Earl of Selbourne, Minister of Economic Warfare, replied for the Government that it was the intention to make the school leaving age fifteen as soon as possible. As far as the voluntary organizations were concerned, the Board of Education was their friend:

"... we are in this dilemma, that the more the State does for youth the greater the danger of a uniform State-ridden system which is really going to have a totalitarian influence.... It can only be avoided through the voluntary organizations, through the community centres, the youth centres, the clubs, the boy scouts, the girl guides, the cadets, the church lads' brigades, and organizations of that nature.... In the post-war England that we are all going to have a hand in building up, we shall do what can be done to provide better health, better employment, better education, better training for the rising generation, but an education and a training that shall be religious, free, individualistic, worthy of democracy and something totally different to that conceived in a totalitarian State."

PART FOUR

"Now we have peace. We aim at no more war. We pray it may never occur again, so that our boys will be able to grow up as citizens of a free country in a peaceful world."

Field-Marshal Montgomery at the Mansion House, 21st May, 1946.

I

Outward Bound

EVEN WHILE WAR WAS BEING WAGED on an unprecedented scale by land, sea and air, plans were being made in Britain for the new Jerusalem when peace came. As early as 1942 the Beveridge Report laid the foundation stone by proposing that the prosperity and happiness of all the people from the cradle to the grave should become the business of the government. R. A. Butler's Education Act of 1944 finally swept away the outmoded idea that secondary education was for an *elite* of boys and girls and this led in 1947 to the raising of the school leaving age to fifteen, something for which boys' club leaders had been fighting for a generation. These reforms were introduced by the Conservatives, but they were not given the chance to implement them; in the popular imagination they were too closely identified with pre-war unemployment. Even Mr. Churchill's immense prestige and popularity as the leader of the nation in war could not save his party from a crushing defeat at the hands of Mr. Attlee and the Labour Party in the General Election of 1945 immediately following Victory in Europe.

Clement Attlee was at the head of the first Labour Government with a working majority, committed publicly to a new Britain and a whole new range of social services, privately to maintaining Britain's role as a world power by developing its own atomic bomb in the belief that here was a weapon which would make war impossible in the future. In the midst of rushing through legislation in an economic crisis, the new Prime Minister found time to attend the launching of a national appeal for boys' clubs at the Grocers' Hall in the City of London.

The appeal had its origins in Oflag 79, a prisoner-of-war camp at Brunswick in Germany, where the senior British officer, Colonel Dunnill, had called a meeting in an upper-storey room without windows and with a hole in the roof. His audience consisted of officers and men, some in the battle-dress they had been wearing when they were captured at Dunkirk, others in khaki drill from the battlefields of the Western Desert. There were Australians, Canadians, Poles, Belgians, Gurkhas and New Zealanders among them. All were hungry because the supply of Red Cross parcels had been stopped.

They listened somewhat sceptically as the colonel made the point that their captivity was a symbol of another captivity—that of unprivileged boys in peacetime who were held captive not by barbed wire but by bad housing and lack of opportunity for recreation and education. He proposed that they should start raising money there and then for a boys' club to give the younger generation a better chance when the war was over.

There were those at the meeting who doubted the relevance of this plan, and said so. But at the critical moment in the discussion a young private in the Parachute Regiment, who had been captured during the airborne assault on the bridge at Arnhem, chimed in: "If that gentleman who has just spoken will forgive me, he is talking poppycock. I know all about boys' clubs. I was a member of one, and believe me we always needed money and you can never have too much money. I owe everything to my boys' club and if you gentlemen endow this boys' club, you will be doing the finest thing you have ever done."

The speaker was Private Flamberg and his interjection turned the scale. Everyone in that dismal prison camp room cheered, and the meeting decided unanimously to support the boys' club idea. During the rest of their time in captivity they collected £13,000 in donations and £700 a year by annual subscription, appointed a committee of management and drew up a trust deed.

In May 1945 a few of the ex-POWs from Oflag 79 arrived at the offices of the National Association of Boys' Clubs in Bedford Square to tell its officials what had been done and invite them to take up the challenge. This they gladly did. The story symbolized the awakening of the social conscience during the war; not for the first time in its history the boys' club movement gained new impetus from the trauma of death and destruction.

Apart from the Prime Minister, the Brunswick appeal was supported by Lord Woolton, who was also proud to describe himself as "an old boys' club man," and Britain's most celebrated soldier, Field-Marshal Montgomery, who had defeated Rommel in North Africa. Monty declared that he intended to devote the rest of his life to the youth movement and threw himself with characteristic vigour into the campaign to raise money for boys' clubs. So successful was it, that the target of £250,000 was exceeded in less than two years.

Three-quarters of this sum was shared with local associations and clubs. With the remainder, the NABC set up a leaders' training centre at St. Pierre, a Norman-Tudor house, standing in 250 acres overlooking the River Severn at Chepstow, a senior boy training centre at Ford Castle, Berwick-on-Tweed, and an arts centre at Bakers Cross, Cranbrook.

Reg Goodwin, who returned to Bedford Square to work with Dr. Eric Piercy, the general secretary, after being invalided out of the Army, looked back thirty years to those days immediately after the war in an interview with the author:

"For the first time we had a training centre for professional leaders because it was becoming apparent that professional leadership would have to be a feature for the future. It was a boom time for club development in all respects. In the years following, associations for 16 more counties were formed. In 1948 the NABC received £30,000 of the gift of £1 million from the people of South Africa—which was handed by Field Marshal Smuts to Clement Attlee—and purchased Nash Court as a camping and training centre. With a similar sum the Scottish Association established Dalguise in Perthshire."

Nor was the post-war concern for the younger generation confined to boys at home who had grown up while their fathers were away at the front. The sufferings of youngsters in a Europe half in ruins cried out for help. In the winter of 1945 the NABC sent two of its field officers to Germany to advise on the problems of setting up a youth service in the British occupied zone. A British Army anti-tank battery in Austria, which had ten boys from Berlin aged between fourteen and seventeen as waiters in the mess and canteen, treated them as a boys' club and some of the soldiers who took a special interest in them were keen to carry on similar work in their spare time when they returned to civilian life. The former members of the Hitler Youth who had been brought up in ignorance of the Christian faith (apart from one Roman Catholic boy) and with a fierce hatred for Jews, were soon playing darts with British Tommies and saying "just the job," "smashing" or "you've had it" in English. They refused, however, to play cricket, which they considered a stupid game.

In Britain the years after the end of the war saw progress in the administration of clubs, with increasing emphasis being placed on giving boys more responsibility for the management of their own affairs. Lord Joicey made available his thirteenth-century crenellated castle at Berwick-on-Tweed, on the Scottish border, for their training. No better site could have been found than Ford Castle, overlooking Flodden Field and its memorial "To the Brave of Both Nations" and the Holy Island of Lindisfarne whence Aidan and Cuthbert brought Christianity to England for the second time.

In 1951 the first National Boys' Club candidates' week was held at Ford Castle. Here for the first time was a national link between able senior boys from clubs all over the country. They were the movement's hope for the future in that they would provide a substantial body of leadership coming up from the grass roots.

Meanwhile, frustrated youth, disappointed with the reality of peace, was getting restive. The *Sunday Pictorial* warned in a headline in March 1947 of "One thousand little gangsters on the loose." Four Battersea boys in a letter to the Prime Minister asking for more recreation and leisure facilities said: "We hope you won't be angry, but we're sick to death of having nowhere to go."

The chief distraction of the young was the cinema, where Abbott and Costello, a latter day Laurel and Hardy, were the comedy rage. According to Martin Parr, who was running the library in a boys' club in Shoreditch, the most popular books were thrillers like *She Was a Lady* by Leslie Charteris, the *Biggles* books by W. E. Johns and Richmal Crompton's *William* series. *Robinson Crusoe, Mr. Midshipman Easy* and *First Steps in Batting* came simply nowhere. The *Times Educational Supplement* noted in 1949 that detective stories were read by 60 per cent of boys in the fourteen to fifteen age group, whereas before the war, when Professor Jenkinson made a survey, the figure was less than 8 per cent. The pre-war taste for boys' adventure stories, many of which centred on the theme of "playing the game," was now being replaced by a desire for stories in which toughness and brutality was glorified. "Twopenny bloods" and the *News of the World* reports on the more sensational court cases involving sex and violence formed the greater part of juvenile reading and very few boys borrowed books regularly either from their school, clubs or the public libraries.

Concern about delinquency and gangs of cosh-boys roaming the streets was widespread and the blame was put on the war and its disruption of education and family life. Would more boys' clubs keep the rising generation in order? Among the most interesting developments were the Stonehouse Gang groups started by Harry Webb in Birmingham. Mr. Webb, a journalist who was also a Sunday school teacher, set out specially just before the war to divert the fascination of the gang idea which landed so many boys in the juvenile court into more constructive channels. The clubs took their name from the Stonehouse council housing estate where the movement began and in the post-war period there were five of them.

Most club leaders took the view that there was more to boys' clubs than keeping lads out of the juvenile courts. Basil Henriques, speaking from experience as chairman of the East London Juvenile Court, wrote in *The Boy* in 1947:

"Probably one of the main reasons for starting clubs in the early history of the movement was to keep boys off the streets and thereby prevent juvenile delinquency. Clubs undoubtedly continue to perform this extremely important function, but to-day the movement has gone far beyond its original purpose. . . . The multifarious causes of juvenile delinquency can be roughly summarized under two headings: either there is something wrong in the make-up of the boy, or else there is something wrong in his environment. The club movement can do very little for those in the former class, for they are either psychopathic personalities—in which case they should be the patients of a psychiatrist—or else they are mentally sub-normal and not likely to fit easily into the social life of the club. The real work of boys' clubs, therefore, with regard to delinquents, lies with those whose environment is bad, and by the word environment is meant not only slums and poverty, but also—and this is of even greater importance—the broken and unhappy homes.... Given the right environment these boys become normal citizens. Clubs can help to supply such an environment."

Mr. Henriques was also much concerned with the effect of National Service on adolescents and wrote a pamphlet entitled *So You're Being Called-up?*, published by the NABC. Between the end of the war and 1960 all able-bodied young men were liable, for the first time in peacetime in Britain, for service in the forces. Since the minimum school leaving age was now fifteen, a boy had at the very least three years before he became a fighting man in uniform. At that impressionable age many youngsters found themselves policing the British occupied zone of Germany at a time when, in conditions of desperate poverty, girls would sell themselves to a soldier for a packet of cigarettes, a bar of chocolate or a pair of nylons.

During this period boys' clubs began to benefit from the goodwill of prominent men, notably in the worlds of sport and show business, who had grown up in the clubs and were glad to acknowledge the part clubs had played in their early lives. Bud Flanagan repaid his debt to the Brady Boys' Club in Whitechapel by organizing an all-star concert at the London Coliseum in 1947 at about the time it was celebrating its jubilee as the oldest Jewish boys' club in London. Benny Hill, the comedian, a former member of the Firefly Boys' Club at Eastleigh in Hampshire; Roger Byrne, captain of Manchester United, from Rider Borough Boys' Club, Manchester; Jim Peters, the marathon champion, of Dagenham Boys' Club; the boxers Joe Erskine (Cardiff Central Boys' Club) and Billy Wells (Broad Street Boys' Club, London); Keith Mason from the Meadows Boys' Club, Nottingham, who stroked Oxford in the 1957 Boat Race; the England and Surrey cricketer Ken Barrington, of Mount Pleasant Youth Club, Reading, and Donald Zec, *Daily Mirror* columnist and former member of Stamford Hill Boys' Club: these were just a few of the famous "old boys" who came forward to help the clubs in the 1950s.

At last austerity was being relieved. A conscious mood of jollity was fostered by the Festival of Britain in 1951 and less than two years later the coronation of the young Queen on the death of her father gave rise to hopes of a brave new Elizabethan era.

In that spirit, boys' clubs were ready to try out new ideas. Club Week, with its opportunities for club members to help the NABC and their local associations, as well as their own clubs, had grown rapidly from its beginning in 1947 with a modest £7,000. By 1970 it had grown to more than £100,000 and no one played a more active part in making it a success than the singer Frankie Vaughan. The reason for his interest in the movement was simple: he had been a member of Lancaster Lads' Club. In 1955 he organized a talent competition among all the clubs taking part in Club Week and donated the royalties from his latest record, "Seventeen" and "Meet Me on the Corner," to the funds. Two years later Club Week was launched with a special boys' club show "Clubs are Trumps" with Bill Cotton, Junior, as the producer and Jack Payne as chief adviser. Pessimists thought boys' clubs were being over-ambitious in booking the Royal Festival Hall, the showpiece of the Festival of Britain site on the south bank of the Thames, but all three thousand seats were sold out in advance.

The show was to become an annual feature at the Festival Hall for the next twenty years, and Frankie Vaughan put all his professional drive and private enthusiasm into it. Star performers appeared alongside the boy acts which made up the greater part of the show—pop groups, classical soloists, folk singers, drum and fife bands, gymnasts and jugglers—the whole spectrum of entertainment was covered.

The post-war generation was much more demanding in its leisure pursuits. In recognition of this, the new arts centre at Bakers Cross in Kent followed the wartime lead of South Wales and in 1948 sent out on a nationwide tour a travelling theatre of boys who had attended drama training courses at the centre. The average age of the company was sixteen. One of the boys who attended the course in 1947 wrote:

"It were smashing! Skipper (he's our club leader) said: 'You ought to learn a bit more about acting for next winter's drama festival and you can have a holiday at the same time, so go to Bakers Cross for a week.' I didn't know what it was all about and kept thinking it had something to do with Hot Cross Buns. Well, there were lads from Plymouth, Stafford, Worcester and all over. One from Scotland did Young Arthur in 'heat me them irons hot' from *King John* what we did at the club last year. And you should have seen . . . being a fairy in *Babes in the Wood!* I split with laughing! But his acting was very good. It was a holiday alright, but not what I expected. Of course there was the swimming pool in Mr. . . .'s back garden and the wood and the stream at the back where Jock collected his tadpoles. But all the acting stuff was so interesting. We did two rehearsals a day when they showed us no end of tips—do you know you've got to walk right before you can really act? Then I went to the lectures about make-up and scenery and all that, which were really for the producers, but Mr. Thomas said I could. On the last night a lot of local big-wigs turned up to make an audience and we had a proper performance of the plays each lot of chaps had rehearsed. It was all done on a real stage with scenery we had built during the week. We had proper costumes and make-up and spot-lights like they have in a real theatre. I don't think I was very good, but it was fun all right and I only wish we could have stayed on another week. All the chaps said that. It's a pity that Bakers Cross isn't big enough to take all the chaps in clubs what do dramatics. It'd make them really keen on their club plays, like it's made me."

Bakers Cross was a country house standing in three acres of garden and woodland just outside Cranbrook in the Weald of Kent. In the autumn of 1945 other boys from clubs were invited to Glyndebourne, the home of country house opera in a wooded hollow of the Sussex Downs, for a week-long drama producers' training course. Throughout the war Glyndebourne had been a London County Council nursery school occupied by hundreds of babies. Now, with the return to peace, the Organ Room echoed once again to the strains of the Trumpet Voluntary.

Drama, music, art and entertainment of all kinds were a flourishing part of the boys' club movement immediately after the war, but sport and adventure still attracted the most recruits. Captain Sammy Cole returned from the Army Physical Training Corps in 1945 to find that the pre-war cult of "physical jerks" was dead. He concentrated instead in building up a wide ranging programme of sporting events and outdoor pursuits.

An international boys' club soccer team developed from a highly successful tour by the first German team to visit England after the war, and both national and county competitions were organized. Boxing remained a major boys' club activity as it had been since the early days of the London Federation and expanded to the point where there were no fewer than seventeen national championships. Cross-country running, cycling, swimming and table tennis were also very popular. But games alone were not enough. Boys wanted adventure and Sammy Cole gave it to them. Despite repeated attempts by public school and university men ever since the days of the Victorian missions to interest boys' clubs in rowing, it had never caught on. Canoeing did. In an interview with the author in 1974, Sammy Cole, by now retired from the post of physical training adviser to the NABC, explained:

"In a canoe you're master of your own craft. You may be in a group but you've got to control that canoe with your own mind, your own body, and keep it under control so that it doesn't tip over. It's not hard to learn but it's tough if you're fighting against the current. When we first did it, just after the war, every boy made his own canoe of canvas, whereas now they're all fibreglass. Some of those early canoes were terrible things—so heavy and cumbersome you could hardly lift them."

With the growing popularity of canoeing, expeditions were organized. The first attempt to cross the Channel from Margate by a score of boys in their frail craft was beaten by rough seas and tides, but the next year they succeeded, and the crossing became an annual event excelling in numbers even the Dunkirk armada of small boats. Another well supported event was the hundred-mile canoe test down the River Wye, which started with just seventeen canoes and built up to six hundred.

The intrepid Captain Cole next turned to the mountains, fells and moors as adventure playgrounds for his boys from the towns. In co-operation with the Ramblers' Association they pioneered the Pennine Way from Derbyshire near Sheffield all the way up to Scotland, finding their own way and mapping the route as they went. They then tracked Offa's Dyke, a mound stretching for mile upon mile over the hills and said to have been built by the King of Mercia to divide Wales from England. With as many as 150 boys from clubs all over the country, he walked every year over the

Roof of Wales from Swansea to Caernarvon Castle and handed over finally to his League of Young Adventurers the leadership of future trips which were to take them abroad as well as exploring their own land. They formed, too, a conservation corps in association with the National Trust and spent five years repairing mountain paths and in a single week built a new track round a lake in Snowdonia.

Captain Cole crossed the Channel in a canoe at the age of sixty-two. Still fit and full of life, he said:

"I don't know what I'd do if I dropped it. I love the comradeship built up among boys from widely different areas and backgrounds out in the open air on the rivers and the sea and in the mountains. It brings out the best or the worst in them. This was all a post-war thing. My opinion is that boys' clubs before the war were for the poor working lad and the club camp and games like football were the only way of bringing out his character. The signs of social levelling-up were very apparent in boys' clubs after the war. A complete revolution in fact."

In a materialistic age, these boys discovered that recreation need not depend on how much money they had in their pockets. The street corner was no longer the best club and the attractions of funfairs, pin-table saloons and the pictures palled. On one of the Roof of Wales trips some boys took £25 and came back with £22.50 after a week.

In 1956 the Duke of Edinburgh, a patron of the London Federation of Boys' Clubs, announced his award scheme, financed by the King George VI Memorial Foundation, and organized by Sir John Hunt, the conqueror of Everest. It included rescue and public service training, expeditions, pursuits and fitness. The awards, which were to be open to boys in the club age-group but regardless of whether they were members of voluntary organizations or not, ranged from commendations for those of fourteen and upwards, through silver awards for those of fifteen and upwards to gold for those over sixteen.

The horizons of the new generation were getting wider all the time, even though some preferred to become the Teddy Boys of the 1950s, affecting long sideburns, Edwardian-style drainpipe trousers and long jackets with velvet collars. For others a hut in the mountains or a cottage on the moors was better than rock 'n' roll at the local Palais. The opportunities were there for those who wanted to take them. The chain of youth hostels had been greatly expanded at home and abroad and membership in 1957 cost only 7s. 6d. a year for boys between sixteen and eighteen and 3s. 6d. for juniors under sixteen. The overnight charge was 2s. in summer and meals cost 2s 3d. for supper, 2s. for breakfast and 1s. for a lunch packet. By the early 1950s youth was on the move all over Europe, by bike and on foot with rucksacks bearing the flags of nations as far away as Australia and New Zealand, with thumbs extended in the hope of a lift from a passing car or lorry. The rumble of gunfire in distant Korea, the ever-present shadow of the mushroom cloud cast by the atomic bomb and the prospect of being called-up at eighteen made them determined to enjoy their heritage of freedom while there was still time.

2

The Shadow
of the State

WITH THE COMING of a State-sponsored youth movement, and the Butler Education Act of 1944, it was felt in some quarters that voluntary organizations like the National Association of Boys' Clubs were rapidly becoming redundant. This was certainly not the view of Mr. (later Lord) Attlee, the leader of the post-war Labour Government and, indeed, in the House of Lords in 1949 Lord Longford (then Lord Pakenham), defining the Government's attitude towards voluntary action, described it as "the life blood of democracy."

Yet within a year Britain's growing economic difficulties resulted in the suspension of capital grants to the voluntary youth movement by the Government, and these were only partially restored five years later. All over the country support from local authorities was reduced. During the 1950s the NABC was forced to close all its residential centres except Nash Court.

Up to 1939 the main object of boys' clubs had been *preventive*: keeping lads off the streets and thereby mitigating juvenile delinquency. During the Second World War the emphasis switched to education and the promotion of the Service of Youth became a recognized State endeavour.

The post-war county colleges (Mr. Butler's act of contrition for the ill-fated day continuation schools set up at the end of the 1914–18 war) were seen not only as a means of part-time education for adolescents beyond the statutory school leaving age but as places where the Ministries of Education and Labour could centralize and co-ordinate the various youth activities. Like Fisher's blueprint of 1918 it came to nothing, and for much the same reason, namely that the nation could not afford to insure its future.

In 1953 the Minister of Education described the youth service as one of the "fringes of education" and cut grants to the headquarters of the voluntary organizations by 10 per cent. These cuts remained for six years. At that time the voluntary organizations were catering for nearly 650,000 boys between the ages of eleven and eighteen, of which 190,000 were members of boys' clubs and 219,000 were Scouts. A far from insignificant fringe.

Boys' clubs still catered largely for boys out at work rather than younger lads who were attracted by the Scouts and Boys' Brigades and the wearing of uniforms. A random sample of 880 boys in fifteen clubs in various parts of England in 1947 showed that clubs in the north had 15 per cent of their members still at school, while those in the south had 19 per cent. This conflicted with a report from a county youth committee quoted in the *Times Educational Supplement* in that year: "Former pupils of grammar schools and some of the better students from modern schools form the core of the clubs ... the poorer sort of adolescent still, in general, prefers the streets, the pictures and the dance halls to any form of organized activity."

Grammar school boys no doubt took a valuable part in the life of many clubs, but the majority of members were working in building and decorating as apprenice plumbers, painters and joiners, as labourers, in engineering works and motor factories and in the distributive trades. Only a very tiny percentage worked on the land.

Boys under sixteen were called upon to work a 44-hour week in industry, with a week's annual holiday; an abrupt change from $27\frac{1}{2}$ hours a week for a total of only 40 weeks a year which they had had at school. But unlike the pre-war years boy labour was in short supply. Thanks to the falling birth rate of those lean years and the raising of the school leaving age to fifteen, there were some 100,000 fewer boys under eighteen available for industry by 1950 than there had been in 1938. More apprenticeships were given. No longer was a boy "thrown in at the deep end" when he left school. In association with Government bodies and local authorities and firms, the boys' club movement launched its "Adjustment to Industry" courses for school leavers in the spring of 1947. Twenty Birmingham boys who were changing their school bag, cap and blazer for lunch-box and overalls were given a week's course on what to expect, including lectures on trade unionism, national service and the complexities of insurance and pay-as-you-earn tax (PAYE). By the mid-1950s these courses had spread to most industrial areas and were an established part of boys' club work, which they remain to this day.

"Adjustment to Industry" is a clear example of a voluntary youth organization supplementing State social service. Yet at the NABC conference in 1956, the chairman, Lord Aberdare, entitled his address "The Youth Service is in Grave Danger" and the delegates decided that his warning should be circulated to all members of both Houses of Parliament. In the following year a sub-committee of the House of Commons Select Committee on Estimates examined the youth service and in its report castigated the Ministry of Education for its indifference and neglect of the voluntary movements.

Another committee was appointed to look at the youth service and the decade of the fifties ended with the result of its deliberations appearing in print as the Albemarle Report. It was denigrating in its references to voluntary workers as "do-gooders" and called for the full-time leader force to be almost doubled from its existing strength of seven hundred.

One paragraph in the White Paper seems to sum up the attitude of the new generation of professional boys' club leaders:

"At a time when many young people feel tempted to reject adult experience and authority it is plain that the Youth Service should not seem to offer something packaged—a 'way of life,' a 'set of values,' a 'code,' as though these were things which came ready-made, upon the asking, without being tested in living experience."

Neville Goodridge, who was deputy general secretary of the NABC at the time, said in an interview with the author: "Responsibility for leadership had been shifted on to the shoulders of those who had themselves been club members in their youth. Up to 1939 clubs had been run for boys by men who on the whole were men of privilege."

In the post-war years these leaders of yesterday were receiving honours and knighthoods—and dying. They were great men in their way, giants even, like Sir Charles Wrench, who served the London Federation of Boys' Clubs for nearly forty years and during the whole of that time appeared as MC at the boxing finals every year. He was hale and hearty enough at the age of sixty to take out a pilot's "A" licence. Sir Basil Henriques and Sir Alec Paterson were others whose pens and personal effort were directed towards helping unprivileged youngsters and particularly those who had fallen foul of the law. Sir Hubert Llewellyn Smith and John Stansfeld, "the Doctor," ended their days at the dawn of the new social era as did many others, too numerous to mention here—some not even known, much less knighted, who had worked tirelessly over the years in the cause.

But now their creed was out of date; a creed based on an interpretation of the Christian ethic which emphasized loyalty, honour, duty and obedience; a creed which embodied the Winchester College motto "Manners Makyth Man." As one of the new leaders, Richard O'Brien, wrote in *The Boy* in the spring of 1947:

"They have stamped the Service of Youth with their own design, and we who follow after must conform. Can we fit in easily? Is our attitude today the same as theirs was yesterday? Questions such as these are now being asked in many clubs up and down the country. In the first place we come from a very different background. We grew up in the period between the two wars. We were, if anything, iconoclasts; we abandoned the old beliefs in King and Country, *noblesse oblige,* and (often) in God Himself. ... We do not feel competent to teach a code because we are not so certain that we are qualified to do so. We do not feel ourselves to be the proud inheritors of a glorious past, but rather we regard ourselves as involved with the rest of mankind in its struggle to find an answer to the problems of the present. ... Do manners make men? Might they not just as easily mar men if taught in the wrong way against an unfamiliar background?"

Predictably, the article provoked a rumble of protest from the old guard, who were suspicious of the Welfare State, planned culture and the pseudopsychological jargon of the new generation of leaders. Some of them were even privately relieved at the cuts in government and local authority grants. In their eyes the mixed clubs which mushroomed all over the country after the war, admitting boys and girls on more or less equal terms, the juke boxes and fish and chip bars were but the first examples of what might emerge from the Trojan horse of State aid.

Yet this was a vital part of the development of boys' clubs after the war: over £4 million spent on five hundred schemes throughout Britain up to the end of the 1960s came from the Government and local authorities. Yet despite the fears of the older generation, there was still a need for self-help. A development fund of £65,000 raised by the NABC in 1954 to help new club schemes went on to provide more than £250,000 in the following two decades.

Moreover the movement was raising its own leaders on a scale never envisaged before. By 1954 the National Boys' Club had 157 members, fifty of whom were on national service, eighty serving apprenticeships and ten studying at college. One was in Korea, another had won his pilot's wings and was learning to fly Varsity aircraft having been rejected for jet aircraft because "my thigh length is too long to allow ejection from the cockpit in an emergency." Fifty of these boys were helping to run their own boys' clubs and three had taken on the leadership of clubs other than their own.

Chris Chataway became chairman of the National Boys' Club in that year and in the following year set up a new British track record over three miles of 13 min. 33 sec., thus beating Gordon Pirie's 1953 record by 21.2 seconds. Another great athlete, Dr. Roger Bannister, the first man to run the mile in under four minutes, became president of the NABC's fitness scheme in the mid-1950s.

Whatever the arguments for and against the increased intervention of the State in everyone's lives, it was generally agreed that the health of British boys and girls had never been better than it was during the period of rationing in wartime and the years which followed. Not only was there a better distribution of meat, eggs and milk, but tooth decay had been restricted along with supplies of sugar and sweets. With the setting up of the National Health Service, medical and dental care no longer came to an abrupt end when youngsters left school. During the 1950s the heaviest boys in the national club boxing championships weighed-in at nearly 12 st. —2 st. heavier than the heavyweights at the championships twenty years before.

3

Boys' Clubs
in the Sixties

THE OFTEN QUOTED REMARK to the British people by their then Prime
Minister, Mr. Macmillan, to the effect that they had "never had it so good,"
sums up the spirit of the affluent age which was ushered in during the
1950s and continued throughout the 1960s. There seemed to be more of
everything: there were nearly 9 million cars and other motor vehicles on
the roads where there had been only just over 2 million when war broke
out, nearly 8 million telephones where there had been only 3.3 million,
twice as many books lent by public libraries and more than twice the number of students in universities and colleges.

By 1965 the majority of British households had a television set, vacuum
cleaner and washing machine, and a third of them had a refrigerator. Two
out of three middle class families owned a car, and among working class
families the ration was one in three. Three times as many people took holidays abroad in 1965 than in 1955. Obesity was becoming a major health
problem as people ate more and consumed the richer foods which came to
them in a variety of frozen, canned, pre-cooked and "instant" forms; they
were furnishing and decorating their homes to previously unheard of
standards.

But if there was more of everything for almost everybody in the material
sense there was also more divorce and more crime: the rate of both was
three times higher in 1960 than it had been twenty years earlier. There was
little unemployment, and a great scarcity of labour. Certain sectors of the
economy—public transport, notably—became dependent on immigrants
from the former colonies. More and more married women and mothers
were employed in industry, and of course unprecedented spending power
was placed in the hands of adolescent working boys and girls.

No longer was adolescence an awkward phase to get through as quickly
as possible. The word teenager came into the language to describe a new
breed of youngster with more money, more freedom and more leisure time
than ever before. The teenager was a power in the land. The teenaged
consumer was a type courted lavishly in expensive advertising campaigns
by the fashion, cosmetics, entertainment and travel industries. Boys could
afford motor-bikes ("ton-up boys" in black leather jackets were a product
of the age) or even cars. After 1960 boys were no longer called up for

military service and through the latter half of the 1960s their hair got progressively longer and longer until shoulder length provoked no public comment or curiosity whatever; indeed boys at public schools or in the army felt embarrassed at having their locks shorn close around their ears and the nape of their neck, and regulations about what was considered properly masculine were considerably relaxed.

The affluent age was a testing time for boys' clubs. In 1962, hot on the heels of the Albemarle Report, the NABC produced in *Boys' Clubs in the Sixties* its own analysis of the situation:

"During these years of growing up there are many influences at work, some of which have much greater influence than in the past. The higher school leaving age has put off the time when the adult responsibility of earning a living and making a career has to be accepted. But the desire for independence that money gives is an ever present spur to earn it at the earliest possible age. When the time does come the opportunities are greater for some and the pecuniary rewards higher for all. The effects of the welfare state on physical growth are resulting in earlier maturity. At the same time the adolescent, with more to spend, is subjected to greater and more compelling propaganda than ever before. His standards and enthusiasms are being conditioned and set to a great extent by commercial agencies and by adult behaviour and attitudes which he can now afford and often has the freedom to adopt. By many means he is being encouraged to accept a materialistic view of life which discounts the importance of religion and in which the simple virtues are of little consequence. Through these many influences boys are being encouraged to behave prematurely like men and to face adult problems and temptations before they are equipped to do so. In these conditions certain relationships are undergoing severe testing and often radical changes. The responsibility of parents is constantly being questioned by the State, by the community at large and by boys and girls themselves. The influence of the family tends, therefore, to be less effective. Authority as represented by schoolmasters and the church has been weakened, and one effect of full employment for this age group is a lessening of discipline in industry."

It was a period when everything was being questioned and nothing was sacred. *The Boy* changed its name to *Challenge*, a title redolent of the publicity-conscious sixties. Under the editorship of Chris Brasher, one of the new breed of abrasive television journalists, *Challenge* was launched in a frenzy of controversy. An article on "The Anatomy of the Do-gooder" brought protests about cynicism and bad taste from some parts of the NABC hierarchy, but the unrepentant editor retorted: "We aim to live up to our first editorial when we said we would challenge long-held values and stale thinking—after all, what is the point of having a journal called *Challenge* if it doesn't do just that?"

So Mr. Brasher pursued his outspoken and provocative course with a survey of teenage spending, an article by the NABC's religious adviser, the Rev. Robert Skillern, on "Sex and love—some notes for teenagers," and an interview between John Gilbert of Sidcup County Boys' Club and Robert (now Lord) Briginshaw, the general secretary of the vast printing union

NATSOPA. There was a good deal of concern at the time about the number of unofficial strikes and allegations of communist influence in the unions and Gilbert innocently asked if it would not be better for the young worker to keep well away from trade unionism: a question which provoked a tirade from Mr. Briginshaw on the subject of unfair publicity and witch-hunting by Fleet Street.

Elitism of any kind was also under attack. The National Boys' Club, after ten years, was being accused by some club leaders and county secretaries of making a hierarchy among boys by holding up the talented few as shining examples, concentrating resources on a small group of boys, who on the whole needed the least attention, and giving them an exaggerated idea of their own importance. Fred Smewin, the secretary, replied that at least half the NBC members returned to their own clubs to give active voluntary help and there was plenty of evidence to suggest that they gained in confidence and usefulness by mixing with other men of character and ability in a national club.

The Duke of Edinburgh's award scheme was not exempt from criticism either. Its director, Sir John Hunt, on a visit to County Durham in the spring of 1963 to see how the scheme was working, was told that it had become nothing more than a prestige symbol. Frank Turnbull, the young superintendent of the Lambton Street Boys' Fellowship Centre in Sunderland, said the bronze, silver and gold awards given under the scheme favoured the tall, athletic youngster rather than the small boy, who had great difficulty in passing them. Many youth clubs had neither the time nor space to complete the necessary courses. Sir John later produced statistics showing that 26 per cent of secondary modern and 25 per cent of secondary technical schools were using the scheme for boys and the percentage of boys taking part who were "C" stream and below had actually gone up slightly between 1961 and 1962. The scheme was also being used in approved schools for delinquents and in schools for handicapped children and Sir John declared: "I believe these indications of the attraction and value of the scheme to the ordinary—in addition to the more gifted—boys will continue to increase."

Public schools found themselves singled out in films, television plays and the media as perpetuators of the class war and nurseries of snobbery and privilege—and yet some of the boys' clubs founded by the Victorian public school missions lived on.

After members of Harrow Boys' Club and Harrow School attended a weekend course at Amersham in the summer of 1962, an article in the school magazine threw some light on contemporary attitudes towards these missions:

"The very word Mission conveys the nature of these institutions which reflect some of the finer aspects of the Victorian spirit of Christian duty, as well as the natural acceptance of those class distinctions which to-day we habitually denounce but seem unable to forget. They were usually specifically Christian in their aims. Some still are, and many have some connection with their local Church. There is still a school of thought which maintains that School Clubs should be built around the idea of Christian training. Others see the Harrow Club in less purposeful light as a place in which boys can find scope for constructive activities, where they can play, relax and talk together, off the street corners and away from the pubs and juke-box cafes. The traditional view of the 'Mission' has been upset by the levelling-up of the 'affluent society', the disintegration of the old concepts of class and the widespread suspicion of Victorian 'charity'.... The welfare state has not eliminated class suspicion; difficulties of communication are, if anything, increased by the new 'status' and 'education' consciousness. The Harrow Club is proud of its association with the School; the School too has reason to be proud of the Club. This pride should not, however, conceal the fact that many past and present Harrovians do not know or care much about the work of the Club ... only a relatively small number of boys are able to go down there during term. Times do not always synchronize; nor do games, for the Club boy plays soccer and he does not play Fives or Squash. It was suggested that there should be more joint activities; not only in the term, boxing, swimming, running matches, but in the holidays, canoeing, climbing and camping. There might be informal concerts occasionally, or visits in small groups to the School. Sometimes they might come, as they sometimes have in the past, to Chapel; Harrow boys in return to the informal Sunday evening services at Latimer Road. The most important thing about the Amersham weekend was not, however, the ideas that were thrown up in debate and discussion. It was just that everybody enjoyed themselves enormously and naturally. There was neither 'do-gooding' nor constraint because Harrow and Latimer Road had found things they wanted to do in common. This is not usual in our divided society...."

The article was signed "Harrovian" and it has a great deal of relevance to the crisis facing the youth movement in Britain in the 1960s. The ad-mass technique of communication had given boys and girls of all classes a new common identity; they liked the same kind of records, the Beatles and the Rolling Stones and other pop music groups, they enjoyed the same television shows, ranging from the "Z-Cars" police serial to the satirical late-night Saturday show "That Was The Week That Was." On radio, the zany "Goon Show" crossed all social frontiers. Out of school (and sometimes even in it) the young of both sexes adopted a uniform of faded blue denim and training shoes which made it virtually impossible to distinguish a Harrow school boy from a Hackney garage mechanic when they were both on a day out. There remained the barrier of speech and accent, but even here the differences were becoming blurred by the influence of "Steptoe & Son" on public school vowels.

In the uneasy thermo-nuclear stalemate between America and Russia, the young showed an overwhelming aversion to militarism, jingoism and all forms of sabre-rattling, as was made clear by the American draft-dodgers and vociferous protests against the Vietnam War. Britain was for a brief period towards the end of the 1960s totally at peace for the first time this century, although the eruption of trouble in Northern Ireland soon brought that happy state of affairs to an end. A male generation was growing to maturity with no experience of military discipline and between 1963 and 1967 the numbers of boys in the combined cadet forces or Army, Navy and RAF sections in public and grammar schools fell from 73,000 to 56,500. In nearly half of these schools service in a military unit was compulsory, but many of the more liberal headmasters were against the idea. When St. Paul's School disbanded its cadet force, Field-Marshal Viscount Montgomery of Alamein (who was a cadet in the school's force in 1902, became an NCO, but was quickly reduced to the ranks) agreed with the decision. Peter Moran, editor of the magazine *Sixth Form Opinion* wrote: "I loathe the whole idea of school cadet forces. It seems quite unnecessary to train boys in the imperialist tradition when the Empire no longer exists."

Cadet forces were scarcely more popular among boys who left school at fifteen and by the mid-1960s there were only 39,000 of them in the Army cadets, 17,800 in the Sea cadets and 28,000 in the Air Training Corps. Younger boys were still attracted to the Boys' Brigades, the Scouts or the Nautical Training Corps, but on the whole the youth movement (whether in or out of uniform) appeared to be teetering on the brink of decline, if not already well on the way down the slope. In some quarters of the National Association of Boys' Clubs it was being argued that girls were the cause, but an article in the movement's news-sheet in November 1961 declared:

"While it is true to say that boys seek the company of the opposite sex it is also true to say that the boy is in the club for so few hours, that he has plenty of time to do his courting elsewhere. The real cankers in the side of the movement are: apathetic leadership, insufficient county secretaries and committees (both management and executive)."

Yet the movement, like most organizations of its kind, was bedevilled by committees at every level, often consisting of old club leaders whose attitudes tended to linger nostalgically between the wars and who would block new ideas on the basis of greater experience. The gulf between social classes of the pre-war era was now being replaced by a growing generation gap.

Fairly typical of this conflict was the experience of Elwyn Rees, appointed as a young man in his mid-twenties as the leader of the Shaftesbury Boys' Club at Birkenhead in the summer of 1962. This professional boys' leader, whose background was the socialism of South Wales valleys in the era of Nye Bevan, clashed with the Old Boys, who were trade unionists but conservative, with a small "c," and traditionalist. Some of them remembered the days of the late founder, William Norrish. Leslie Bibby, who was chairman, says: "Rees was young enough to understand the minds of the senior boys and fit enough to take them on expeditions and join in their games just at a time when long hair and pop music were beginning to divide the generations and to strain relations between them as never before."

Rees taught the boys to build canoes, took them on adventures on the rivers and across the English Channel, and replaced gym with judo and kendo taught by professional teachers. His plea for a more flexible attitude on the part of the committee towards the admission of girls to the club (heresy in the eyes of some) again reflects a trend throughout the country. The Ministry of Education, proposing in 1961 to build a £36,000 mixed club at Withywood, Bristol, says in "Building Bulletin No. 20" that this is a prototype of a specially designed building providing "an uninterrupted space or series of linked spaces, sub-divided by partial or discontinuous screens, within which social, practical, physical and cultural activities can be pursued in harmony." Moreover, the traditional gymnasium was firmly out of favour since it was not, according to the Ministry, "the right kind of space for the physical activities of a general mixed club."

This was the State-planned youth club of the future, something which sent a shiver down the spines of old boys' club men. Yet, as Bibby admits, despite structural improvements and the installation of television, his club and others "still in many ways looked like a workhouse, and sometimes behaved like one too." Membership was falling in the 1960s as families moved away from the old part of the town to the new estates. Boys with well-filled bellies were no longer attracted by the free tea and buns at the traditional annual festival party given by the president. Third-rate panto-mime or a conjurer could not compete with the television set at home. Boys' clubs found it more difficult than ever to provide effective counter-attractions to brightly lit coffee bars and dance halls with their tempting arrays of juke-boxes and one-arm bandits.

Mixed clubs appeared to some to be the answer but, as a Nottingham magistrate said, they could become little more than dance halls and picking-up centres supported out of the local rates. Alec Muir, the chief constable of County Durham and chairman of the Durham Association of Boys' Clubs, attacked the philosophy of "Don't give them what is good for them, give them what they want" in the association's annual report for 1964. Unscrupulous adults were making large sums of money out of young people through films, records, paperbacks and other forms of mass media, he claimed:

"Writers in the Press are quick to apportion blame; pastors, parents, teachers, youth leaders and officialdom, quick to present solutions—birch them, conscript them, discipline them. Few have the courage to suggest that we are all to blame, for this is the age of adult apathy. Time and time again it is left to a small band to run our clubs, and too often we depend on the same people to form the management committees of our voluntary organizations."

Wealthy men gave considerable sums of money to the boys' club move-ment but what was needed as much if not more than funds was adult leadership and participation. When the Singlegate Boys' Club at Colliers Wood in Surrey was forced to close in 1962, Cyril Wentzel, the county association's development officer, said:

"It's a death for which the whole community must share the blame, for it has been caused entirely by public apathy and neglect. The club has been far more than merely 'something to get 'em off the streets'. It was a place where boys had the opportunities to direct their energy and high spirits into the right channels. It has also been a place where they have benefited from genuine adult sympathy and help in the difficult business of growing up.... Mr. Robinson ran it for many years and devoted practically every minute of his spare time to it. But not one single man in the whole district could be found to help him out with the work."

Religion was no longer in the 1960s the prime motivation of the boys' club movement. The NABC's annual conference in Newcastle in 1965 was told that of 600 replies received to a questionnaire on religious attitudes, 200 boys said they said prayers privately, more than half the boys' parents never went to church at all and 135 went only once a year. The youth service as a whole did not reach more than 40 per cent of youngsters, and on the remaining 60 per cent the main pressures were commercial and material. The NABC's religious training adviser, the Rev. Skillern, told a parents' meeting in 1965:

"There is a very sad trend in girls and boys to promiscuity, and a large increase in sexual diseases—nearly 35 per cent over six years. But from all my reports, and from reports throughout the whole country, it is clear that, when young people are banded together in voluntary organizations, in clubs, we have had very little trouble—something like 0.01 per cent."

Trying to keep up with the times, the NABC asked the public relations experts what was wrong with its image, and was told by one of them: "If you called yourselves the National Association for the Prevention of Young Criminals you wouldn't get many people coming in. Yet this is how many of you see yourselves."

The 1960s saw a spate of reports on education, heralding another rise in the school leaving age, this time to sixteen, the ending of examinations at eleven-plus which determined whether a child went to a grammar or a secondary modern school, and increasing emphasis on comprehensive secondary education for all under one roof. By the early 1970s the gap between leaving school and attaining the age of majority (at eighteen) had been reduced to a mere two years. One of the government reports on secondary education was called *Half Our Future* and it was especially concerned with children of average and less than average ability.

The NABC was the only youth organization to call together a working party to advise on the implications of the famous Newson Report, and it did so because it wanted to know whether in the light of developments in State education there was any future at all for boys' clubs. The report of the working party was widely circulated and its chairman, Leslie Tait, emphasized its conclusion that there was definitely a future role, and an important one, for the movement:

"It is obvious that difficulties will increase, that the voluntary system will have to struggle to maintain its existence, that the clubs which are oblivious to the changes taking place around them will find it hard to keep their place. The strength of the NABC at club, city, county, national level is the vast support it has from the efforts of voluntary workers in all walks of life. The future of the clubs will depend on the maintenance and increase of this splendid heritage of voluntary help."

Reports, working parties and committees all seemed somewhat remote from the life of the youngsters they were discussing; the warring factions of Mods and Rockers (a latter day version of the Peaky Blinders and the Bermondsey Yobboes), the Top Twenty, Beatle hair-cuts and tight trousers, coffee bars, football and fast motor-bikes.

Disc-jockeys were the oracles of the age. Jimmy Savile appeared on the platform at the 1967 NABC conference wearing thigh-high brown suede boots and a Chairman Mao jacket. Sitting casually on the edge of a table he told the three hundred delegates how he had been fired by "a vision of Beverley Hills and E-type Jags" after he had gone to work down the pit at fourteen. He said he had worked hard to stop teenagers taking drugs but the recent prosecution of the Rolling Stones pop group had made drugs more fashionable than ever.

A survey among seventy-eight members of the old-established St. Andrew's Club in Westminster in 1964 showed another side of the picture. More than half the boys were non-smokers and hardly any of the boys under sixteen drank at all. The majority of those over sixteen liked a pint of beer, but averaged no more than seven a week. The boys considered that smoking was more harmful to the health than drinking. Needless to say, none of them was on drugs. About a third of the St. Andrew's Club boys attended church at least once a month and two-thirds considered themselves Christians, but their belief tended to be less definite as they grew older. At fourteen, 100 per cent considered themselves Christian, but between seventeen and nineteen the figure fell to 54 per cent. As many as 67 per cent took no interest whatever in politics and the most popular newspaper reading was the *Daily Mirror* or *Daily Express, News of the World, Sunday Mirror* or *Sunday People*.

Westminster, of course, was not necessarily typical of the rest of the country, or even the rest of London. But there were hopeful indications for the future of boys' clubs in the latter part of the 1960s. Tom Moore, director of the McCormick Boys' Club in Chicago, was impressed during a tour of British clubs, particularly by the NABC's Adjustment to Industry scheme, consisting of week-long residential courses for apprentices and boys not long out of school: "Boys in the United States are often stamped as drop-outs if they leave school early, but in Britain a boy fresh out of school is regarded as being on the threshold of a career . . . we have a major social problem in America dealing with these boys."

So, despite the all-embracing spread of State education, training and welfare, boys' clubs were still catering for the social needs of working youngsters, and as growing numbers of adolescents emerged from the schools there were serious problems of unemployment, particularly in the north-east.

Yet the main emphasis in boys' clubs in the 1960s was less on education and welfare than on leisure, sport and recreation. And like their elders in the working men's clubs, boys demanded television, one-arm bandits and draught beer on tap. Their leisure tastes had become, however, somewhat more sophisticated than their fathers', and included go-karting, building canoes and sailing dinghies, making wet suits and forming pop groups. The singlesticks described by Russell in *Working Lads' Clubs* had been replaced by kendo, a 500-year-old form of fencing from Japan using a weapon called a shinai made from bamboo and leather. Traditional boxing was giving way in some clubs to karate. This was the new face of the boys' club movement in Britain as the 1970s dawned.

4

Now More Than Ever

ONE OF THE LESSONS of social history is that we are never as advanced as we think we are. In 1880 the great Victorian reformer Lord Shaftesbury declared: "The great mass of the people are no longer in need of Friends and Champions: they can, and they do, defend themselves." He was, of course, somewhat previous. Nearly a hundred years later, in the 1970s, the raising of the school leaving age to sixteen and the lowering of the age of majority to eighteen did not result in any noticeable lessening of problems as far as adolescents were concerned. On the contrary, truancy, violence, vandalism and juvenile crime were all growing. At some schools truancy reached 50 per cent among fifteen-year-olds. Forty-one headmasters in the Bristol area wrote jointly to the *Times Educational Supplement* in 1974 describing the raising of the school leaving age as "a mistake with deplorable effects" and the National Association of Head Teachers called on the Government to reconsider its decision.

A survey by the Manchester social services department in 1974 concluded that the extra year at school might actually be driving some children to crime. Certainly in London during that year juvenile crime rose by 15 per cent and 32,000 children between the ages of ten and sixteen were detained by the police. The offences were mainly thefts, but also included muggings, robbery and burglaries. London Transport reported that large gangs of youths were terrorizing and even robbing passengers in certain sections of the capital's Underground. Colin Woods, the Assistant Commissioner (Crimes) at Scotland Yard, declared that juvenile offences were closely linked with truancy.

Charles Russell wrote in *Working Lads' Clubs*: "It was not until the latter decades of the nineteenth century, when ruffianism of youths had reached such pitch as to become an absolute danger to the community that attention was thoroughly aroused, and men who had the welfare of their city and country at heart grew apprehensive and began to cast about for some means of checking so alarming a development." Was history repeating itself a hundred years on? If so, where were the men with the welfare of their city and country at heart?

Only a few years earlier the Youth Service Development Council—one of those all-knowing, all-seeing Whitehall organizations—had published a report entitled "Youth and Community Work in the 70s", which pooh-poohed the work of volunteers, decried the traditional idea that youth leaders should attempt to give any kind of lead to the young and argued that in any case clubs were no longer valid because they isolated a particular age group from the community. A large number of local authorities adopted the council's thinking, including their recommendation that future grants should favour mixed clubs rather than those for boys and girls separately. The NABC was moved to retort:

"The association believes that the adults in boys' clubs and throughout the association recognize that the contribution of boys' clubs to society depends on the positive qualities of leadership, that adults cannot abdicate their responsibility for standards and must be prepared to lead by example. No less important is the association's conviction that society, including young people, look to adults to do just this."

This counter-blast against the so-called permissive society was not a fashionable one, nor did it accord with the views of trendy sociologists, but in any event Mrs. Thatcher, the Conservative Secretary of State for Education and Science, announced in Parliament in 1971 that the recommendations of the Youth Service Development Council were not acceptable to the government and she disbanded that organization.

This was a victory for the voluntary youth movement, and in particular the boys' clubs, which had reached a plateau after all the building and development of the 1950s and 1960s. Sir Reginald Goodwin, shortly to retire as general secretary of the NABC and become Labour leader of the Greater London Council, told the annual conference at Reading in the summer of 1972:

"I believe that a youth service or any part of it which is content with a formula of fun and freedom, and reckons success in numbers of attendance, is begging the whole question of what leadership is. To be a service rather than a disservice to the nation and to its young people, it must be a preparation not merely for living but for living a good life."

Fortunately, there were still leaders in the boys' club movement who, like the Victorian founders, were prepared to lead and expected no financial reward. Neville Goodridge, then retired from his post as deputy general secretary of the NABC but still helping to promote clubs in the expanding new town of Basingstoke in Hampshire, told the author in 1974:

"We discovered there that no sooner do you get a new neighbourhood built, where you've got lots of families dumped down in an area almost whilst the mushrooms are still growing, you get the embryo boys' club emerging from a football team, or a canoeing club or some other activity. The voluntary leadership comes from a dad, who perhaps wants to get his lads and other lads from the neighbourhood playing football, or the local curate, or a young schoolmaster who's a hero with the lads because he happens to be a bit of a sportsman, or sometimes it's a young policeman. They help to bring out the latent leadership among the boys themselves. Boys need more now than before to feel that they're running their own show but unless you have the wise, experienced and mature leadership which comes from an enthusiastic young adult, boys' leadership so often becomes *ringleadership*. There's no doubt that there's more, not less, need for boys' clubs as the age of maturation comes down physically and in a way psychologically, while at the same time the age of dependence is being extended by the higher school leaving age. These factors create terrible crises in young people's lives around the age of 15 and 16 and it's in that period that they need the support of a spontaneous gang or group."

When the Duke of Gloucester died in the summer of 1974 it ended almost fifty years of unstinted effort for the boys' club movement. He became president of the NABC in 1926, the year after it was formed, and through him the interst and support of the royal family was maintained down the years. He was no mere figurehead, but travelled the country visiting scores of clubs and talking to hundreds of boys. His son, Richard, has succeeded him as president of the NABC.

During the years of the Duke of Gloucester's presidency the National Association of Boys' Clubs had grown from a couple of typists in a small office to a great national organization with the support of the State and industry, bringing together the efforts of professional youth workers, enthusiastic volunteers and the boys themselves. The NABC ran a fitness scheme with awards rising from one-star to five-star and national championships in virtually every sport from basket ball to lawn tennis, and each week some three thousand boys' club football teams took to the field. It had its League of Young Adventurers, bringing together young men with a love of outdoor life and an interest in conserving mountains and rivers, and its National Boys' Club, composed of outstanding members of clubs from all over the country.

Expeditions and courses in boxing, football and coaching formed a major part of the national programme. But not all the activities were physical: there were festivals and national competitions for drama and films made by boys in the clubs, for young writers, artists and photographers, and the boys' club national chess championships.

Nor had the NABC lost its concern for the working environment of its club members. Adjustment to industry courses were run at Nash Court, a large Georgian house set in beautiful Shropshire parkland, for lads between sixteen and eighteen who had just started work. More than twenty thousand workers in a wide range of industries had attended since the courses were started in 1948.

Up and down the country, the affiliated associations ran their own adventure and training centres, from Dalguise House in Perthshire to Drake's Island at Plymouth, from the oldest, the Boys' Village at St. Athan in Wales, to the newest, Hindleap Warren, in the forests of Sussex only thirty miles from London.

Every year during Club Week over £100,000 was raised for boys' clubs and many individual clubs managed to collect over £1,000 in a frenzy of peanut pushing, leap-frogging, billiard cue balancing, sponsored walks and marathons of all kinds, including darts, football, badminton and guitar-playing. The memory of the Shoeblacks' Brigade of Queen Victoria's day stirred with attempts at shoe-shine records, sponsored by a manufacturer of shoe polish. The annual boys' club show at the Festival Hall also included the occasional drum-and-fife band among all the pop groups formed in the clubs.

A steel band formed by West Indian boys at a club in Leyton made an appearance at the Festival Hall in the early 1970s, a small indication of an important new role for the clubs among the communities of immigrants from the former colonies of Britain. In South London there was considerable tension between black youths and the police and in many of the ghettoes of the major cities bitterness grew among the immigrants over what they felt to be discrimination against them and lack of opportunity. One voluntary boys' club leader who made his own modest contribution towards easing racial tension was Tom Curran, of the Ladywood Boys' Club in Birmingham. In 1970 he started a Wednesday evening club for forty Sikh lads after intervening in a quarrel between some of them playing football in a local park.

The enemy of boys growing up in Victorian industrial England was poverty; today the enemy is boredom. William Norrish started his Shaftesbury Club for Street Boys and Working Lads in 1886 to keep half-clad boys away from the street corners. The members of the new Shaftesbury Club opened by Lord Leverhulme in October 1971 were, without exception, better nourished and better educated, clean and well-clothed, yet as Leslie Bibby says in his history of the club:

"Cultural poverty, some may say, has taken the place of material poverty.... If you were to call a member of to-day a 'street-boy' or a 'working lad' he would be likely to laugh in your face or clobber you.... Leisure is now a more plentiful commodity, and will become more plentiful still during the lifetime of present members, and yet most people are singularly ill-equipped to use it. Much of the work that young people have to do is repetitive and boring too, and fails either to satisfy their needs or to absorb their energies. I see the Youth Service as providing opportunities for constructive recreation, adventure, organized sport, for training for enjoyable and creative leisure and, hopefully, as providing a little much-needed discipline too, away from the formalized atmosphere of the school class-room or the restrictions of the place of work."

The men who created the first boys' clubs and later the NABC, did so because they perceived a social need. I would like to close with a thought for their grandchildren and their great-grandchildren who "never had it so good," who have been educated and supposedly coddled by the State, and yet are trapped on the assembly line. The comprehensive schools have not proved to be the salvation of this generation. Many of those who have been pronounced "too thick to take O-levels" have been left with a sense of inferiority, of being the rejects of society. Now more than ever they need somewhere to go and something to do in their spare time if they are not to become an embittered and shiftless older generation of tomorrow.

Officers of the National Association of Boys' Clubs

Presidents

1926–1974   H.R.H. The Duke of Gloucester, KG, KT

1974–   H.R.H. The Duke of Gloucester, GCVO

Chairmen

1925–1930   J. Heron Eccles, JP

1930–1935   Lt. Col. J. M. Mitchell, CBE, MC

1935–1943   Sir Hubert Llewellyn-Smith, GCB

1943–1957   The Lord Aberdare, GBE

1958–1963   Admiral The Hon. Sir Guy Russell, GBE, KCB, DSO

1963–   Captain The Viscount Althorp, MVO, DL

Hon. Secretaries

1925–1930   Colonel R. B. Campbell, CBE, DSO ⎫
                            Captain L. F. Ellis, DSO, MC ⎬ Joint
                                                    ⎭

Secretaries

1927–1930   R. F. Millard

1930–1945   Dr. E. F. Piercy, OBE

1945–1973   Sir Reginald Goodwin, CBE, DL

1973–   Brigadier E. G. B. Davies-Scourfield, CBE, MC

INDEX